Machine Learning Engineering

Andriy Burkov

Copyeditor: Aida E. Roig-Compton

Illustrators: Koen Van den Eeckhout, Andriy Burkov

Cover designer: Cristina Eleutério Alves Augusto

Publisher: True Positive Inc.

ISBN 978-1-9995795-7-9

To my parents:
Tatiana and Valeriy

and to my family:
daughters Catherine and Eva,
and brother Dmitriy

"In theory, there is no difference between theory and practice. But in practice, there is."
— *Benjamin Brewster*

"The perfect project plan is possible if one first documents a list of all the unknowns."
— *Bill Langley*

"When you're fundraising, it's AI. When you're hiring, it's ML. When you're implementing, it's linear regression. When you're debugging, it's printf()."
— *Baron Schwartz*

The book is distributed on the "read-first, buy-later" principle.

Contents

Foreword

Foreword by **Cassie Kozyrkov**, Chief Decision Scientist at Google, author of the course *Making Friends with Machine Learning* on Google Cloud Platform

I'd like to let you in on a secret: when people say "machine learning" it sounds like there's only one discipline here. Surprise! There are actually two machine learnings, and they are as different as innovating in food recipes and inventing new kitchen appliances. Both are noble callings, as long as you don't get them confused; imagine hiring a pastry chef to build you an oven or an electrical engineer to bake bread for you!

The bad news is that almost everyone does mix these two machine learnings up. No wonder so many businesses fail at machine learning as a result. What no one seems to tell beginners is that most machine learning courses and textbooks are about Machine Learning Research — how to build ovens (and microwaves, blenders, toasters, kettles... the kitchen sink!) from scratch, not how to cook things and innovate with recipes at enormous scale. In other words, if you're looking for opportunities to create innovative ML-based solutions to business problems, you want the discipline called Applied Machine Learning, not Machine Learning Research, so most books won't suit your needs.

And now for the good news! You're looking at one of the few true Applied Machine Learning books out there. That's right, you found one! A real applied needle in the haystack of research-oriented stuff. Excellent job, dear reader... unless what you were actually looking for is a book to help you learn the skills to design general purpose algorithms, in which case I hope the author won't be too upset with me for telling you to flee now and go pick up pretty much any other machine learning book. This one is different.

When I created Making Friends with Machine Learning in 2016, Google's Applied Machine Learning course loved by more than ten thousand of our engineers and leaders, I gave it a very similar structure to the one in this book. That's because doing things in the right order is crucial in the applied space. As you use your newfound data powers, tackling certain steps before you've completed others can lead to anything from wasted effort to a project-demolishing kablooie. In fact, the similarity in table of contents between this book and my course is what originally convinced me to give this book a read. In a clear case of convergent evolution, I saw in the author a fellow thinker kept up at night by the lack of available resources on Applied Machine Learning, one of the most potentially-useful yet horribly-misunderstood areas of engineering, enough to want to do something about it. So, if you're about to close this book, how about you do me a quick favor and at least ponder why the Table of Contents is arranged the way it is. You'll learn something good just from that, I promise.

So, what's in the rest of the book? The machine learning equivalent of a bumper guide to innovating in recipes to make food at scale. Since you haven't read the book yet, I'll put it in culinary terms: you'll need to figure out what's worth cooking / what the objectives are (*decision-making and product management*), understand the suppliers and the customers (*domain expertise and business acumen*), how to process ingredients at scale (*data engineering and analysis*), how to try many different ingredient-appliance combinations quickly to generate potential recipes (*prototype phase ML engineering*), how to check that the quality of the recipe is good enough to serve (*statistics*), how to turn a potential recipe into millions of dishes served efficiently (*production phase ML engineering*), and how to ensure that your dishes stay top notch even if the delivery truck brings you a ton of potatoes instead of the rice you ordered (*reliability engineering*). This book is one of the few to offer perspectives on each step of the end-to-end process.

Now would be a good moment for me to be blunt with you, dear reader. This book *is* pretty good. It is. Really. But it's not perfect. It cuts corners on occasion — just like a professional machine learning engineer is wont to do — though on the whole it gets its message right. And, since it covers an area with rapidly-evolving best practices, it doesn't pretend to offer the last word on the subject. But even if it were terribly sloppy, it would still be worth reading. Given how few comprehensive guides to Applied Machine Learning are out there, a coherent introduction to these topics is worth its weight in gold. I'm so glad this one is here!

One of my favorite things about this book is how fully it embraces the most important thing you need to know about machine learning: mistakes are possible... and sometimes they hurt. As my colleagues in site reliability engineering love to say, "Hope is not a strategy." Hoping that there will be no mistakes is the worst approach you can take. This book does so much better. It promptly shatters any false sense of security you were tempted to have about building an AI system that is more "intelligent" than you are. (Um, no. Just no.) Then it diligently takes you through a survey of all kinds of things that can go wrong in practice and how to prevent/detect/handle them. This book does a great job of outlining the importance of monitoring, how to approach model maintenance, what to do when things go wrong, how to think about fallback strategies for the kinds of mistakes you can't anticipate, how to deal with adversaries who try to exploit your system, and how to manage the expectations of your human users (there's also a section on what to do when your, er, users are machines). These are hugely important topics in practical machine learning, but they're so often neglected in other books. Not here.

If you intend to use machine learning to solve business problems at scale, I'm delighted you got your hands on this book. Enjoy!

Cassie Kozyrkov

September 2020

Preface

During the past several years, machine learning (ML), for many, has become a synonym for artificial intelligence. Even though machine learning, as a field of science, has existed for several decades, only a handful of organizations in the world have fully harnessed its potential. Despite the availability of modern open-source machine learning libraries, packages and frameworks supported by the leading organizations and broad communities of scientists and software engineers, most organizations are still struggling to apply machine learning for solving practical business problems.

One difficulty lies in the scarcity of talent. However, even when they have access to talented machine learning engineers and data analysts, in 2020, most organizations[1] still spend between 31 and 90 days deploying one model, while 18 percent of companies are taking longer than 90 days — some spending more than a year productionizing. The main challenges organizations face when developing ML capabilities, such as model version control, reproducibility, and scaling, are rather engineering than scientific.

There are plenty of good books on machine learning, both theoretical and hands-on. From a typical machine learning book, you can learn the types of machine learning, major families of algorithms, how they work, and how to build models from data using those algorithms.

A typical machine learning book is less concerned with the engineering aspects of implementing machine learning projects. Such questions as data collection, storage, preprocessing, feature engineering, as well as testing and debugging of models, their deployment to and retirement from production, runtime and post-production maintenance, are often left outside the scope of machine learning books.

This book intends to fill that gap.

Who This Book is For

I assume that the reader of this book understands machine learning basics and is capable of building a model, given a properly formatted dataset using a favorite programming

---

[1] "2020 state of enterprise machine learning", Algorithmia, 2019.

language or a machine learning library. If you don't feel comfortable applying machine learning algorithms to data and don't clearly see the difference between logistic regression, support vector machine, and random forest, I recommend starting your journey with The Hundred-Page Machine Learning Book, and then move to this book.

The target audience of this book is data analysts who lean towards a machine learning engineering role, machine learning engineers who want to bring more structure to their work, machine learning engineering students, as well as software architects who happen to deal with models provided by data analysts and machine learning engineers.

How to Use This Book

This book is a comprehensive review of machine learning engineering best practices and design patterns. I recommend reading it from beginning to end. However, you can read chapters in any order as they cover distinct aspects of the machine learning project lifecycle and do not have direct dependencies.

Should You Buy This Book?

Like its companion and precursor The Hundred-Page Machine Learning Book, this book is distributed on the "read-first, buy-later" principle. I firmly believe that readers must be able to read a book before paying for it; otherwise, they buy a pig in a poke.

The "read-first, buy-later" principle implies that you can freely download the book, read it, and share it with your friends and colleagues. If you read and liked the book, or found it helpful or useful in your work, business, or studies, then buy it.

Now you are all set. Enjoy your reading!

Andriy Burkov

Chapter 1

Introduction

Though the reader of this book should have a basic understanding of machine learning, it is still important to start with definitions, so that we are sure that we have a common understanding of the terms used throughout the book.

Below, I repeat some of the definitions from Chapter 2 of The Hundred-Page Machine Learning Book and also give several new ones. If you read my first book, some parts of this chapter might sound familiar.

After reading this chapter, we will understand the same way such concepts as supervised and unsupervised learning. We will agree on the data terminology, such as data used directly and indirectly, raw and tidy data, training and holdout data.

We will know when to use machine learning, when not to use it, and various forms of machine learning such as model- and instance-based, deep and shallow, classification and regression, and others.

Finally, we will define the scope of machine learning engineering and introduce the machine learning project lifecycle.

1.1   Notation and Definitions

Let's start by stating the basic mathematical notation and define the terms and notions, to which we will often have recourse in this book.

1.1.1 Data Structures

A **scalar**[1] is a simple numerical value, like 15 or -3.25. Variables or constants that take scalar values are denoted by an italic letter, like x or a.

A **vector** is an ordered list of scalar values, called attributes. We denote a vector as a bold character, for example, $\mathbf{x}$ or $\mathbf{w}$. Vectors can be visualized as arrows that point to some directions as well as points in a multi-dimensional space. Illustrations of three two-dimensional vectors, $\mathbf{a} = [2, 3]$, $\mathbf{b} = [-2, 5]$, and $\mathbf{c} = [1, 0]$ are given in Figure 1.1. We denote an attribute of a vector as an italic value with an index, like this: $w^{(j)}$ or $x^{(j)}$. The index j denotes a specific **dimension** of the vector, the position of an attribute in the list. For instance, in the vector $\mathbf{a}$ shown in red in Figure 1.1, $a^{(1)} = 2$ and $a^{(2)} = 3$.

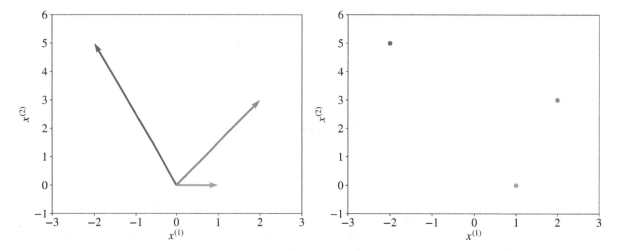

Figure 1.1: Three vectors visualized as directions and as points.

The notation $x^{(j)}$ should not be confused with the power operator, such as the 2 in x^2 (squared) or 3 in x^3 (cubed). If we want to apply a power operator, say squared, to an indexed attribute of a vector, we write like this: $(x^{(j)})^2$.

A variable can have two or more indices, like this: $x_i^{(j)}$ or like this $x_{i,j}^{(k)}$. For example, in neural networks, we denote as $x_{l,u}^{(j)}$ the input feature j of unit u in layer l.

A **matrix** is a rectangular array of numbers arranged in rows and columns. Below is an example of a matrix with two rows and three columns,

$$\mathbf{A} = \begin{bmatrix} 2 & -2 & 1 \\ 3 & 5 & 0 \end{bmatrix}.$$

---

[1]If a term is **in bold**, that means that the term can be found in the index at the end of the book.

Matrices are denoted with bold capital letters, such as $\mathbf{A}$ or $\mathbf{W}$. You can notice from the above example of matrix $\mathbf{A}$ that matrices can be seen as regular structures composed of vectors. Indeed, the columns of matrix $\mathbf{A}$ above are vectors $\mathbf{a}$, $\mathbf{b}$, and $\mathbf{c}$ illustrated in Figure 1.1.

A **set** is an unordered collection of unique elements. We denote a set as a calligraphic capital character, for example, $\mathcal{S}$. A set of numbers can be finite (include a fixed amount of values). In this case, it is denoted using accolades, for example, $\{1, 3, 18, 23, 235\}$ or $\{x_1, x_2, x_3, x_4, \ldots, x_n\}$. Alternatively, a set can be infinite and include all values in some interval. If a set includes all values between a and b, including a and b, it is denoted using brackets as $[a, b]$. If the set doesn't include the values a and b, such a set is denoted using parentheses like this: (a, b). For example, the set $[0, 1]$ includes such values as 0, 0.0001, 0.25, 0.784, 0.9995, and 1.0. A special set denoted $\mathbb{R}$ includes all numbers from minus infinity to plus infinity.

When an element x belongs to a set $\mathcal{S}$, we write $x \in \mathcal{S}$. We can obtain a new set $\mathcal{S}_3$ as an **intersection** of two sets $\mathcal{S}_1$ and $\mathcal{S}_2$. In this case, we write $\mathcal{S}_3 \leftarrow \mathcal{S}_1 \cap \mathcal{S}_2$. For example $\{1, 3, 5, 8\} \cap \{1, 8, 4\}$ gives the new set $\{1, 8\}$.

We can obtain a new set $\mathcal{S}_3$ as a **union** of two sets $\mathcal{S}_1$ and $\mathcal{S}_2$. In this case, we write $\mathcal{S}_3 \leftarrow \mathcal{S}_1 \cup \mathcal{S}_2$. For example $\{1, 3, 5, 8\} \cup \{1, 8, 4\}$ gives the new set $\{1, 3, 5, 8, 4\}$.

The notation $|\mathcal{S}|$ means the size of set $\mathcal{S}$, that is, the number of elements it contains.

1.1.2 Capital Sigma Notation

The summation over a collection $\mathcal{X} = \{x_1, x_2, \ldots, x_{n-1}, x_n\}$ or over the attributes of a vector $\mathbf{x} = [x^{(1)}, x^{(2)}, \ldots, x^{(m-1)}, x^{(m)}]$ is denoted like this:

$$\sum_{i=1}^{n} x_i \stackrel{\text{def}}{=} x_1 + x_2 + \ldots + x_{n-1} + x_n, \text{ or else: } \sum_{j=1}^{m} x^{(j)} \stackrel{\text{def}}{=} x^{(1)} + x^{(2)} + \ldots + x^{(m-1)} + x^{(m)}.$$

The notation $\stackrel{\text{def}}{=}$ means "is defined as".

The **Euclidean norm** of a vector $\mathbf{x}$, denoted by $\|\mathbf{x}\|$, characterizes the "size" or the "length" of the vector. It's given by $\sqrt{\sum_{j=1}^{D} \left(x^{(j)}\right)^2}$.

The distance between two vectors $\mathbf{a}$ and $\mathbf{b}$ is given by the **Euclidean distance**:

$$\|a - b\| \stackrel{\text{def}}{=} \sqrt{\sum_{i=1}^{N} \left(a^{(i)} - b^{(i)}\right)^2}.$$

1.2 What is Machine Learning

Machine learning is a subfield of computer science that is concerned with building algorithms that, to be useful, rely on a collection of examples of some phenomenon. These examples can come from nature, be handcrafted by humans, or generated by another algorithm.

Machine learning can also be defined as the process of solving a practical problem by,

1) collecting a dataset, and
2) algorithmically training a **statistical model** based on that dataset.

That statistical model is assumed to be used somehow to solve the practical problem. To save keystrokes, I use the terms "learning" and "machine learning" interchangeably. For the same reason, I often say "model" referring to a statistical model.

Learning can be supervised, semi-supervised, unsupervised, and reinforcement.

1.2.1 Supervised Learning

In **supervised learning**, the data analyst works with a collection of **labeled examples** $\{(\mathbf{x}_1, y_1), (\mathbf{x}_2, y_2), \ldots, (\mathbf{x}_N, y_N)\}$. Each element $\mathbf{x}_i$ among N is called a **feature vector**. In computer science, a vector is a one-dimensional array. A one-dimensional array, in turn, is an ordered and indexed sequence of values. The length of that sequence of values, D, is called the vector's **dimensionality**.

A feature vector is a vector in which each dimension j from 1 to D contains a value that describes the example. Each such value is called a **feature** and is denoted as $x^{(j)}$. For instance, if each example $\mathbf{x}$ in our collection represents a person, then the first feature, $x^{(1)}$, could contain height in cm, the second feature, $x^{(2)}$, could contain weight in kg, $x^{(3)}$ could contain gender, and so on. For all examples in the dataset, the feature at position j in the feature vector always contains the same kind of information. It means that if $x_i^{(2)}$ contains weight in kg in some example $\mathbf{x}_i$, then $x_k^{(2)}$ will also contain weight in kg in every example $\mathbf{x}_k$, for all k from 1 to N. The **label** y_i can be either an element belonging to a finite set of **classes** $\{1, 2, \ldots, C\}$, or a real number, or a more complex structure, like a vector, a matrix, a tree, or a graph. Unless otherwise stated, in this book y_i is either one of a finite set of classes or a real number.[2] You can think of a class as a category to which an example belongs.

For instance, if your examples are email messages and your problem is spam detection, then you have two classes: spam and not_spam. In supervised learning, the problem of predicting a class is called **classification**, while the problem of predicting a real number is called **regression**. The value that has to be predicted by a supervised model is called a **target**. An example of regression is a problem of predicting the salary of an employee given their work experience

---

[2]A real number is a quantity that can represent a distance along a line. Examples: $0, -256.34, 1000, 1000.2$.

and knowledge. An example of classification is when a doctor enters the characteristics of a patient into a software application, and the application returns the diagnosis.

The difference between classification and regression is shown in Figure 1.2. In classification, the learning algorithm looks for a line (or, more generally, a hypersurface) that separates examples of different classes from one another. In regression, on the other hand, the learning algorithm looks to find a line or a hypersurface that closely follows the training examples.

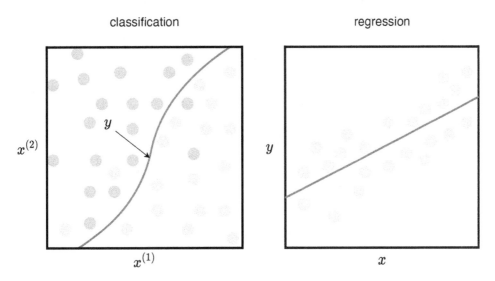

Figure 1.2: Difference between classification and regression.

The goal of a **supervised learning algorithm** is to use a dataset to produce a model that takes a feature vector $\mathbf{x}$ as input and outputs information that allows deducing a label for this feature vector. For instance, a model created using a dataset of patients could take as input a feature vector describing a patient and output a probability that the patient has cancer.

Even if the model is typically a mathematical function, when thinking about what the model does with the input, it is convenient to think that the model "looks" at the values of some features in the input and, based on experience with similar examples, outputs a value. That output value is a number or a class "the most similar" to the labels seen in the past in the examples with similar values of features. It looks simplistic, but the decision tree model and the k-nearest neighbors algorithm work almost like that.

1.2.2 Unsupervised Learning

In **unsupervised learning**, the dataset is a collection of **unlabeled examples** $\{\mathbf{x}_1, \mathbf{x}_2, \ldots, \mathbf{x}_N\}$. Again, $\mathbf{x}$ is a feature vector, and the goal of an **unsupervised learning algorithm** is to create a model that takes a feature vector **x** as input and either transforms it into another vector or into a value that can be used to solve a practical problem. For example, in **clustering**, the model returns the ID of the cluster for each feature vector in the dataset. Clustering is useful for finding groups of similar objects in a large collection of objects, such as images or text documents. By using clustering, for example, the analyst can sample a sufficiently representative yet small subset of unlabeled examples from a large collection of examples for manual labeling: a few examples are sampled from each cluster instead of sampling directly from the large collection and risking only sampling examples very similar to one another.

In **dimensionality reduction**, the model's output is a feature vector with fewer dimensions than the input. For example, the scientist has a feature vector that is too complex to visualize (it has more than three dimensions). The dimensionality reduction model can transform that feature vector into a new feature vector (by preserving the information up to some extent) with only two or three dimensions. This new feature vector can be plotted on a graph.

In **outlier detection**, the output is a real number that indicates how the input feature vector is different from a "typical" example in the dataset. Outlier detection is useful for solving a network intrusion problem (by detecting abnormal network packets that are different from a typical packet in "normal" traffic) or detecting novelty (such as a document different from the existing documents in a collection).

1.2.3 Semi-Supervised Learning

In **semi-supervised learning**, the dataset contains both labeled and unlabeled examples. Usually, the quantity of unlabeled examples is much higher than the number of labeled examples. The goal of a **semi-supervised learning algorithm** is the same as the goal of the supervised learning algorithm. The hope here is that, by using many unlabeled examples, a learning algorithm can find (we might say "produce" or "compute") a better model.

1.2.4 Reinforcement Learning

Reinforcement learning is a subfield of machine learning where the machine (called an agent) "lives'' in an environment and is capable of perceiving the state of that environment as a vector of features. The machine can execute actions in non-terminal states. Different actions bring different rewards and could also move the machine to another state of the environment. A common goal of a reinforcement learning algorithm is to learn an optimal **policy**.

An optimal policy is a function (similar to the model in supervised learning) that takes the feature vector of a state as input and outputs an optimal action to execute in that state. The action is optimal if it maximizes the expected average long-term reward.

Reinforcement learning solves a particular problem where decision making is sequential, and the goal is long-term, such as game playing, robotics, resource management, or logistics.

In this book, for simplicity, most explanations are limited to supervised learning. However, all the material presented in the book is applicable to other types of machine learning.

1.3 Data and Machine Learning Terminology

Now let's introduce the common data terminology (such as data used directly and indirectly, raw and tidy data, training and holdout data) and the terminology related to machine learning (such as baseline, hyperparameter, pipeline, and others).

1.3.1 Data Used Directly and Indirectly

The data you will work with in your machine learning project can be used to form the examples **x** **directly** or **indirectly**.

Imagine that we build a named entity recognition system. The input of the model is a sequence of words; the output is the sequence of labels[3] of the same length as the input. To make the data readable by a machine learning algorithm, we have to transform each natural language word into a machine-readable array of attributes, which we call a feature vector.[4] Some features in the feature vector may contain the information that distinguishes that specific word from other words in the dictionary. Other features can contain additional attributes of the word in that specific sequence, such as its shape (lowercase, uppercase, capitalized, and so on). Or it can be binary attributes indicating whether this word is the first word of some human name or the last word of the name of some location or organization. To create these latter binary features, we may decide to use some dictionaries, lookup tables, gazetteers, or other machine learning models making predictions about words.

You could already have noticed that the collection of word sequences is the data used to form training examples directly, while the data contained in dictionaries, lookup tables, and gazetteers is used indirectly: we can use it to extend feature vectors with additional features, but we cannot use it to create new feature vectors.

1.3.2 Raw and Tidy Data

As we just discussed, directly used data is a collection of entities that constitute the basis of a dataset. Each entity in that collection can be transformed into a training example. **Raw data** is a collection of entities in their natural form; they cannot always be directly employable for

---

[3] Labels can be, for example, values from the set {"Location", "Organization", "Person", "Other"}.

[4] The terms "attribute" and "feature" are often used interchangeably. In this book, I use the term "attribute" to describe a specific property of an example, while the term "feature" refers to value $x^{(j)}$ at position j in the feature vector **x** used by a machine learning algorithm.

machine learning. For instance, a Word document or a JPEG file are pieces of raw data; they cannot be directly used by a machine learning algorithm.[5]

To be employable in machine learning, a necessary (but not sufficient) condition for the data is to be tidy. **Tidy data** can be seen as a spreadsheet, in which each row represents one example, and columns represent various **attributes** of an example, as shown in Figure 1.3. Sometimes raw data can be tidy, e.g., provided to you in the form of a spreadsheet. However, in practice, to obtain tidy data from raw data, data analysts often resort to the procedure called **feature engineering**, which is applied to the direct and, optionally, indirect data with the goal to transform each raw example into a feature vector **x**. Chapter 4 is devoted entirely to feature engineering.

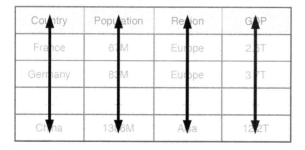
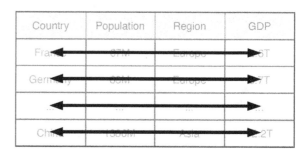

Figure 1.3: Tidy data: examples are rows and attributes are columns.

It's important to note here that for some tasks, an example used by a learning algorithm can have a form of a sequence of vectors, a matrix, or a sequence of matrices. The notion of data tidiness for such algorithms is defined similarly: you only replace "row of fixed width in a spreadsheet" by a matrix of fixed width and height, or a generalization of matrices to a higher dimension called a **tensor**.

The term "tidy data" was coined by Hadley Wickham in his paper with the same title.[6]

As I mentioned at the beginning of this subsection, data can be tidy, but still not usable by a particular machine learning algorithm. Most machine learning algorithms, in fact, only accept training data in the form of a collection of numerical feature vectors. Consider the data shown in Figure 1.3. The attribute "Region" is categorical and not numerical. The decision tree learning algorithm can work with categorical values of attributes, but most learning

---

[5]The term "unstructured data" is often used to designate a data element that contains information whose type was not formally defined. Examples of unstructured data are photos, images, videos, text messages, social media posts, PDFs, text documents, and emails. The term "semi-structured data" refers to data elements whose structure helps deriving types of some information encoded in those data elements. Examples of semi-structured data include log files, comma- and tab-delimited text files, as well as documents in JSON and XML formats.

[6]Wickham, Hadley. "Tidy data." Journal of Statistical Software 59.10 (2014): 1-23.

algorithms cannot. In Section 4.2 of Chapter 4, we will see how to transform a categorical attribute into a numerical feature.

Note that in the academic machine learning literature, the word "example" typically refers to a tidy data example with an optionally assigned label. However, during the stage of data collection and labeling, which we consider in the next chapter, examples can still be in the raw form: images, texts, or rows with categorical attributes in a spreadsheet. In this book, when it's important to highlight the difference, I will say **raw example** to indicate that a piece of data was not transformed into a feature vector yet. Otherwise, assume that examples have the form of feature vectors.

1.3.3   Training and Holdout Sets

In practice, data analysts work with three distinct sets of examples:

1) training set,
2) validation set,[7] and
3) test set.

Once you have got the data in the form of a collection of examples, the first thing you do in your machine learning project is shuffle the examples and split the dataset into three distinct sets: **training**, **validation**, and **test**. The training set is usually the biggest one; the learning algorithm uses the training set to produce the model. The validation and test sets are roughly the same size, much smaller than the size of the training set. The learning algorithm is not allowed to use examples from the validation or test sets to train the model. That is why those two sets are also called **holdout sets**.

The reason to have three sets, and not one, is simple: when we train a model, we don't want the model to only do well at predicting labels of examples the learning algorithm has already seen. A trivial algorithm that simply memorizes all training examples and then uses the memory to "predict" their labels will make no mistakes when asked to predict the labels of the training examples. However, such an algorithm would be useless in practice. What we really want is a model that is good at predicting examples that the learning algorithm didn't see. In other words, we want good performance on a holdout set.[8]

We need two holdout sets and not one because we use the validation set to 1) choose the learning algorithm, and 2) find the best configuration values for that learning algorithm (known as **hyperparameters**). We use the test set to assess the model before delivering it

---

[7]In some literature, the validation set can also be called "development set." Sometimes, when the labeled examples are scarce, analysts can decide to work without a validation set, as we will see in Chapter 5 in the section on **cross-validation**.

[8]To be precise, we want the model to do well on most random samples from the statistical distribution to which our data belongs. We assume that if the model demonstrates good performance on a holdout set, randomly drawn from the unknown distribution of our data, there are high chances that our model will do well on other random samples of our data.

to the client or putting it in production. That is why it's important to make sure that no information from the validation or test sets is exposed to the learning algorithm. Otherwise, the validation and test results will most likely be too optimistic. This can indeed happen due to **data leakage**, an important phenomenon we consider in Section 3.2.8 of Chapter 3 and subsequent chapters.

1.3.4 Baseline

In machine learning, a **baseline** is a simple algorithm for solving a problem, usually based on a heuristic, simple summary statistics, randomization, or very basic machine learning algorithm. For example, if your problem is classification, you can pick a baseline classifier and measure its performance. This baseline performance will then become what you compare any future model to (usually, built using a more sophisticated approach).

1.3.5 Machine Learning Pipeline

A machine learning **pipeline** is a sequence of operations on the dataset that goes from its initial state to the model.

A pipeline can include, among others, such stages as data partitioning, missing data imputation, feature extraction, data augmentation, class imbalance reduction, dimensionality reduction, and model training.

In practice, when we deploy a model in production, we usually deploy an entire pipeline. Furthermore, an entire pipeline is usually optimized when hyperparameters are tuned.

1.3.6 Parameters vs. Hyperparameters

Hyperparameters are inputs of machine learning algorithms or pipelines that influence the performance of the model. They don't belong to the training data and cannot be learned from it. For example, the maximum depth of the tree in the decision tree learning algorithm, the misclassification penalty in support vector machines, k in the k-nearest neighbors algorithm, the target dimensionality in dimensionality reduction, and the choice of the missing data imputation technique are all examples of hyperparameters.

Parameters, on the other hand, are variables that define the model trained by the learning algorithm. Parameters are directly modified by the learning algorithm based on the training data. The goal of learning is to find such values of parameters that make the model optimal in a certain sense. Examples of parameters are w and b in the equation of linear regression $y = wx + b$. In this equation, x is the input of the model, and y is its output (the prediction).

1.3.7 Classification vs. Regression

Classification is a problem of automatically assigning a **label** to an **unlabeled example**. Spam detection is a famous example of classification.

In machine learning, the classification problem is solved by a **classification learning algorithm** that takes a collection of **labeled examples** as inputs and produces a **model** that can take an unlabeled example as input and either directly output a label or output a number that can be used by the analyst to deduce the label. An example of such a number is a probability of an input data element to have a specific label.

In a classification problem, a label is a member of a finite set of **classes**. If the size of the set of classes is two ("sick"/"healthy", "spam"/"not_spam"), we talk about **binary classification** (also called **binomial** in some sources). **Multiclass classification** (also called **multinomial**) is a classification problem with three or more classes.[9]

While some learning algorithms naturally allow for more than two classes, others are by nature binary classification algorithms. There are strategies to turn a binary classification learning algorithm into a multiclass one. I talk about one of them, **one-versus-rest**, in Section 6.5 of Chapter 6.

Regression is a problem of predicting a real-valued quantity given an unlabeled example. Estimating house price valuation based on house features, such as area, number of bedrooms, location, and so on, is a famous example of regression.

The regression problem is solved by a **regression learning algorithm** that takes a collection of labeled examples as inputs and produces a model that can take an unlabeled example as input and output a target.

1.3.8 Model-Based vs. Instance-Based Learning

Most supervised learning algorithms are **model-based**. A typical **model** is a **support vector machine (SVM)**. Model-based learning algorithms use the training data to create a model with **parameters** learned from the training data. In SVM, the two parameters are **w** (a vector) and b (a real number). After the model is trained, it can be saved on disk while the training data can be discarded.

Instance-based learning algorithms use the whole dataset as the model. One instance-based algorithm frequently used in practice is **k-Nearest Neighbors** (kNN). In classification, to predict a label for an input example, the kNN algorithm looks at the close neighborhood of the input example in the space of feature vectors and outputs the label that it saw most often in this close neighborhood.

---

[9]There's still one label per example, though.

1.3.9 Shallow vs. Deep Learning

A **shallow learning** algorithm learns the parameters of the model directly from the features of the training examples. Most machine learning algorithms are shallow. The notorious exceptions are **neural network** learning algorithms, specifically those that build neural networks with more than one **layer** between input and output. Such neural networks are called **deep neural networks**. In deep neural network learning (or, simply, **deep learning**), contrary to shallow learning, most model parameters are learned not directly from the features of the training examples, but from the outputs of the preceding layers.

1.3.10 Training vs. Scoring

When we apply a machine learning algorithm to a dataset in order to obtain a model, we talk about **model training** or simply training.

When we apply a trained model to an input example (or, sometimes, a sequence of examples) in order to obtain a prediction (or, predictions) or to somehow transform an input, we talk about **scoring**.

1.4 When to Use Machine Learning

Machine learning is a powerful tool for solving practical problems. However, like any tool, it should be used in the right context. Trying to solve all problems using machine learning would be a mistake.

You should consider using machine learning in one of the following situations.

1.4.1 When the Problem Is Too Complex for Coding

In a situation where the problem is so complex or big that you cannot hope to write all the rules to solve it and where a partial solution is viable and interesting, you can try to solve the problem with machine learning.

One example is spam detection: it's impossible to write the code that will implement such a logic that will effectively detect spam messages and let genuine messages reach the inbox. There are just too many factors to consider. For instance, if you program your spam filter to reject all messages from people who are not in your contacts, you risk losing messages from someone who has got your business card at a conference. If you make an exception for messages containing specific keywords related to your work, you will probably miss a message from your child's teacher, and so on.

If you still decide to directly program a solution to that complex problem, with time, you will have in your programming code so many conditions and exceptions from those conditions that maintaining that code will eventually become infeasible. In this situation, training a classifier on examples "spam"/"not_spam" seems logical and the only viable choice.

Another difficulty for writing code to solve a problem lies in the fact that humans have a hard time with prediction problems based on input that has too many parameters; it's especially true when those parameters are **correlated** in unknown ways. For example, take the problem of predicting whether a borrower will repay a loan. Hundreds of numbers represent each borrower: age, salary, account balance, frequency of past payments, married or not, number of children, make and year of the car, mortgage balance, and so on. Some of those numbers may be important to make the decision, some may be less important alone, but become more important if considered in combination with some other numbers.

Writing code that will make such decisions is hard because, even for an expert, it's not clear how to combine, in an optimal way, all the attributes describing a person into a prediction.

1.4.2   When the Problem Is Constantly Changing

Some problems may continuously change with time so that the programming code must be regularly updated. That results in the frustration of software engineers working on the problem, an increased chance of introducing errors, difficulties of combining "previous" and "new" logic, and significant overhead of testing and deploying updated solutions.

For example, you can have a task of scraping specific data elements from a collection of webpages. Let's say that for each webpage in that collection, you write a set of fixed data extraction rules in the following form: "pick the third <p> element from <body> and then pick the data from the second <div> inside that <p>." If a website owner changes the design of a webpage, the data you scrape may end up in the second or the fourth <p> element, making your extraction rule wrong. If the collection of webpages you scrape is large (thousands of URLs), every day you will have rules that become wrong; you will end up endlessly fixing those rules. Needless to say that very few software engineers would love to do such work on a daily basis.

1.4.3   When It Is a Perceptive Problem

Today, it's hard to imagine someone trying to solve **perceptive problems** such as speech, image, and video recognition without using machine learning. Consider an image. It's represented by millions of pixels. Each pixel is given by three numbers: the intensity of red, green, and blue channels. In the past, engineers tried to solve the problem of image recognition (detecting what's on the picture) by applying handcrafted "filters" to square patches of pixels. If one filter, for example, the one that was designed to "detect" grass, generates a high value when applied to many pixel patches, while another filter, designed to detect brown fur, also returns high values for many patches, then we can say that there are high chances that the image represents a cow in a field (I'm simplifying a bit).

Today, perceptive problems are effectively solved using machine learning models, such as neural networks. We consider the problem of training neural networks in Chapter 6.

1.4.4   When It Is an Unstudied Phenomenon

If we need to be able to make predictions of some phenomenon that is not well-studied scientifically, but examples of it are observable, then machine learning might be an appropriate (and, in some cases, the only available) option. For example, machine learning can be used to generate personalized mental health medication options based on the patient's genetic and sensory data. Doctors might not necessarily be able to interpret such data to make an optimal recommendation, while a machine can discover patterns in data by analyzing thousands of patients and predicting which molecule has the highest chance to help a given patient.

Another example of observable but unstudied phenomena are logs of a complex computing system or a network. Such logs are generated by multiple independent or interdependent processes. For a human, it's hard to make predictions about the future state of the system based on logs alone without having a model of each process and their interdependency. If the number of examples of historical log records is high enough (which is often the case), the machine can learn patterns hidden in logs and be able to make predictions without knowing anything about each process.

Finally, making predictions about people based on their observed behavior is hard. In this problem, we obviously cannot have a model of a person's brain, but we have readily available examples of expressions of the person's ideas (in the form of online posts, comments, and other activities). Based on those expressions alone, a machine learning model deployed in a social network can recommend the content or other people to connect with.

1.4.5   When the Problem Has a Simple Objective

Machine learning is especially suitable for solving problems that you can formulate as a problem with a simple objective: such as yes/no decisions or a single number. In contrast, you cannot use machine learning to build a model that works as a general video game, like Mario, or a word processing software, like Word. This is due to too many different decisions to make: what to display, where and when, what should happen as a reaction to the user's input, what to write to or read from the hard drive, and so on; getting examples that illustrate all (or even most) of those decisions is practically infeasible.

1.4.6   When It Is Cost-Effective

Three major sources of cost in machine learning are:

- collecting, preparing, and cleaning the data,

- training the model,
- building and running the infrastructure to serve and and monitor the model, as well as labor resources to maintain it.

The cost of training the model includes human labor and, in some cases, the expensive hardware needed to train deep models. Model maintenance includes continuously monitoring the model and collecting additional data to keep the model up to date.

1.5 When Not to Use Machine Learning

There are plenty of problems that cannot be solved using machine learning; it's hard to characterize all of them. Here we only consider several hints.

You probably should not use machine learning when:

- every action of the system or a decision made by it must be explainable,
- every change in the system's behavior compared to its past behavior in a similar situation must be explainable,
- the cost of an error made by the system is too high,
- you want to get to the market as fast as possible,
- getting the right data is too hard or impossible,
- you can solve the problem using traditional software development at a lower cost,
- a simple heuristic would work reasonably well,
- the phenomenon has too many outcomes while you cannot get a sufficient amount of examples to represent them (like in video games or word processing software),
- you build a system that will not have to be improved frequently over time,
- you can manually fill an exhaustive lookup table by providing the expected output for any input (that is, the number of possible input values is not too large, or getting outputs is fast and cheap).

1.6 What is Machine Learning Engineering

Machine learning engineering (MLE) is the use of scientific principles, tools, and techniques of machine learning and traditional software engineering to design and build complex computing systems. MLE encompasses all stages from data collection, to model training, to making the model available for use by the product or the customers.

Typically, a data analyst[10] is concerned with understanding the business problem, building a model to solve it, and evaluating the model in a restricted development environment. A

---

[10] Since circa 2013, data scientist has become a popular job title. Unfortunately, companies and experts don't have an agreement on the definition of the term. Instead, I use the term "data analyst" by referring to a person capable of applying numerical or statistical analysis to data ready for analysis.

machine learning engineer, in turn, is concerned with sourcing the data from various systems and locations and preprocessing it, programming features, training an effective model that will run in the production environment, coexist well with other production processes, be stable, maintainable, and easily accessible by different types of users with different use cases.

In other words, MLE includes any activity that lets machine learning algorithms be implemented as a part of an effective production system.

In practice, machine learning engineers might be employed in such activities as rewriting a data analyst's code from rather slow R and Python[11] into more efficient Java or C++, scaling this code and making it more robust, packaging the code into an easy-to-deploy versioned package, optimizing the machine learning algorithm to make sure that it generates a model compatible with, and running correctly in, the organization's production environment.

In many organizations, data analysts execute some of the MLE tasks, such as data collection, transformation, and feature engineering. On the other hand, machine learning engineers often execute some of the data analysis tasks, including learning algorithm selection, hyperparameter tuning, and model evaluation.

Working on a machine learning project is different from working on a typical software engineering project. Unlike traditional software, where a program's behavior usually is deterministic, machine learning applications incorporate models whose behavior may naturally degrade over time, or they can start behaving abnormally. Such abnormal behavior of the model might be explained by various reasons, including a fundamental change in the input data or an updated feature extractor that now returns a different distribution of values or values of a different type. They often say that machine learning systems "fail silently." A machine learning engineer must be capable of preventing such failures or, when it's impossible to prevent them entirely, know how to detect and handle them when they happen.

1.7 Machine Learning Project Life Cycle

A machine learning project starts with understanding the business objective. Usually, a business analyst works with the client[12] and the data analyst to transform a business problem into an engineering project. The engineering project may or may not have a machine learning part. In this book, we, of course, consider engineering projects that have some machine learning involved.

Once an engineering project is defined, this is where the scope of the machine learning engineering starts. In the scope of a broader engineering project, machine learning must first have a well-defined **goal**. The goal of machine learning is a specification of what a

---

[11]Many scientific modules in Python are indeed implemented in fast C/C++; however, data analyst's own Python code can still be slow.

[12]If the machine learning project supports a product developed and sold by the organization, then the business analyst works with the product owner.

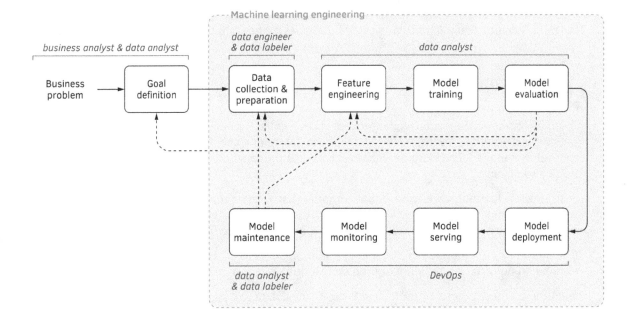

Figure 1.4: Machine learning project life cycle.

statistical model receives as input, what it generates as output, and the criteria of acceptable (or unacceptable) behavior of the model.

The goal of machine learning is not necessarily the same as the business objective. The business objective is what the organization wants to achieve. For example, the business objective of Google with Gmail can be to make Gmail the most-used email service in the world. Google might create multiple machine learning engineering projects to achieve that business objective. The goal of one of those machine learning projects can be to distinguish Primary emails from Promotions with accuracy above 90%.

Overall, a machine learning project life cycle, illustrated in Figure 1.4, consists of the following stages: 1) goal definition, 2) data collection and preparation, 3) feature engineering, 4) model training, 5) model evaluation, 6) model deployment, 7) model serving, 8) model monitoring, and 9) model maintenance.

In Figure 1.4, the scope of machine learning engineering (and the scope of this book) is limited by the blue zone. The solid arrows show a typical flow of the project stages. The dashed arrows indicate that at some stages, a decision can be made to go back in the process and either collect more data or collect different data, and revise features (by decommissioning some of them and engineering new ones).

Every stage mentioned above will be considered in one of the book's chapters. But first, let's discuss how to prioritize machine learning projects, define the project's goal, and structure a machine learning team. The next chapter is devoted to these three questions.

1.8 Summary

A model-based machine learning algorithm takes a collection of training examples as input and outputs a model. An instance-based machine learning algorithm uses the entire training dataset as a model. The training data is exposed to the machine learning algorithm, while holdout data isn't.

A supervised learning algorithm builds a model that takes a feature vector and outputs a prediction about that feature vector. An unsupervised learning algorithm builds a model that takes a feature vector as input and transforms it into something useful.

Classification is the problem of predicting, for an input example, one of a finite set of classes. Regression, in turn, is a problem of predicting a numerical target.

Data can be used directly or indirectly. Directly-used data is a basis for forming a dataset of examples. Indirectly-used data is used to enrich those examples.

The data for machine learning must be tidy. A tidy dataset can be seen as a spreadsheet where each row is an example, and each column is one of the properties of an example. In addition to being tidy, most machine learning algorithms require numerical data, as opposed to categorical. Feature engineering is the process of transforming data into a form that machine learning algorithms can use.

A baseline is essential to make sure that the model works better than a simple heuristic.

In practice, machine learning is implemented as a pipeline that contains chained stages of data transformation, from data partitioning to missing-data imputation, to class imbalance and dimensionality reduction, to model training. The hyperparameters of the entire pipeline are usually optimized; the entire pipeline can be deployed and used for predictions.

Parameters of the model are optimized by the learning algorithm based on the training data. The values of hyperparameters cannot be learned by the learning algorithm and are, in turn, tuned by using the validation dataset. The test set is only used to assess the model's performance and report it to the client or product owner.

A shallow learning algorithm trains a model that makes predictions directly from the input features. A deep learning algorithm trains a layered model, in which each layer generates outputs by taking the outputs of the preceding layer as inputs.

You should consider using machine learning to solve a business problem when the problem is too complex for coding, the problem is constantly changing, it is a perceptive problem, it is an unstudied phenomenon, the problem has a simple objective, and it is cost-effective.

There are many situations when machine learning should, probably, not be used: when explainability is needed, when errors are intolerable, when traditional software engineering is a less expensive option, when all inputs and outputs can be enumerated and saved in a database, and when data is hard to get or too expensive.

Machine learning engineering (MLE) is the use of scientific principles, tools, and techniques of machine learning and traditional software engineering to design and build complex computing systems. MLE encompasses all stages from data collection, to model training, to making the model available for use by the product or the consumers.

A machine learning project life cycle consists of the following stages: 1) goal definition, 2) data collection and preparation, 3) feature engineering, 4) model training, 5) model evaluation, 6) model deployment, 7) model serving, 8) model monitoring, and 9) model maintenance.

Every stage will be considered in one of the book's chapters.

Chapter 2

Before the Project Starts

Before a machine learning project starts, it must be prioritized. Prioritization is inevitable: the team and equipment capacity is limited, while the organization's backlog of projects could be very long.

To prioritize a project, one has to estimate its complexity. With machine learning, accurate complexity estimation is rarely possible because of major unknowns, such as whether the required model quality is attainable in practice, how much data is needed, and what, and how many features are necessary.

Furthermore, a machine learning project must have a well-defined goal. Based on the goal of the project, the team could be adequately adjusted and resources provisioned.

In this chapter, we consider these and related activities that must be taken care of before a machine learning project starts.

2.1 Prioritization of Machine Learning Projects

The key considerations in the prioritization of a machine learning project, are impact and cost.

2.1.1 Impact of Machine Learning

The impact of using machine learning in a broader engineering project is high when, 1) machine learning can replace a complex part in your engineering project or 2) there's a great benefit in getting inexpensive (but probably imperfect) predictions.

For example, a complex part of an existing system can be rule-based, with many nested rules and exceptions. Building and maintaining such a system can be extremely difficult, time-consuming, and error-prone. It can also be a source of significant frustration for software engineers when they are asked to maintain that part of the system. Can the rules be learned instead of programming them? Can an existing system be used to generate labeled data easily? If yes, such a machine learning project would have a high impact and low cost.

Inexpensive and imperfect predictions can be valuable, for example, in a system that dispatches a large number of requests. Let's say many such requests are "easy" and can be solved quickly using some existing automation. The remaining requests are considered "difficult" and must be addressed manually.

A machine learning-based system that recognizes "easy" tasks and dispatches them to the automation will save a lot of time for humans who will only concentrate their effort and time on difficult requests. Even if the dispatcher makes an error in prediction, the difficult request will reach the automation, the automation will fail on it, and the human will eventually receive that request. If the human gets an easy request by mistake, there's no problem either: that easy request can still be sent to the automation or processed by the human.

2.1.2   Cost of Machine Learning

Three factors highly influence the cost of a machine learning project:

- the difficulty of the problem,
- the cost of data, and
- the need for accuracy.

Getting the right data in the right amount can be very costly, especially if manual labeling is involved. The need for high accuracy can translate into the requirement of getting more data or training a more complex model, such as a unique **architecture** of a deep neural network or a nontrivial **ensembling** architecture.

When you think about the problem's difficulty, the primary considerations are:

- whether an implemented algorithm or a software library capable of solving the problem is available (if yes, the problem is greatly simplified),
- whether significant computation power is needed to build the model or to run it in the production environment.

The second driver of the cost is data. The following considerations have to be made:

- can data be generated automatically (if yes, the problem is greatly simplified),
- what is the cost of manual **annotation** of the data (i.e., assigning labels to unlabeled examples),
- how many examples are needed (usually, that cannot be known in advance, but can be estimated from known published results or the organization's own experience).

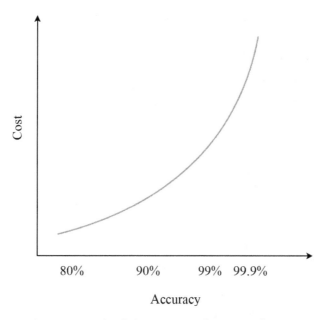

Figure 2.1: Superlinear growth of the cost as a function of accuracy requirement.

Finally, one of the most influential cost factors is the desired accuracy of the model. The machine learning project's cost grows superlinearly with the accuracy requirement, as illustrated in Figure 2.1. Low accuracy can also be a source of significant loss when the model is deployed in the production environment. The considerations to make:

- how costly is each wrong prediction, and
- what is the lowest accuracy level below which the model becomes impractical.

2.2 Estimating Complexity of a Machine Learning Project

There is no standard complexity estimation method for a machine learning project, other than by comparison with other projects executed by the organization or reported in the literature.

2.2.1 The Unknowns

There are several major unknowns that are almost impossible to guess with confidence unless you worked on a similar project in the past or read about such a project. The unknowns are:

- whether the required quality is attainable in practice,
- how much data you will need to reach the required quality,

- what features and how many features are necessary so that the model can learn and generalize sufficiently,
- how large the model should be (especially relevant for neural networks and ensemble architectures), and
- how long will it take to train one model (in other words, how much time is needed to run one **experiment**) and how many experiments will be required to reach the desired level of performance.

One thing you can almost be sure of: if the required level of model **accuracy** (one of the popular model quality metrics we consider in Section 5.5 of Chapter 5) is above 99%, you can expect complications related to an insufficient quantity of labeled data. In some problems, even 95% accuracy is considered very hard to reach. (Here we assume, of course, that the data is balanced, that is, there's no **class imbalance**. We will discuss class imbalance in Section 3.9 of the next chapter.)

Another useful reference is the human performance on the task. This is typically a hard problem if you want your model to perform as well as a human.

2.2.2   Simplifying the Problem

One way to make a more educated guess is to simplify the problem and solve a simpler problem first. For example, assume that the problem is that of classifying a set of documents into 1000 topics. Run a pilot project by focusing on 10 topics first, by considering documents belonging to other 990 topics as "Other."[1] Manually label the data for these 11 classes (10 real topics, plus "Other"). The logic here is that it's much simpler for a human to keep in mind the definitions of only 10 topics compared to memorizing the difference between 1000 topics[2].

Once you have simplified your problem to 11 classes, solve it, and measure time on every stage. Once you see that the problem for 11 classes is solvable, you can reasonably hope that it will be solvable for 1000 classes as well. Your saved measurements can then be used to estimate the time required to solve the full problem, though you cannot simply multiply this time by 100 to get an accurate estimate. The quantity of data needed to learn to distinguish between more classes usually grows superlinearly with the number of classes.

An alternative way of obtaining a simpler problem from a potentially complex one is to split the problem into several simple ones by using the natural slices in the available data. For example, let an organization have customers in multiple locations. If we want to train a model that predicts something about the customers, we can try to solve that problem only for one location, or for customers in a specific age range.

---

[1]Putting examples belonging to 990 classes in one class will likely create a highly imbalanced dataset. If it's the case, you would prefer to **undersample** the data in the class "Other." We consider data undersampling in Section 3.9 of the next chapter.

[2]To save even more time, apply clustering to the whole collection of unlabeled documents and only manually label documents belonging to one or a few clusters.

2.2.3   Nonlinear Progress

The progress of a machine learning project is nonlinear. The prediction error usually decreases fast in the beginning, but then the progress gradually slows down.[3] Sometimes you see no progress and decide to add additional features that could potentially depend on external databases or knowledge bases. While you are working on a new feature or labeling more data (or outsourcing this task), no progress in model performance is happening.

Because of this nonlinearity of progress, you should make sure that the product owner (or the client) understands the constraints and risks. Carefully log every activity and track the time it took. This will help not only in reporting, but also in the estimation of the complexity of similar projects in the future.

2.3   Defining the Goal of a Machine Learning Project

The **goal** of a machine learning project is to build a model that solves, or helps solve, a business problem. Within a project, the model is often seen as a black box described by the structure of its input (or inputs) and output (or outputs), and the minimum acceptable level of performance (as measured by accuracy of prediction or another **performance metric**).

2.3.1   What a Model Can Do

The model is typically used as a part of a system that serves some purpose. In particular, the model can be used within a broader system to:

- automate (for example, by taking action on the user's behalf or by starting or stopping a specific activity on a server),
- alert or prompt (for example, by asking the user if an action should be taken or by asking a system administrator if the traffic seems suspicious),
- organize, by presenting a set of items in an order that might be useful for a user (for example, by sorting pictures or documents in the order of similarity to a query or according to the user's preferences),
- annotate (for instance, by adding contextual annotations to displayed information, or by highlighting, in a text, phrases relevant to the user's task),
- extract (for example, by detecting smaller pieces of relevant information in a larger input, such as named entities in the text: proper names, companies, or locations),
- recommend (for example, by detecting and showing to a user highly relevant items in a large collection based on item's content or user's reaction to the past recommendations),
- classify (for example, by dispatching input examples into one, or several, of a predefined set of distinctly-named groups),

---

[3]The 80/20 rule of thumb often applies: 80% of progress is made using the first 20% of resources.

- quantify (for example, by assigning a number, such as a price, to an object, such as a house),
- synthesize (for example, by generating new text, image, sound, or another object similar to the objects in a collection),
- answer an explicit question (for example, "Does this text describe that image?" or "Are these two images similar?"),
- transform its input (for example, by reducing its dimensionality for visualization purposes, paraphrasing a long text as a short abstract, translating a sentence into another language, or augmenting an image by applying a filter to it),
- detect a novelty or an anomaly.

Almost any business problem solvable with machine learning can be defined in a form similar to one from the above list. If you cannot define your business problem in such a form, likely, machine learning is not the best solution in your case.

2.3.2   Properties of a Successful Model

A successful model has the following four properties:

- it respects the input and output specifications and the performance requirement,
- it benefits the organization (measured via cost reduction, increased sales or profit),
- it helps the user (measured via productivity, engagement, and sentiment),
- it is scientifically rigorous.

A scientifically rigorous model is characterized by a predictable behavior (for the input examples that are similar to the examples that were used for training) and is reproducible. The former property (predictability) means that if input feature vectors come from the same distribution of values as the training data, then the model, on average, has to make the same percentage of errors as observed on the holdout data when the model was trained. The latter property (reproducibility) means that a model with similar properties can be easily built once again from the same training data using the same algorithm and values of hyperparameters. The word "easily" means that no additional analysis, labeling, or coding is necessary to rebuild the model, only the compute power.

When defining the goal of machine learning, make sure you solve the right problem. To give an example of an incorrectly defined goal, imagine your client has a cat and a dog and needs a system that lets their cat in the house but keeps their dog out. You might decide to train the model to distinguish cats from dogs. However, this model will also let *any cat* in and not just *their* cat. Alternatively, you may decide that because the client only has two animals, you will train a model that distinguishes between those two. In this case, because your classification model is binary, a raccoon will be classified as either the dog or the cat. If it's classified as the cat, it will be let in the house.[4]

---

[4]This is why having the class "Other" your classification problems is almost always a good idea.

Defining a single goal for a machine learning project could be challenging. Usually, within an organization, there will be multiple stakeholders having interest towards your project. An obvious stakeholder is the product owner. Let their objective be to increase the time the user spends on an online platform by at least 15%. At the same time, the executive VP would like to increase the revenue from advertisements by 20%. Furthermore, the finance team would like to reduce the monthly cloud bill by 10%. When defining the goal of your machine learning project, you should find the right balance between those possibly conflicting requirements and translate them into the choice of the model's input and output, **cost function**, and **performance metric**.

2.4 Structuring a Machine Learning Team

There are two cultures of structuring a machine learning team, depending on the organization.

2.4.1 Two Cultures

One culture says that a machine learning team has to be composed of data analysts who collaborate closely with software engineers. In such a culture, a software engineer doesn't need to have deep expertise in machine learning, but has to understand the vocabulary of their fellow data analysts.

According to other culture, all engineers in a machine learning team must have a combination of machine learning and software engineering skills.

There are pros and cons in each culture. The proponents of the former say that each team member must be the best in what they do. A data analyst must be an expert in many machine learning techniques and have a deep understanding of the theory to come up with an effective solution to most problems, fast and with minimal effort. Similarly, a software engineer must have a deep understanding of various computing frameworks and be capable of writing efficient and maintainable code.

The proponents of the latter say that scientists are hard to integrate with software engineering teams. Scientists care more about how accurate their solution is and often come up with solutions that are impractical and cannot be effectively executed in the production environment. Also, because scientists don't usually write efficient, well-structured code, the latter has to be rewritten into production code by a software engineer; depending on the project, that can turn out to be a daunting task.

2.4.2 Members of a Machine Learning Team

Besides machine learning and software engineering skills, a machine learning team may include experts in data engineering (also known as data engineers) and experts in data labeling.

Data engineers are software engineers responsible for ETL (for Extract, Transform, Load). These three conceptual steps are part of a typical data pipeline. Data engineers use ETL techniques and create an automated pipeline, in which raw data is transformed into analysis-ready data. Data engineers design how to structure the data and how to integrate it from various resources. They write on-demand queries on that data, or wrap the most frequent queries into fast application programming interfaces (APIs) to make sure that the data is easily accessible by analysts and other data consumers. Typically, data engineers are not expected to know any machine learning.

In most big companies, data engineers work separately from machine learning engineers in a data engineering team.

Experts in data labeling are responsible for four activities:

- manually or semi-automatically assign labels to unlabeled examples according to the specification provided by data analysts,
- build labeling tools,
- manage outsourced labelers, and
- validate labeled examples for quality.

A **labeler** is person responsible for assigning labels to unlabeled examples. Again, in big companies, data labeling experts may be organized in two or three different teams: one or two teams of labelers (for example, one local and one outsourced) and a team of software engineers, plus a user experience (UX) specialist, responsible for building labeling tools.

When possible, invite domain experts to work closely with scientists and engineers. Employ domain experts in your decision making about the inputs, outputs, and features of your model. Ask them what they think your model should predict. Just the fact that the data you can get access to can allow you to predict some quantity doesn't mean the model will be useful for the business.

Discuss with the domain experts what they look for in the data to make a specific business decision; that will help you with feature engineering. Discuss also what clients pay for and what is a deal-breaker for them; that will help you to translate a business problem into a machine learning problem.

Finally, there are DevOps engineers. They work closely with machine learning engineers to automate model deployment, loading, monitoring, and occasional or regular model maintenance. In smaller companies and startups, a DevOps engineer may be part of the machine learning team, or a machine learning engineer could be responsible for the DevOps activities. In big companies, DevOps engineers employed in machine learning projects usually work in a larger DevOps team. Some companies introduced the MLOps role, whose responsibility is to deploy machine learning models in production, upgrade those models, and build data processing pipelines involving machine learning models.

2.5 Why Machine Learning Projects Fail

According to various estimates made between 2017 and 2020, from 74% to 87% of machine learning and advanced analytics projects fail or don't reach production. The reasons for a failure range from organizational to engineering. In this section, we consider the most impactful of them.

2.5.1 Lack of Experienced Talent

As of 2020, both data science and machine learning engineering are relatively new disciplines. There's still no standard way to teach them. Most organizations don't know how to hire experts in machine learning and how to compare them. Most of the available talent on the market are people who completed one or several online courses and who don't possess significant practical experience. A significant fraction of the workforce has superficial expertise in machine learning obtained on toy datasets in a classroom context. Many don't have experience with the entire machine learning project life cycle. On the other hand, experienced software engineers that might exist in an organization don't have expertise in handling data and machine learning models appropriately.

2.5.2 Lack of Support by the Leadership

As discussed in the previous section on the two cultures, scientists and software engineers often have different goals, motivations, and success criteria. They also work very differently. In a typical Agile organization, software engineering teams work in sprints with clearly defined expected deliverables and little uncertainty.

Scientists, on the other hand, work in high uncertainty and move ahead with multiple experiments. Most of such experiments don't result in any deliverable and, thus, can be seen by inexperienced leaders as no progress. Sometimes, after the model is built and deployed, the entire process has to start over because the model doesn't result in the expected increase of the metric the business cares about. Again, this can lead to the perception of the scientist's work by the leadership as wasted time and resources.

Furthermore, in many organizations, leaders responsible for data science and artificial intelligence (AI), especially at the vice-president level, have a non-scientific or even non-engineering background. They don't know how AI works, or have a very superficial or overly optimistic understanding of it drawn from popular sources. They might have such a mindset that with enough resources, technical and human, AI can solve any problem in a short amount of time. When fast progress doesn't happen, they easily blame scientists or entirely lose interest in AI as an ineffective tool with hard-to-predict and uncertain results.

Often, the problem lies in the inability of scientists to communicate the results and challenges to upper management. Because they don't share the vocabulary and have very different levels of technical expertise, even a success presented badly can be seen as a failure.

This is why, in successful organizations, data scientists are good popularizers, while top-level managers, responsible for AI and analytics, often have a technical or scientific background.

2.5.3 Missing Data Infrastructure

Data analysts and scientists work with data. The quality of the data is crucial for a machine learning project's success. Enterprise data infrastructure must provide the analyst with simple ways to get quality data for training models. At the same time, the infrastructure must make sure that similar quality data will be available once the model is deployed in production.

However, in practice, this is often not the case. Scientists obtain the data for training by using various ad-hoc scripts; they also use different scripts and tools to combine various data sources. Once the model is ready, it turns out that it's impossible, by using the available production infrastructure, to generate input examples for the model fast enough (or at all). We extensively talk about storing data and features in Chapters 3 and 4.

2.5.4 Data Labeling Challenge

In most machine learning projects, analysts use labeled data. This data is usually custom, so labeling is executed specifically for each project. As of 2019, according to some reports,[5] as many as 76% AI and data science teams label training data on their own, while 63% build their own labeling and annotation automation technology.

This results in a significant time spent by skilled data scientists on data labeling and labeling tool development. This is a major challenge for the effective execution of an AI project.

Some companies outsource data labeling to third-party vendors. However, without proper quality validation, such labeled data can turn out to be of low quality or entirely wrong. Organizations, in order to maintain quality and consistency across datasets, have to invest in formal and standardized training of internal or third-party labelers. This, in turn, can slow down machine learning projects. Though, according to the same reports, companies that outsource data labeling are more likely to get their machine learning projects up to production.

2.5.5 Siloed Organizations and Lack of Collaboration

Data needed for a machine learning project often resides within an organization in different places with different ownership, security constraints, and in different formats. In siloed organizations, people responsible for different data assets might not know one another. Lack of trust and collaboration results in friction when one department needs access to the data stored in a different department. Furthermore, different branches of one organization often

---

[5]Alegion and Dimensional Research, "What data scientists tell us about AI model training today," 2019.

have their own budgets, so collaboration becomes complicated because no side has an interest in spending their budget helping to the other side.

Even within one branch of an organization, there are often several teams involved in a machine learning project at different stages. For example, the data engineering team provides access to the data or individual features, the data science team works on modeling, ETL or DevOps work on the engineering aspects of deployment and monitoring, while the automation and internal tools teams develop tools and processes for a continuous model update. Lack of collaboration between any pair of the involved teams might result in the project being frozen for a long time. Typical reasons for mistrust between teams is the lack of understanding by the engineers of the tools and approaches used by the scientists and the lack of knowledge (or plain ignorance) by the scientists of software engineering good practices and design patterns.

2.5.6 Technically Infeasible Projects

Because of the high cost of many machine learning projects (due to high expertise and infrastructure cost) some organizations, to "recoup the investment," might target very ambitious goals: to completely transform the organization or the product or provide unrealistic return or investment. This results in very large-scale projects, involving collaboration between multiple teams, departments, and third-parties, and pushing those teams to their limits.

As a result, such overly ambitious projects could take months or even years to complete; some key players, including leaders and key scientists, might lose interest in the project or even leave the organization. The project could eventually be deprioritized, or, even when completed, be too late to the market. It is best, at least in the beginning, to focus on achievable projects, involving simple collaboration between teams, easy to scope, and targeting a simple business objective.

2.5.7 Lack of Alignment Between Technical and Business Teams

Many machine learning projects start without a clear understanding, by the technical team, of the business objective. Scientists usually frame the problem as classification or regression with a technical objective, such as high accuracy or low mean squared error. Without continuous feedback from the business team on the achievement of a business objective (such as an increased click-through rate or user retention), the scientists often reach an initial level of model performance (according to the technical objective), and then they are not sure if they are making any useful progress and whether an additional effort is worth it. In such situations, the projects end up being put on the shelf because time and resources were spent but the business team didn't accept the result.

2.6 Summary

Before a machine learning project starts, it must be prioritized, and the team working on the project must be built. The key considerations in the prioritization of a machine learning project, are impact and cost.

The impact of using machine learning is high when, 1) machine learning can replace a complex part in your engineering project, or 2) there's a great benefit in getting inexpensive (but probably imperfect) predictions.

The cost of the machine learning project is highly influenced by three factors: 1) the difficulty of the problem, 2) the cost of data, and 3) the needed model performance quality.

There is no standard method of estimation of how complex a machine learning project is other than by comparison with other projects executed by the organization or reported in the literature. There are several major unknowns that are almost impossible to guess: whether the required level of model performance is attainable in practice, how much data you will need to reach that level of performance, what features and how many features are needed, how large the model should be, and how long will it take to run one experiment and how many experiments will be needed to reach the desired level of performance.

One way to make a more educated guess is to simplify the problem and solve a simpler one.

The progress of a machine learning project is nonlinear. The error usually decreases fast in the beginning, but then the progress slows down. Because of this nonlinearity of progress, it's better to make sure that the client understands the constraints and the risks. Carefully log every activity and track the time it took. This will help not only in reporting but also in estimating complexity for similar projects in the future.

The goal of a machine learning project is to build a model that solves some business problem. In particular, the model can be used within a broader system to automate, alert or prompt, organize, annotate, extract, recommend, classify, quantify, synthesize, answer an explicit question, transform its input, and detect novelty or an anomaly. If you cannot frame the goal of machine learning in one of these forms, likely, machine learning is not the best solution.

A successful model 1) respects the input and output specifications and the minimum performance requirement, 2) benefits the organization and the user, and 3) is scientifically rigorous.

There are two cultures of structuring a machine learning team, depending on the organization. One culture says that a machine learning team has to be composed of data analysts who collaborate closely with software engineers. In such a culture, a software engineer doesn't need to have profound expertise in machine learning but has to understand the vocabulary of their fellow data analysts or scientists. According to the other culture, all engineers in a machine learning team must have a combination of machine learning and software engineering skills.

Besides having machine learning and software engineering skills, a machine learning team may include experts in data labeling and data engineering experts. DevOps engineers work closely with machine learning engineers to automate model deployment, loading, monitoring, and occasional or regular model maintenance.

A machine learning projects can fail for many reasons, and most actually do. Typical reasons for a failure are:

- lack of experienced talent,
- lack of support by the leadership,
- missing data infrastructure,
- data labeling challenge,
- siloed organizations and lack of collaboration,
- technically infeasible projects, and
- lack of alignment between technical and business teams.

Chapter 3

Data Collection and Preparation

Before any machine learning activity can start, the analyst must collect and prepare the data. The data available to the analyst is not always "right" and is not always in a form that a machine learning algorithm can use. This chapter focuses on the second stage in the machine learning project life cycle, as shown below:

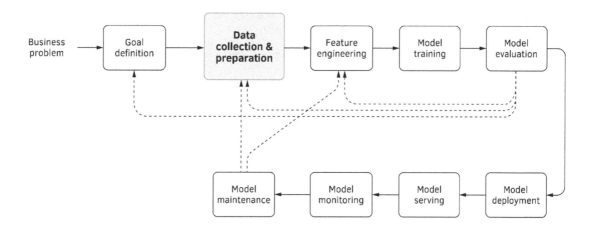

Figure 3.1: Machine learning project life cycle.

In particular, we talk about the properties of good quality data, typical problems a dataset can have, and ways to prepare and store data for machine learning.

3.1 Questions About the Data

Now that you have a machine learning goal with well-defined model input, output, and success criteria, you can start collecting the data needed to train your model. However, before you start collecting the data, there are some questions to answer.

3.1.1 Is the Data Accessible?

Does the data you need already exist? If yes, is it accessible (physically, contractually, ethically, or from a cost perspective)? If you are purchasing or re-using someone else's data sources, have you considered how that data might be used or shared? Do you need to negotiate a new licensing agreement with the original supplier?

If the data is accessible, is it protected by copyright or other legal norms? If so, have you established who owns the copyright in your data? Might there be joint copyright?

Is the data sensitive (e.g., concerning your organization's projects, clients, or partners, or it is classified by the government), and are there any potential privacy issues? If so, have you discussed data sharing with the respondents from whom you collected the data? Can you preserve personal information for a long-term so that it can be used in the future?

Do you need to share the data along with the model? If so, do you need to get written consent from owners or respondents?

Do you need to anonymize data,[1] for example, to remove **personally identifiable information (PII)**, during analysis or in preparation for sharing?

Even if it's physically possible to get the data you need, don't work with it until all the above questions are resolved.

3.1.2 Is the Data Sizeable?

The question for which you would like to have a definitive answer is whether there's enough data. However, as we already found out, it's usually not known how much data is needed to reach your goal, especially if the minimum model quality requirement is stringent.

If you have doubts about the immediate availability of sufficient data, find out how frequently new data gets generated. For some projects, you can start with what's initially available and, while you are working on feature engineering, modeling, and solving other relevant technical problems, new data might gradually come in. It can come in naturally, as the result of some

---

[1] An illustrative example is the content redistribution policy of Twitter. The policy restricts the sharing of tweet information other than tweet IDs and user IDs. Twitter wants the analysts always to pull fresh data using Twitter API. One possible explanation of such a restriction is that some users might want to delete a particular tweet because they changed their mind or found it too controversial. If that tweet has already been pulled and is shared on a public domain, then it might make that user vulnerable.

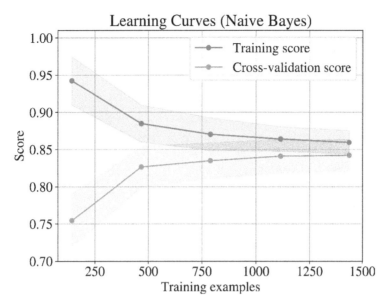

Figure 3.2: Learning curves for the Naïve Bayes learning algorithm applied to the standard "digits" dataset of scikit-learn.

observable or measurable process, or progressively be provided by your data labeling experts or a third-party data provider.

Consider the estimated time needed to accomplish the project. Will a sufficiently large dataset[2] be gathered during this time? Base your answer on the experience working on similar projects or results reported in the literature.

One practical way to find out if you have collected sufficient data is to plot **learning curves**. More specifically, plot the training and validation scores of your learning algorithm for varying numbers of training examples, as shown in Figure 3.2.

By looking at the learning curves, you will see your model's performance will plateau after you reach a certain number of training examples. Upon reaching that number of training examples, you will begin to experience diminishing returns from additional examples.

If you observe the performance of the learning algorithm plateaued, it might be a sign that collecting more data will not help in training a better model. I used the expression "might be" because two other explanations are possible:

- you didn't have enough informative features that your learning algorithm can leverage to build a more performant model, or

---

[2]Don't forget, in your estimates, that you need not just training but also holdout data to validate the model performance on the examples it wasn't trained on. That holdout data also has to be sizeable to provide reliable, in a statistical sense, model quality estimates.

- you used a learning algorithm incapable of training a complex enough model using the data you have.

In the former case, you might think about engineering additional features by combining the existing features in some clever ways, or by using information from indirect data sources, such as lookup tables and gazetteers. We consider techniques for synthesizing features in Section 4.6 of Chapter 4.

In the latter case, one possible approach would be to use an ensemble learning method or train a deep neural network. However, deep neural networks usually require more training data compared to shallow learning algorithms.

Some practitioners use rules of thumb to estimate the number of training examples needed for a problem. Usually, they are using scaling factors applied to either,

- number of features, or
- number of classes, or
- number of trainable parameters in the model.

Such rules of thumb often work, but they are different for different problem domains. Each analyst adjusts the numbers based on experience. While you would discover by experience those "magical" scaling factors that work for you, the most frequently cited numbers in various online sources are:

- 10 times the amount of features (this often exaggerates the size of the training set, but works well as an upper bound),
- 100 or 1000 times the number of classes (this often underestimates the size), or
- ten times the number of trainable parameters (usually applied to neural networks).

Keep in mind that just because you have big data does not mean that you should use all of it. A smaller sample of big data can give good results in practice and accelerate the search for a better model. It's important to ensure, though, that the sample is representative of the whole big dataset. Sampling strategies such as **stratified** and **systematic sampling** can lead to better results. We consider data sampling strategies in Section 3.10.

3.1.3   Is the Data Useable?

The data quality is one of the major factors affecting the model performance. Imagine that you want to train a model that predicts a person's gender, given their name. You might acquire a dataset of people that contains gender information. However, if you use this dataset blindly, you might realize that no matter how hard you try to improve the quality of your model, its performance on new data is low. What is the reason for such a weak performance?

The answer could be that the gender information was not factual but obtained using a rather low-quality statistical classifier. In this case, the best you can achieve with your model is the performance of that low-quality classifier.

If the dataset comes in the form of a spreadsheet, the first thing to check is if the data in the spreadsheet is tidy. As discussed in the introduction, the dataset used for machine learning must be tidy. If it's not the case for your data, you must transform it into tidy data using, as already mentioned, feature engineering.

A tidy dataset can have **missing values**. Consider **data imputation** techniques to fill the missing values. We will discuss several such techniques in Section 3.7.

One frequent problem with datasets compiled by a human is that people can decide to indicate missing values with some **magic number** like 9999 or −1. Such situations must be spotted during the visual analysis of the data, and those magic numbers have to be replaced using an appropriate data imputation technique.

Another property to validate is whether the dataset contains **duplicates**. Usually, duplicates are removed, unless you added them on purpose to balance an **imbalanced problem**. We consider this problem and methods to alleviate it in Section 3.9.

Data can be **expired** or be significantly not up to date. For example, let your goal be to train a model that recognizes abnormality in the behavior of a complex piece of electronic appliance, such as a printer. You have measurements taken during the normal and abnormal functioning of a printer. However, these measurements have been recorded for a previous generation of printers, while the new generation has received several significant upgrades since then. The model trained using such expired data from an older printer generation might perform worse when deployed on the new generation of printers.

Finally, data can be **incomplete** or **unrepresentative** of the phenomenon. For example, a dataset of animal photos might contain pictures taken only during the summer or in a specific geography. A dataset of pedestrians for self-driving car systems might be created with engineers posing as pedestrians; in such a dataset, most situations would include only younger men, while children, women, and the elderly would be underrepresented or entirely absent.

A company working on facial expression recognition might have the research and development office in a predominantly white location, so the dataset would only show faces of white men and women, while black or Asian people would be underrepresented. Engineers developing a posture recognition model for a camera might build the training dataset by taking pictures of people indoors, while the customers would typically use the camera outdoors.

In practice, data can only become useable for modeling after preprocessing; hence the importance of visual analysis of the dataset before you start modeling. Let's say you work on a problem of predicting the topic in news articles. It's likely you will scrape your data from news websites. It's also likely that download dates would be saved in the same document as the news article text. Imagine also that the data engineer decides to loop over news topics mentioned on the websites and scrape one topic at a time. So, on Monday the arts-related articles were scraped, on Tuesday — sports, on Wednesday — technology, and so on.

If you don't preprocess such data by removing the dates, the model can learn the date-topic correlation, and such a model will be of no practical use.

3.1.4   Is the Data Understandable?

As demonstrated in gender prediction, it's crucial to understand from where each attribute in the dataset came. It is equally important to understand what each attribute exactly represents. One frequent problem observed in practice is when the variable that the analyst tries to predict is found among the features in the feature vector. How could that happen?

Imagine that you work on the problem of predicting the price of a house from its attributes such as the number of bedrooms, surface, location, year of construction, and so on. The attributes of each house were provided to you by the client, a large online real estate sales platform. The data has the form of an Excel spreadsheet. Without spending too much time analyzing each column, you remove only the transaction price from the attributes and use that value as the target you want to learn to predict. Very quickly you realize that the model is almost perfect: it predicts the transaction price with accuracy near 100%. You deliver the model to the client, they deploy it in production, and the tests show that the model is wrong most of the time. What happened?

What did happen is called **data leakage** (also known as **target leakage**). After a more careful examination of the dataset, you realize that one of the columns in the spreadsheet contained the real estate agent's commission. Of course, the model easily learned to convert this attribute into the house price perfectly. However, this information is not available in the production environment before the house is sold, because the commission depends on the selling price. In Section 3.2.8, we will consider the problem of data leakage in more detail.

3.1.5   Is the Data Reliable?

The reliability of a dataset varies depending on the procedure used to gather that dataset. Can you trust the labels? If the data was produced by the workers on Mechanical Turk (so-called "turkers"), then the reliability of such data might be very low. In some cases, the labels assigned to feature vectors might be obtained as a majority vote (or an average) of several turkers. If that's the case, the data can be considered more reliable. However, it's better to do additional validation of quality on a small random sample of the dataset.

On the other hand, if the data represents measurements made by some measuring devices, you can find the details of each measurement's accuracy in the technical documentation of the corresponding measuring device.

The reliability of labels can also be affected by the **delayed** or **indirect** nature of the label. The label is considered delayed when the feature vector to which the label was assigned represents something that happened significantly earlier than the time of label observation.

To be more concrete, take the **churn prediction** problem. Here, we have a feature vector describing a customer, and we want to predict whether the customer will leave at some point in the future (typically six months to one year from now). The feature vector represents what we know about the customer now, but the label ("left" or "stayed") will be assigned in the future. This is an important property, because between now and the future, many events, not reflected in our feature vector might happen which would affect the customer's decision to stay or leave. Therefore delayed labels make our data less reliable.

Whether a label is direct or indirect also affects reliability, depending, of course, on what we are trying to predict. For example, let's say our goal is to predict whether the website visitor will be interested in a webpage. We might acquire a certain dataset containing information about users, webpages, and labels "interested"/"not_interested" reflecting whether a specific user was interested in a particular webpage. A direct label would indeed indicate interest, while an indirect label could suggest <u>some</u> interest. For example, if the user pressed the "Like" button, we have the direct indicator of interest. However, if the user only clicked on the link, this could be an indicator of some interest, but it's an indirect indicator. The user could have clicked by mistake, or because the link text was a clickbait, we cannot know for sure. If the label is indirect, this also makes such data less reliable. Of course, it's less reliable for predicting the interest, but can be perfectly reliable for predicting clicks.

Another source of unreliability in the data is feedback loops. A **feedback loop** is a property in the system design when the data used to train the model is obtained using the model itself. Again, imagine that you work on a problem of predicting whether a specific user of a website will like the content, and you only have indirect labels – clicks. If the model is already deployed on the website and the users click on links recommended by the model, this means that the new data indirectly reflects not only the interest of users to the content, but also how intensively the model recommended that content. If the model decided that a specific link is important enough to recommend to many users, more users would likely click on that link, especially if the recommendation was made repeatedly during several days or weeks.

3.2 Common Problems With Data

As we have just seen, the data you will work with can have problems. In this section, we cite the most important of these problems and what you can do to alleviate them.

3.2.1 High Cost

Getting unlabeled data can be expensive; however, labeling data is the most expensive work, especially if the work is done manually.

Getting unlabeled data becomes expensive when it nust be gathered specifically for your problem. Let's say your goal is to know where different types of commerce are located in a city. The best solution would be to buy this data from a government agency. However, for various reasons it can be complicated or even impossible: the government database may be incomplete or outdated. To get up-to-date data, you may decide to send cars equipped with cameras on the streets of a given city. They would take pictures of all buildings on the streets.

| Original photo | Labeled photo |

Figure 3.3: The unlabeled and labeled aerial photo. Photo credit: Tom Fisk.

As you might imagine, such an enterprise is not cheap. Collecting pictures of the buildings is not enough. We need the type of commerce in every building. Now we need labeled data: "coffee house," "bank," "grocery," "drug store," "gas station," etc. These must be assigned manually, and paying someone to do that work is expensive. By the way, Google has a clever technique outsourcing the labeling to random people with its free reCAPTCHA service. reCAPTCHA thus solves two problems: reducing spam on the Web and providing cheap labeled data to Google.

In Figure 3.3, you can see the work needed to label one image. The goal here is to segment a picture by assigning labels to every pixel from the following: "heavy truck," "car or light truck," "boat," "building," "container," "other." Labeling image in Figure 3.3 took me about 30 minutes. If there were more types, for example "motorcycle," "tree," "road," it would take longer, and the labeling cost would be higher.

Well-designed labeling tools will minimize mouse use (including menus activated by mouse clicks), maximize hotkeys, and reduce costs by increasing the speed of data labeling.

Whenever possible, reduce decision-making to a yes/no answer. Instead of asking "Find all prices in this text", extract all numbers from the text and then display each number, one by one, asking, "Is this number a price?" as shown in 3.4. If the labeler clicks "Not Sure," you can save this example to analyze later or simply not use such examples for training the model.

Another trick allowing for accelerated labeling is **noisy pre-labeling** consisting of pre-labeling the example using the current best model. In this scenario, you start by labeling a certain quantity of examples "from scratch" (that is, without using any support). Then you build the first model that works reasonably well, using this initial set of labeled examples. Next, use the current model and label each new example in place of the human labeler.[3] Ask whether the

---

[3]This is why it's called a "noisy" pre-labeling: the labels assigned to examples using a sub-optimal model would

automatically assigned label is correct. If the labeler clicks "Yes," save this example as usual. If they click "No," then ask to label this example manually. See the workflow chart illustrating this process in Figure 3.5. The goal of a good labeling process design is to make the labeling as streamlined as possible. Keeping the labeler engaged is also key. Show progress in the number of labels added, as well as the quality of the current best model. This engages the labeler and adds purpose to the labeling task.

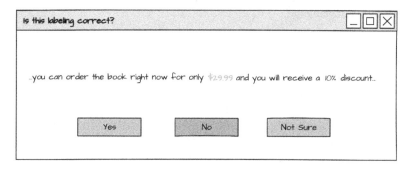

Figure 3.4: An example of simple labeling interface.

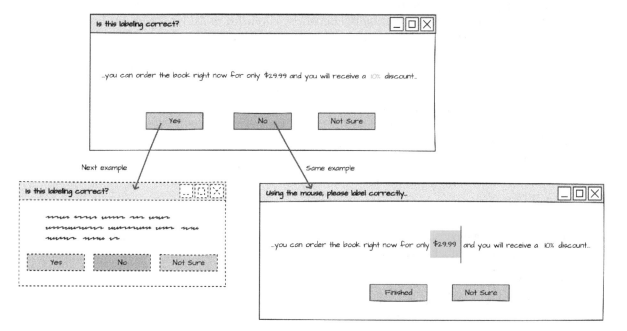

Figure 3.5: An example of noisy pre-labeling workflow.

---

not all be accurate and require a human validation.

3.2.2 Bad Quality

Remember that data quality is one of the major factors affecting the performance of the model. I cannot stress it strongly enough.

Data quality has two components: raw data quality and labeling quality.

Some common problems with raw data are noise, bias, low predictive power, outdated examples, outliers, and leakage.

3.2.3 Noise

Noise in data is a corruption of examples. Images can be blurry or incomplete. Text can lose formatting, which makes some words concatenated or split. Audio data can have noise in the background. Poll answers can be incomplete or have missing attributes, such as the responder's age or gender. Noise is often a random process that corrupts each example independently of other examples in the collection.

If tidy data has missing attributes, **data imputation** techniques can help in guessing values for those attributes. We will consider data imputation techniques in Section 3.7.1.

Blurred images can be deblurred using specific image deblurring algorithms, though deep machine learning models, such as neural networks, can learn to deblur if needed. The same can be said about noise in audio data: it can be algorithmically suppressed.

Noise is more a problem when the dataset is relatively small (thousands of examples or less), because the presence of noise can lead to **overfitting**: the algorithm may learn to model the noise contained in the training data, which is undesirable. In the big data context, on the other hand, noise, if it's randomly applied to each example independently of other examples in the dataset, is typically "averaged out" over multiple examples. In that latter context, noise can bring a regularization effect as it prevents the learning algorithm from relying too much on a small subset of input features.[4]

3.2.4 Bias

Bias in data is an inconsistency with the phenomenon that data represents. This inconsistency may occur for a number of reasons (which are not mutually exclusive).

Types of Bias

Selection bias is the tendency to skew your choice of data sources to those that are easily available, convenient, and/or cost-effective. For example, you might want to know the opinion of the readers on your new book. You decide to send several initial chapters to the

---

[4]This is, by the way, the rationale behind the increase in performance brought by the **dropout** regularization technique in **deep learning**.

mailing list of your previous book's readers. It's very likely this select group will like your new book. However, this information doesn't tell you much about a general reader.

A real-life example of selection bias is an image generated by the Photo Upsampling via Latent Space Exploration (**PULSE**) algorithm that uses a neural network model to upscale (increase the resolution) of images. When Internet users tested it, they discovered that an upscaled image of a black person could, in some cases, represent a white person, as illustrated by Barack Obama's upscaled photo shown in Figure 3.6.

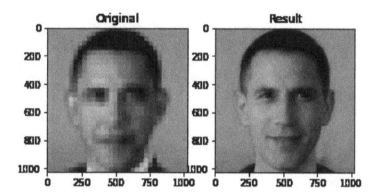

Figure 3.6: An illustration of the effect the selection bias can have on the trained model. Image: Twitter / @Chicken3gg.

The above example shows that it cannot be assumed that machine learning model is correct, simply because machine learning algorithms are impartial and the trained models are based on data. If the data has a bias, it will most likely be reflected in the model.

Self-selection bias is a form of selection bias where you get the data from sources that "volunteered" to provide it. Most poll data has this type of bias. For example, you want to train a model that predicts the behavior of successful entrepreneurs. You decide to first ask entrepreneurs whether they are successful or not. Then you only keep the data obtained from those who declared themselves successful. The problem here is that most likely, really successful entrepreneurs don't have time to answer your questions, while those who claim themselves successful can be wrong on that matter.

Here's another example. Let's say, you want to train a model that predicts whether a book will be liked by the readers. You can use the rating users gave to similar books in the past. However, it turns out that unhappy users tend to provide disproportionally low ratings. The data will be biased towards too many very low ratings as compared to the quantity of mid-range ratings, as shown in Figure 3.7. The bias is compounded by the fact that we tend to rate only when the experience was either very good or very bad.

Customer reviews

 4 out of 5 ⌄

617 customer ratings

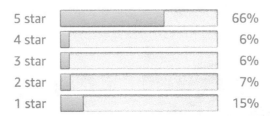

5 star	66%
4 star	6%
3 star	6%
2 star	7%
1 star	15%

Figure 3.7: The distribution of ratings given by the readers to a popular AI book on Amazon.

Omitted variable bias happens when your featurized data doesn't have a feature necessary for accurate prediction. For example, let's assume that you are working on a churn prediction model and you want to predict whether a customer cancels their subscription within six months. You train a model, and it's accurate enough; however, several weeks after deployment you see many unexpected false negatives. You investigate the decreased model performance and discover a new competitor now offers a very similar service for a lower price. This feature wasn't initially available to your model, therefore important information for accurate prediction was missing.

Sponsorship or **funding bias** affects the data produced by a sponsored agency. For example, let a famous video game company sponsor a news agency to provide news about the video game industry. If you try to make a prediction about the video game industry, you might include in your data the story produced by this sponsored agency.

However, sponsored news agencies tend to suppress bad news about their sponsor and exaggerate their achievements. As a result, the model's performance will be suboptimal.

Sampling bias (also known as **distribution shift**) occurs when the distribution of examples used for training doesn't reflect the distribution of the inputs the model will receive in production. This type of bias is frequently observed in practice. For example, you are working on a system that classifies documents according to a taxonomy of several hundred topics. You might decide to create a collection of documents in which an equal amount of documents represents each topic. Once you finish the work on the model, you observe 5% error. Soon after deployment, you see the wrong assignment to about 30% of documents. Why did this happen?

One of the possible reasons is sampling bias: one or two frequent topics in production data might account for 80% of all input. If your model doesn't perform well for these frequent topics, then your system will make more errors in production than you initially expected.

Prejudice or **stereotype bias** is often observed in data obtained from historical sources, such as books or photo archives, or from online activity such as social media, online forums, and comments to online publications.

Using a photo archive to train a model that distinguishes men from women might show, for example, men more frequently in work or outdoor contexts, and women more often at home indoors. If we use such biased data, our model will have more difficulty recognizing a woman outdoors or a man at home.

A famous example of this type of bias is looking for associations for words using **word embeddings** trained with an algorithm like **word2vec**. The model predicts that king − man + woman ≈ queen, but at the same time, that programmer − man + woman ≈ homemaker.

Systematic value distortion is bias usually occurring with the device making measurements or observations. This results in a machine learning model making suboptimal predictions when deployed in the production environment.

For example, the training data is gathered using a camera with a white balance which makes white look yellowish. In production, however, engineers decide to use a higher-quality camera which "sees" white as white. Because your model was trained on lower-quality pictures, the predictions using higher-quality input will be suboptimal.

This should not be confused with noisy data. Noise is the result of a random process that distorts the data. When you have a sufficiently large dataset, noise becomes less of a problem because it might average out. On the other hand, if the measurements are consistently skewed in one direction, then it damages training data, and ultimately results in a poor-quality model.

Experimenter bias is the tendency to search for, interpret, favor, or recall information in a way that affirms one's prior beliefs or hypotheses. Applied to machine learning, experimenter bias often occurs when each example in the dataset is obtained from the answers to a survey given by a particular person, one example per person.

Usually, each survey contains multiple questions. The form of those questions can significantly affect the responses. The simplest way for a question to affect the response is to provide limited response options: "Which kind of pizza do you like: pepperoni, all meats, or vegetarian?" This doesn't leave the choice of giving a different answer, or even "Other."

Alternatively, a survey question might be constructed with a built-in slant. Instead of asking, "Do you recycle?" an analyst with a experimenter bias might ask, "Do you dodge from recycling?" In the former case, the respondent is more likely to give an honest answer, compared to the latter.

Furthermore, experimenter bias might happen when the analyst is briefed in advance to support a particular conclusion (for example, the one in favor of doing "business as usual"). In that situation, they can exclude specific variables from the analysis as unreliable or noisy.

Labeling bias happens when labels are assigned to unlabeled examples by a biased process or person. For example, if you ask several labelers to assign a topic to a document by reading the document, some labelers can indeed read the document entirely and assign well-thought labels. In contrast, others could just try to quickly "scan" the text, spot some keyphrases and choose the topic that corresponds the best to the selected keyphrases. Because each person's brain pays more attention to keyphrases from a specific domain or domains and less to others, the labels assigned by labelers who scan the text without reading will be biased.

Alternatively, some labelers would be more interested in reading documents on some topics that they personally prefer. If it's the case, a labeler might skip uninteresting documents, and the latter will be underrepresented in your data.

Ways to Avoid Bias

It is usually impossible to know exactly what biases are present in a dataset. Furthermore, even knowing there are biases, avoiding them is a challenging task. First of all, be prepared.

A good habit is to question everything: who created the data, what were their motivations and quality criteria, and more importantly, how and why the data was created. If the data is a result of some research, question the research method and make sure that it doesn't contribute to any of the biases described above.

Selection bias can be avoided by systematically questioning the reason why a specific data source was chosen. If the reason is simplicity or low cost, then pay careful attention. Recall the example whether a specific customer would subscribe to your new offering. Training the model using only the data about your current customers is likely a bad idea, because your existing customers are more loyal to your brand than a random potential customer. Your estimates of model's quality will be overly optimistic.

Self-selection bias cannot be completely eliminated. It usually appears in surveys; the mere consent of the responder to answer the questions represents self-selection bias. The longer the survey, the less likely the respondent will answer with a high degree of attention. Therefore, keep your survey short and provide an incentive to give quality answers.

Pre-select responders to reduce self-selection. Don't ask entrepreneurs whether they consider themselves successful. Rather, build a list based on references from experts or publications, and only contact those individuals.

It's tough to avoid the **omitted variable bias** completely, because, as they say, "we don't know what we don't know." One approach is to use all available information, that is, to include in your feature vector as many features as possible, even those you deem unnecessary. This could make your feature vector very wide (i.e., of many dimensions) and sparse (i.e., when the values in most dimensions are zero). Still, if you use a well-tuned regularization, your model will "decide" which features are important, and which ones aren't.

Alternatively, let us suspect that a particular variable would be important for accurate predictions, and leaving it out of our model could result in an omitted variable bias. Suppose getting that data is problematic. Try using a proxy variable in lieu of the omitted variable. For instance, if we want to train a model that predicts the price of a used car, and we cannot get the car's age, use, instead, the length of ownership by its current owner. The amount of time the current owner owned the car can be taken as a proxy for the age of the vehicle.

Sponsorship bias can be reduced by carefully investigating the data source, specifically the source owner's incentive to provide the data. For example, it's known that publications on tobacco and pharmaceutical drugs are very often sponsored by tobacco and pharmaceutical companies, or their opponents. The same can be said about news companies, especially those that depend on the advertisement revenue or have an undisclosed business model.

Sampling bias can be avoided by researching the real proportion of various properties in the data that will be observed in production, and then sampling the training data by keeping similar proportions.

Prejudice or **stereotype bias** can be controlled. When developing the training model to distinguish pictures of women from men, a data analyst could choose to under-sample the number of women indoors, or oversample the number of men at home. In other words, prejudice or stereotype bias is reduced by exposing the learning algorithm to a more even-handed distribution of examples.

Systematic value distortion bias can be alleviated by having multiple measuring devices, or hiring humans trained to compare the output of measuring or observing devices.

Experimenter bias can be avoided by letting multiple people validate the questions asked in the survey. Ask yourself: "Do I feel uncomfortable or constrained answering this question?"

Furthermore, despite more difficulties in analysis, opt for open-ended questions rather than yes/no or multiple-choice questions. If you still prefer to give responders a choice of answers, include the option "Other" and a place to write a different answer.

Labeling bias can be avoided by asking several labelers to identify the same example. Ask the labelers why they decided to assign a specific label to examples that produced different results. If you see that some labelers refer to certain keyphrases, rather than trying to paraphrase the entire document, you can identify those who are quickly scanning instead of reading.

You can also compare the frequency of skipped documents for different labelers. If you see that a labeler skips documents more often than the average, ask if they encountered technical problems, or simply were not interested in some topics.

You cannot entirely avoid bias in data. There's no silver bullet. As a general rule, keep a human in the loop, especially if your model affects people's lives.

Recall that there is a temptation among the data analysts to assume that machine learning models are inherently fair because they make decisions based on evidence and math, as opposed to often messy or irrational human judgments. This is, unfortunately, not always the case: inevitably, a model trained on biased data will produce biased results.

It is the duty of people training the model to ensure that the output is fair. But what's fair, you may ask? Unfortunately, again, there is no silver bullet measurement that would always detect unfairness. Choosing an appropriate definition of model fairness is always problem-specific and requires human judgment. In Section 7.6 of Chapter 7, we consider several definitions of **fairness** in machine learning.

Human involvement in all stages of data gathering and preparation is the best approach to make sure that the possible damage caused by machine learning is minimized.

3.2.5   Low Predictive Power

Low predictive power is an issue that you often don't consider until you have spent fruitless energy trying to train a good model. Does the model underperform because it is not expressive enough? Does the data not contain enough information from which to learn? You don't know.

Suppose the goal is to predict whether a listener will like a new song on a music streaming service. Your data is the name of the artist, the song title, lyrics, and whether that song is in their playlist. The model you train with this data will be far from perfect.

Artists who are not in the listener's playlist are unlikely to receive a high score from the model. Furthermore, many users will only add some songs of a specific artist to their playlist. Their musical preferences are significantly influenced by the song arrangement, choice of instruments, sound effects, tone of voice, and subtle changes in tonality, rhythm, and beat. These are properties of songs that cannot be found in lyrics, title, or the artist's name; they have to be extracted from the sound file.

On the other hand, extracting these relevant features from an audio file is challenging. Even with modern neural networks, recommending songs based on how they sound is considered a hard task for artificial intelligence. Typically, song recommendations are developed by comparing playlists of different listeners and finding those with similar compositions.

Consider a different example of low predictive power. Let's say we want to train a model that will predict where to point the telescope and observe something interesting. Our data are photos of various regions of the sky where something unusual was captured in the past. Based on these photos alone, it's very unlikely that we will be able to train a model that accurately predicts such an event. However, if we add to this data the measurements of various sensors, such as those measuring radiofrequency signals from different zones, or particle bursts, it is more likely we will be able to make better predictions.

Your work may be especially challenging the first time working with the dataset. If you cannot obtain acceptable results, no matter how complex the model becomes, it may be time to consider the problem of low predictive power. Engineer as many additional features as possible (apply your creativity!). Consider indirect data sources to enrich feature vectors.

3.2.6   Outdated Examples

Once you build the model and deploy it in production, the model usually performs well for some time. This period depends entirely on the phenomenon you are modeling.

Typically, as we will discuss in Section 9.4 of Chapter 9, a certain model quality monitoring procedure is deployed in the production environment. Once an erratic behavior is detected, new training data is added to adjust the model; the model is then retrained and redeployed.

Often, the cause of an error is explained by the finiteness of the training set. In such cases, additional training examples will solidify the model. However, in many practical scenarios, the model starts to make errors because of **concept drift**. Concept drift is a fundamental change in the statistical relationship between the features and the label.

Imagine your model predicts whether a user will like certain content on a website. Over time, the preferences of some users may start to change, perhaps due to aging, or because a user discovers something new (I didn't listen to jazz three years ago, now I do!). The examples added to the training data in the past no longer reflect some user's preferences and start hurting the model performance, rather than contributing to it. This is concept drift. Consider it if you see a decreasing trend in model performance on new data.

Correct the model by removing the outdated examples from the training data. Sort your training examples, most recent first. Define an additional hyperparameter — what percentage of the most recent examples to use to retrain the model — and tune it using **grid search**, or another hyperparameter tuning technique.

Concept drift is an example of a broader problem known as **distribution shift**. We consider hyperparameter tuning and other types of distribution shift in Sections 5.6 and 6.3.

3.2.7 Outliers

Outliers are examples that look dissimilar to the majority of examples from the dataset. It's up to the data analyst to define "dissimilar." Typically, dissimilarity is measured by some distance metric, such as **Euclidean distance**.

In practice, however, what seems to be an outlier in the original feature vector space can be a typical example in a feature vector space transformed using tools such as a **kernel function**. Feature space transformation is often explicitly done by a kernel-based model, such as **support vector machine** (SVM), or implicitly by a deep neural network.

Shallow algorithms, such as linear or logistic regression, and some ensemble methods, such as AdaBoost, are particularly sensitive to outliers. SVM has one definition that is less sensitive to outliers: a special penalty hyperparameter regulates the influence of misclassified examples (which often happen to be outliers) on the **decision boundary**. If this penalty value is low, the SVM algorithm may completely ignore outliers from consideration when drawing the decision boundary (an imaginary hyperplane separating positive and negative examples). If it's too low, even some regular examples can end up on the wrong side of the decision boundary. The best value for that hyperparameter should be found by the analyst using a hyperparameter tuning technique.

A sufficiently complex neural network can learn to behave differently for each outlier in the dataset and, at the same time, still work well for the regular examples. It's not the desired outcome, as the model becomes unnecessarily complex for the task. More complexity results in longer training and prediction time, and poorer generalization after production deployment.

Whether to exclude outliers from the training data, or to use machine learning algorithms and models robust to outliers, is debatable. Deleting examples from a dataset is not considered scientifically or methodologically sound, especially in small datasets. In the big data context, on the other hand, outliers don't typically have a significant influence on the model.

From a practical standpoint, if excluding some training examples results in better performance of the model on the holdout data, the exclusion may be justified. Which examples to consider for exclusion can be decided based on a certain similarity measure. A modern approach to getting such a measure is to build an **autoencoder** and use the reconstruction error[5] as the measure of (dis)similarity: the higher the reconstruction error for a given example, the more dissimilar it is to the dataset.

3.2.8   Data Leakage

Data leakage, also called **target leakage**, is a problem affecting several stages of the machine learning life cycle, from data collection to model evaluation. In this section, I will only describe how this problem manifests itself at the data collection and preparation stages. In the subsequent chapters, I will describe its other forms.

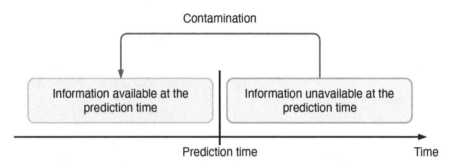

Figure 3.8: Data leakage in a nutshell.

Data leakage in supervised learning is the unintentional introduction of information about the target that should not be made available. We call it "contamination" (Figure 3.8). Training on contaminated data leads to overly optimistic expectations about the model performance.

3.3   What Is Good Data

We already considered questions to answer about the data before to start collecting it and the common problems with the data an analyst might encounter. But what constitutes good data

---

[5]An autoencoder model is trained to reconstruct its input from an **embedding** vector. The hyperparameters of the autoencoder are tuned to minimize the reconstruction error of the holdout data.

for a machine learning project? Below we take a look at several properties of good data.

3.3.1   Good Data Is Informative

Good data contains enough information that can be used for modeling. For example, if you want to train a model that predicts whether the customer will buy a specific product, you will need to possess both the properties of the product in question and the properties of the products customers purchased in the past. If you only have the properties of the product and a customer's location and name, then the predictions will be the same for all users from the same location.

If you have enough training examples, then the model can potentially derive the gender and ethnicity from the name and make different predictions for men, women, locations, and ethnicities, but not to each customer individually.

3.3.2   Good Data Has Good Coverage

Good data has good coverage of what you want to do with the model. For example, if you're going to use the model to classify web pages by topic and you have a thousand topics of interest, then your data has to contain examples of documents on each of the thousand topics in quantity sufficient for the algorithm to be able to learn the difference between topics.

Imagine a different situation. Let's say that for a particular topic, you only have one or a couple of documents. Let each document contain a unique ID in the text. In such a scenario, the learning algorithm will not be sure what it must look at in each document to understand to which topic it belongs. Maybe the IDs? They look like good differentiators. If the algorithm decides to use IDs to separate these couple examples from the rest of the dataset, then the learned model will not be able to generalize: it will not see any of those IDs ever again.

3.3.3   Good Data Reflects Real Inputs

Good data reflects real inputs that the model will see in production. For example, if you build a system that recognizes cars on the road and all pictures you have were taken during the working hours, then it's unlikely that you will have many examples of night pictures. Once you deploy the model in production, pictures will start coming from all times of the day, and your model will more frequently make errors on night pictures. Also, remember the problem of a cat, a dog, and a raccoon: if your model doesn't know anything about raccoons, it will predict their pictures as either dogs or cats.

3.3.4 Good Data Is Unbiased

Good data is as unbiased as possible. This property can look similar to the previous one. Still, bias can be present in both the data you use for training and the data that the model is applied to in the production environment.

We discussed several sources of bias in data and how to deal with it in Section 3.2. A user interface can also be a source of bias. For example, you want to predict the popularity of a news article, and use the click rate as a feature. If some news article was displayed on the top of the page, the number of clicks it got would often be higher compared to another news article displayed on the bottom, even if the latter is more engaging.

3.3.5 Good Data Is Not a Result of a Feedback Loop

Good data is not a result of the model itself. This echoes the problem of the **feedback loop** discussed above. For example, you cannot train a model that predicts the gender of a person from their name, and then use the prediction to label a new training example.

Alternatively, if you use the model to decide which email messages are important to the user and highlight those important messages, you should not directly take the clicks on those emails as a signal that the email is important. The user might have clicked on them because the model highlighted them.

3.3.6 Good Data Has Consistent Labels

Good data has consistent labels. Inconsistency in labeling can come from several sources:

- Different people do labeling according to different criteria. Even if people believe that they use the same criteria, different people often interpret the same criteria differently.[6]
- The definition of some classes evolved over time. This results in a situation when two very similar feature vectors receive two different labels.
- Misinterpretation of user's motives. For example, assume that the user ignored a recommended news article. As a consequence, this news article receives a negative label. However, the motive of the user for ignoring this recommendation might be that they already knew the story and not that they are uninterested in the topic of the story.

3.3.7 Good Data Is Big Enough

Good data is big enough to allow generalization. Sometimes, nothing can be done to increase the accuracy of the model. No matter how much data you throw on the learning algorithm:

---

[6]Recall the example of Mechanical Turk we considered in Section 3.1. To improve the reliability of labels assigned by different people, one can use a majority vote (or an average) of several labelers.

the information contained in the data has low predictive power for your problem. However, more often, you can get a very accurate model if you pass from thousands of examples to millions or hundreds of millions. You cannot know how much data you need before you start working on your problem and see the progress.

3.3.8 Summary of Good Data

For the convenience of future reference, let me once again repeat the properties of good data:

- it contains enough information that can be used for modeling,
- it has good coverage of what you want to do with the model,
- it reflects real inputs that the model will see in production,
- it is as unbiased as possible,
- it is not a result of the model itself,
- it has consistent labels, and
- it is big enough to allow generalization.

3.4 Dealing With Interaction Data

Interaction data is the data you can collect from user interactions with the system your model supports. You are considered lucky if you can gather good data from interactions of the user with the system.

Good interaction data contains information on three aspects:

- context of interaction,
- action of the user in that context, and
- outcome of interaction.

As an example, assume that you build a search engine, and your model reranks search results for each user individually. A reranking model takes as input the list of links returned by the search engine, based on keywords provided by the user and outputs another list in which the items change order. Usually, a reranked model "knows" something about the user and their preferences and can reorder the generic search results for each user individually according to that user's learned preferences. The context here is the search query and the hundred documents presented to the user in a specific order. The action is a click of the user on a particular document link. The outcome is how much time the user spent reading the document and whether the user hit "back." Another action is the click on the "next page" link.

The intuition is that the ranking was good if the user clicked on some link and spent significant time reading the page. The ranking was not so good if the user clicked on a link to a result and then hit "back" quickly. The ranking was bad if the user clicked on the "next page" link. This data can be used to improve the ranking algorithm and make it more personalized.

Country	Population	Region	...	GDP per capita	GDP
France	67M	Europe	...	38,800	2.6T
Germany	83M	Europe	...	44,578	3.7T
...	...	...	...	...	...
China	1386M	Asia	...	8,802	12.2T

Figure 3.9: An example of the target (GDP) being a simple function of two features: Population and GDP per capita.

3.5   Causes of Data Leakage

Let's discuss the three most frequent causes of **data leakage** that can happen during data collection and preparation: 1) target being a function of a feature, 2) feature hiding the target, and 3) feature coming from the future.

3.5.1   Target is a Function of a Feature

Gross Domestic Product (GDP) is defined as the monetary measure of all finished goods and services in a country within a specific period. Let our goal be to predict a country's GDP based on various attributes: area, population, geographic region, and so on. An example of such data is shown in Figure 3.9. If you don't do a careful analysis of each attribute and its relation to GDP, you might let a leakage happen: in the data in Figure 3.9, two columns, Population and GDP per capita, multiplied, equal GDP. The model you will train will perfectly predict GDP by looking at these two columns only. The fact that you let GDP be one of the features, though in a slightly modified form (devised by the population), constitutes contamination and, therefore, leads to data leakage.

A simpler example is when you have a copy of the target among features, just put in a different format. Imagine you train a model to predict the yearly salary, given the attributes of an employee. The training data is a table that contains both monthly and yearly salary, among many other attributes. If you forget to remove the monthly salary from the list of features, that attribute alone will perfectly predict the yearly salary, making you believe your model is perfect. Once the model is put in production, it will likely stop receiving information about a person's monthly salary: otherwise, the modeling would not be needed.

Customer ID	Group	Yearly Spendings	Yearly Pageviews	...	Gender
1	M18-25	1350	11,987	...	M
2	F25-35	2365	8,543	...	F
...	...	...	...	...	...
18879	F65+	3653	6,775	...	F

Figure 3.10: An example of the target being hidden in one of the features.

3.5.2   Feature Hides the Target

Sometimes the target is not a function of one or more features, but rather is "hidden" in one of the features. Consider the dataset in Figure 3.10.

In this scenario, you use customer data to predict their gender. Look at the column Group. If you closely investigate the data in the column Group, you will see that it represents a demographic value to which each existing customer was related in the past. If the data about a customer's gender and age is factual (as opposed to being guessed by another model that might be available in production), then the column Group constitutes a form of data leakage, when the value you want to predict is "hidden" in the value of a feature.

On the other hand, if the Group values are predictions provided by another, possibly less accurate model, then you can use this attribute to build a potentially stronger model. This is called **model stacking**, and we will consider this topic in Section 6.2 in Chapter 6.

3.5.3   Feature From the Future

Feature from the future is a kind of data leakage that is hard to catch if you don't have a clear understanding of the business goal. Imagine a client asked you to train a model that predicts whether a borrower will pay back the loan, based on attributes such as age, gender, education, salary, marital status, and so on. An example of such data is shown in Figure 3.11.

If you don't make an effort to understand the business context in which your model will be used, you might decide to use all available attributes to predict the value in the column Will Pay Loan, including the data from the column Late Payment Reminders. Your model will look accurate at testing time and you send it to the client, who will later report that the model doesn't work well in the production environment.

After investigation, you find out that, in the production environment, the value of Late Payment Reminders is always zero. This makes sense because the client uses your model <u>before</u> the borrower gets the credit, so no reminders have yet been made! However, your

Borrower ID	Demographic Group	Education	...	Late Payment Reminders	Will Pay Loan
1	M35-50	High school	...	0	Y
2	F25-35	Master's	...	1	N
...	...	...	...	...	...
65723	M25-35	Master's	...	3	N

Figure 3.11: A feature unavailable at the prediction time: Late Payment Reminders.

model most likely learned to make the "No" prediction when Late Payment Reminders is 1 or more and pays less attention to the other features.

Here is another example. Let's say you have a news website and you want to predict the ranking of news you serve to the user, so as to maximize the number of clicks on stories. If in your training data, you have positional features for each news item served in the past (e.g., the $x - y$ position of the title, and the abstract block on the webpage), such information will not be available on the serving time, because you don't know the positions of articles on the page before you rank them.

Understanding the business context in which the model will be used is, thus, crucial to avoid data leakage.

3.6 Data Partitioning

As discussed in Section 1.3.3 of the first chapter, in practical machine learning, we typically use three disjoint sets of examples: training set, validation set, and test set.

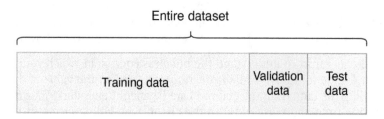

Figure 3.12: The entire dataset partitioned into a training, validation and test sets.

The **training set** is used by the machine learning algorithm to train the model.

The **validation set** is needed to find the best values for the hyperparameters of the machine learning pipeline. The analyst tries different combinations of hyperparameter values one by one, trains a model by using each combination, and notes the model performance on the validation set. The hyperparameters that maximize the model performance are then used to train the model for production. We consider techniques of hyperparameter tuning in more detail in Section 5.6 of Chapter 5.

The **test set** is used for reporting: once you have your best model, you test its performance on the test set and report the results.

Validation and test sets are often referred to as **holdout sets**: they contain the examples that the learning algorithm is not allowed to see.

To obtain good partitions of your entire dataset into these three disjoint sets, as schematically illustrated in Figure 3.12, partitioning has to satisfy several conditions.

Condition 1: Split was applied to raw data.
Once you have access to raw examples, and before everything else, do the split. This will allow avoiding data leakage, as we will see later.

Condition 2: Data was randomized before the split.
Randomly shuffle your examples first, then do the split.

Condition 3: Validation and test sets follow the same distribution.
When you select the best values of hyperparameters using the validation set, you want that this selection yields a model that works well in production. The examples in the test set are your best representatives of the production data. Hence the need for the validation and test sets to follow the same distribution.

Condition 4: Leakage during the split was avoided.
Data leakage can happen even during the data partitioning. Below, we will see what forms of leakage can happen at that stage.

There is no ideal ratio for the split. In older literature (pre-big data), you might find the recommended splits of either 70%/15%/15% or 80%/10%/10% (for training, validation, and test sets, respectively, in proportion to the entire dataset).

Today, in the era of the Internet and cheap labor (e.g., Mechanical Turk or crowdsourcing), organizations, scientists, and even enthusiasts at home can get access to millions of training examples. That makes it wasteful only to use 70% or 80% of the available data for training.

The validation and test data are only used to calculate statistics reflecting the performance of the model. Those two sets just need to be large enough to provide reliable statistics. How much is debatable. As a rule of thumb, having a dozen examples per class is a desirable minimum. If you can have a hundred examples per class in each of the two holdout sets, you have a solid setup and the statistics calculated based on such sets are reliable.

The percentage of the split can also be dependent on the chosen machine learning algorithm or model. Deep learning models tend to significantly improve when exposed to more training data. This is less true for shallow algorithms and models.

Your proportions may depend on the size of the dataset. A small dataset of less than a thousand examples would do best with 90% of the data used for training. In this case, you might decide to not have a distinct validation set, and instead simulate with the **cross-validation** technique. We will talk more about that in Section 5.6.5 in Chapter 5.

It's worth mentioning that when you split **time-series data** into the three datasets, you must execute the split so that the order of observations in each example is preserved during the shuffling. Otherwise, for most predictive problems, your data will be broken, and no learning will be possible. We talk more about time series in Section 4.2.6 in Chapter 4.

3.6.1 Leakage During Partitioning

As you already know, data leakage may happen at any stage, from data collection to model evaluation. The data partitioning stage is no exception.

Group leakage may occur during partitioning. Imagine you have magnetic resonance images of the brains of multiple patients. Each image is labeled with certain brain disease, and the same patient may be represented by several images taken at different times. If you apply the partitioning technique discussed above (shuffle, then split), images of the same patient might appear in both the training and holdout data.

The model might learn from the particularities of the patient rather than the disease. The model would remember that patient A's brain has specific brain convolutions, and if they have a specific disease in the training data, the model successfully predicts this disease in the validation data by recognizing patient A from just the brain convolutions.

The solution to group leakage is **group partitioning**. It consists of keeping all patient examples together in one set: either training or holdout. Once again, you can see how important it is for the data analyst to know as much as possible about the data.

3.7 Dealing with Missing Attributes

Sometimes, the data comes to the analyst in a tidy form, such as an Excel spreadsheet,[7] but you might find some attributes missing. This often happens when the dataset was handcrafted, and the person forgot to fill some values or didn't get them measured.

The list of typical approaches of dealing with missing values for an attribute include:

---

[7]The fact that your raw dataset is contained in an Excel spreadsheet doesn't guarantee that the data is tidy. One property of tidiness is that each row represents one example.

- removing the examples with missing attributes from the dataset (this can be done if your dataset is big enough to safely sacrifice some data);
- using a learning algorithm that can deal with missing attribute values (such as the decision tree learning algorithm);
- using a **data imputation** technique.

3.7.1 Data Imputation Techniques

To impute the value of a missing numerical attribute, one technique consists in replacing the missing value by the average value of this attribute in the rest of the dataset. Mathematically it looks as follows. Let j be an attribute that is missing in some examples in the original dataset, and let $\mathcal{S}^{(j)}$ be the set of size $N^{(j)}$ that contains only those examples from the original dataset in which the value of the attribute j is present. Then the missing value $\hat{x}^{(j)}$ of the attribute j is given by,

$$\hat{x}^{(j)} \leftarrow \frac{1}{N^{(j)}} \sum_{i \in \mathcal{S}^{(j)}} x_i^{(j)},$$

where $N^{(j)} < N$ and the summation is made only over those examples where the value of the attribute j is present. An illustration of this technique is given in Figure 3.13, where two examples (at row 1 and 3) have the Height attribute missing. The average value, 177, will be imputed in the empty cells.

Row	Age	Weight	Height	Salary
1	18	70		35,000
2	43	65	175	26,900
3	34	87		76,500
4	21	66	187	94,800
5	65	60	169	19,000

$$Hei\hat{g}ht \leftarrow \frac{1}{3}(175 + 187 + 169) = 177$$

Figure 3.13: Replacing the missing value by an average value of this attribute in the dataset.

Another technique is to replace the missing value with a value outside the normal range of values. For example, if the regular range is $[0, 1]$, you can set the missing value to 2 or -1; if the attribute is categorical, such as days of the week, then a missing value can be replaced by the value "Unknown." Here, the learning algorithm learns what to do when the attribute has a value different from regular values. If the attribute is numerical, another technique is replacing the missing value with a value in the middle of the range. For example, if the range for an attribute is $[-1, 1]$, you can set the missing value to be equal to 0. Here, the idea is that the value in the middle of the range will not significantly affect the prediction.

A more advanced technique is to use the missing value as the target variable for a regression problem. (In this case, we assume all attributes are numerical.) You can use the remaining attributes $[x_i^{(1)}, x_i^{(2)}, \ldots, x_i^{(j-1)}, x_i^{(j+1)}, \ldots, x_i^{(D)}]$ to form a feature vector $\hat{\mathbf{x}}_i$, set $\hat{y}_i \leftarrow x_i^{(j)}$, where j is the attribute with a missing value. Then you build a regression model to predict $\hat{y}$ from $\hat{\mathbf{x}}$. Of course, to build training examples $(\hat{\mathbf{x}}, \hat{y})$, you only use those examples from the original dataset, in which the value of attribute j is present.

Finally, if you have a significantly large dataset and just a few attributes with missing values, you can add a synthetic binary indicator attribute for each original attribute with missing values. Let's say that examples in your dataset are D-dimensional, and attribute at position $j = 12$ has missing values. For each example $\mathbf{x}$, you then add the attribute at position $j = D + 1$, which is equal to 1 if the value of the attribute at position 12 is present in $\mathbf{x}$ and 0 otherwise. The missing value then can be replaced by 0 or any value of your choice.

At prediction time, if your example is not complete, you should use the same data imputation technique to fill the missing values as the technique you used to complete the training data.

Before you start working on the learning problem, you cannot tell which data imputation technique will work best. Try several techniques, build several models, and select the one that works best (using the validation set to compare models).

3.7.2   Leakage During Imputation

If you use the imputation techniques that compute some statistic of one attribute (such as average) or several attributes (by solving the regression problem), the leakage happens if you use the whole dataset to compute this statistic. Using all available examples, you contaminate the training data with information obtained from the validation and test examples.

This type of leakage is not as significant as other types discussed earlier. However, you still have to be aware of it and avoid it by partitioning first, and then computing the imputation statistic only on the training set.

3.8   Data Augmentation

For some types of data, it's quite easy to get more labeled examples without additional labeling. The strategy is called **data augmentation**, and it's most effective when applied to images. It consists of applying simple operations, such as crop or flip, to the original images to obtain new images.

original	flip	rotation
crop	color shift	noise addition
perspective change	contrast change	loss

Figure 3.14: Examples of data augmentation techniques. Photo credit: Alfonso Escalante.

3.8.1 Data Augmentation for Images

In Figure 3.14, you can see examples of operations that can be easily applied to a given image to obtain one or more new images: flip, rotation, crop, color shift, noise addition, perspective change, contrast change, and information loss.

Flipping, of course, has to be done only with respect to the axis for which the meaning of the image is preserved. If it's a football, you can flip with respect to both axes,[8] but if it's a car or a pedestrian, then you should only flip with respect to the vertical axis.

Rotation should be applied with slight angles to simulate an incorrect horizon calibration. You can rotate an image in both directions.

Crops can be randomly applied multiple times to the same image by keeping a significant part of the object(s) of interest in the cropped images.

---

[8]Unless the context, like grass, makes flipping according to the horizontal axis irrelevant.

In color shift, nuances of red-green-blue (RGB) are slightly changed to simulate different lighting conditions. Contrast change (both decreasing and increasing) and **Gaussian noise** of different intensity can also be applied multiple times to the same image.

By randomly removing parts of an image, we can simulate situations when an object is recognizable but not entirely visible because of an obstacle.

Another popular technique of data augmentation that seems counterintuitive, but works very well in practice, is **mixup**. As the name suggests, the technique consists of training the model on a mix of the images from the training set. More precisely, instead of training the model on the raw images, we take two images (that could be of the same class or not) and use for training their linear combination:

$$\text{mixup\_image} = t \times \text{image}_1 + (1 - t) \times \text{image}_2,$$

where t is a real number between 0 and 1. The target of that mixup image is a combination of the original targets obtained using the same value of t:

$$\text{mixup\_target} = t \times \text{target}_1 + (1 - t) \times \text{target}_2.$$

Experiments[9] on the **ImageNet-2012**, **CIFAR-10**, and several other datasets showed that mixup improves the generalization of neural network models. The authors of the mixup also found that it increases the robustness to **adversarial examples** and stabilizes the training of **generative adversarial networks** (GANs).

In addition to the techniques shown in Figure 3.14, if you expect the input images in your production system will come overcompressed, you can simulate overcompression by using some frequently used lossy compression methods and file formats, such as JPEG or GIF.

Only training data undergoes augmentation. Of course, it's impractical to generate all these additional examples in advance and store them. In practice, the data augmentation techniques are applied to the original data on-the-fly during training.

3.8.2   Data Augmentation for Text

When it comes to text data augmentations, it is not as straightforward. We need to use appropriate transformation techniques to preserve the contextual and grammatical structure of natural language texts.

One technique involves replacing random words in a sentence with their close **synonyms**. For the sentence, "The car stopped near a shopping mall." some equivalent sentences are:

> "The automobile stopped near a shopping mall."

---

[9]More details on the mixup technique can be found in Zhang, Hongyi, Moustapha Cisse, Yann N. Dauphin, and David Lopez-Paz. "mixup: Beyond empirical risk minimization." arXiv preprint arXiv:1710.09412 (2017).

"The car stopped near a shopping center."

"The auto stopped near a mall."

A similar technique uses **hypernyms** instead of synonyms. A hypernym is a word that has more general meaning. For example, "mammal" is a hypernym for "whale" and "cat"; "vehicle" is a hypernym for "car" and "bus." From our example above, we could create the following sentences:

"The vehicle stopped near a shopping mall."

"The car stopped near a building."

If you represent words or documents in your dataset using **word** or **document embeddings**, you can apply slight Gaussian noise to randomly chosen embedding features to make a variation of the same word or document. You can tune the number of features to modify and the noise intensity as hyperparameters by optimizing the performance on validation data.

Alternatively, to replace a given word w in the sentence, you can find k nearest neighbors to the word w in the word embedding space and generate k new sentences by replacing the word w with its respective neighbor. The nearest neighbors can be found using a measure such as **cosine similarity** or **Euclidean distance**. The choice of the measure and the value of k, can be tuned as hyperparameters.

A modern alternative to the k-nearest-neighbors approach described above is to use a deep pre-trained model such as Bidirectional Encoder Representations from Transformers (**BERT**). Models like BERT are trained to predict a masked word given other words in a sentence. One can use BERT to generate k most likely predictions for a masked word and then use them as synonyms for data augmentation.

Similarly, if your problem is document classification, and you have a large corpus of unlabeled documents, but only a small corpus of labeled documents, you can do as follows. First, build document embeddings for all documents in your large corpus. Use **doc2vec** or any other technique of document embedding. Then, for each labeled document d in your dataset, find k closest unlabeled documents in the document embedding space and label them with the same label as d. Again, tune k on the validation data.

Another useful text data augmentation technique is **back translation**. To create a new example from a text written in English (it can be a sentence or a document), first translate it into another language l using a machine translation system. Then translate it back from l into English. If the text obtained through back translation is different from the original text, you add it to the dataset by assigning the same label as the original text.

There are also data augmentation techniques for other data types, such as audio and video: addition of noise, shifting an audio or a video clip in time, slowing it down or accelerating, changing pitch for audio and color balance for video, to name a few. Describing these techniques in detail is out of the scope of this book. You should just be aware that data augmentation can be applied to any media data, and not only images and text.

3.9 Dealing With Imbalanced Data

Class imbalance is a condition in the data that can significantly affect the performance of the model, independently of the chosen learning algorithm. The problem is a very uneven distribution of labels in the training data.

This is the case, for example, when your classifier has to distinguish between genuine and fraudulent e-commerce transactions: the examples of genuine transactions are much more frequent. Typically, a machine learning algorithm tries to classify most training examples correctly. The algorithm is pushed to do so because it needs to minimize a **cost function** that typically assigns a positive loss value to each misclassified example. If the loss is the same for the misclassification of a minority class example as it is for the misclassification of a majority class, then it's very likely that the learning algorithm decides to "give up" on many minority class examples in order to make fewer mistakes in the majority class.

While there is no formal definition of **imbalanced data**, consider the following rule of thumb. If there are two classes, then balanced data would mean half of the dataset representing each class. A slight class imbalance is usually not a problem. So, if 60% examples belong to one class and 40% belong to the other, and you use a popular machine learning algorithm in its standard formulation, it should not cause any significant performance degradation. However, when the class imbalance is high, for example when 90% examples are of one class, and 10% are of the other, using the standard formulation of the learning algorithm that usually equally weights errors made in both classes may not be as effective and would need modification.

3.9.1 Oversampling

A technique used frequently to mitigate class imbalance is **oversampling**. By making multiple copies of minority class examples, it increases their weight, as illustrated in Figure 3.15a. You might also create synthetic examples by sampling feature values of several examples of the minority class and combining them to obtain a new example of that class. Two popular algorithms that oversample the minority class by creating synthetic examples: Synthetic Minority Oversampling Technique (**SMOTE**) and Adaptive Synthetic Sampling Method (**ADASYN**).

SMOTE and ADASYN work similarly in many ways. For a given example $\mathbf{x}_i$ of the minority class, they pick k nearest neighbors. Let's denote this set of k examples as $\mathcal{S}_k$. The synthetic example $\mathbf{x}_{new}$ is defined as $\mathbf{x}_i + \lambda(\mathbf{x}_{zi} - \mathbf{x}_i)$, where $\mathbf{x}_{zi}$ is an example of the minority class chosen randomly from $\mathcal{S}_k$. The interpolation hyperparameter λ is an arbitrary number in the range $[0, 1]$. (See an illustration for $\lambda = 0.5$ in Figure 3.16.)

Both SMOTE and ADASYN randomly pick among all possible $\mathbf{x}_i$ in the dataset. In ADASYN, the number of synthetic examples generated for each $\mathbf{x}_i$ is proportional to the number of examples in $\mathcal{S}_k$, which are not from the minority class. Therefore, more synthetic examples are generated in the area where the minority class examples are rare.

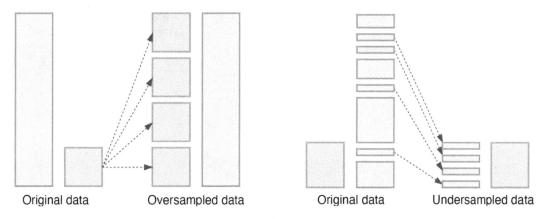

| Original data | Oversampled data | Original data | Undersampled data |

Figure 3.15: Undersampling (left) and oversampling (right).

3.9.2 Undersampling

An opposite approach, **undersampling**, is to remove from the training set some examples of the majority class (Figure 3.15b).

The undersampling can be done randomly; that is, the examples to remove from the majority class can be chosen at random. Alternatively, examples to withdraw from the majority class can be selected based on some property. One such property is **Tomek links**. A Tomek link exists between two examples x_i and x_j belonging to two different classes if there's no other example x_k in the dataset closer to either x_i or x_j than the latter two are to each other. The closeness can be defined using a metric such as **cosine similarity** or **Euclidean distance**.

In Figure 3.17, you can see how removing examples from the majority class based on Tomek links helps to establish a clear margin between examples of two classes.

Cluster-based undersampling works as follows. Decide on the number of examples you want to have in the majority class resulting from undersampling. Let that number be k. Run a **centroid-based clustering algorithm** on the majority examples only with k being the desired number of clusters. Then replace all examples in the majority classes with the k centroids. An example of a centroid-based clustering algorithm is **k-nearest neighbors**.

3.9.3 Hybrid Strategies

You can develop your hybrid strategies (by combining both over- and undersampling) and possibly get better results. One such strategy consists of using ADASYN to oversample, and then Tomek links to undersample.

Another possible strategy consists of combining cluster-based undersampling with SMOTE.

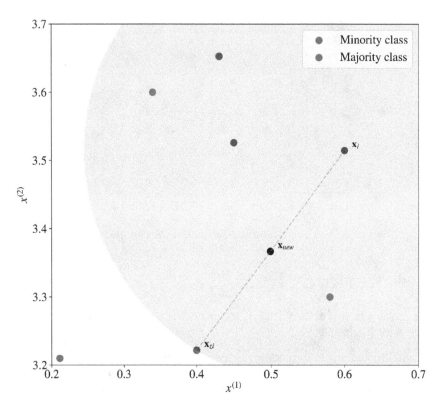

Figure 3.16: An illustration of a synthetic example generation for SMOTE and ADASYN. (Built using a script adapted from Guillaume Lemaitre.)

3.10 Data Sampling Strategies

When you have a large data asset, so-called big data, it's not always practical or necessary to work with the entire data asset. Instead, you can draw a smaller data sample that contains enough information for learning.

Similarly, when you undersample the majority class to adjust for data imbalance, the smaller data sample should be representative of the entire majority class. In this section, we discuss several sampling strategies, their properties, advantages, and drawbacks.

There are two main strategies: probability sampling and nonprobability sampling. In **probability sampling**, all examples have a chance to be selected. These techniques involve randomness.

Nonprobability sampling is not random. To build a sample, it follows a fixed deterministic sequence of heuristic actions. This means that some examples don't have a chance of being

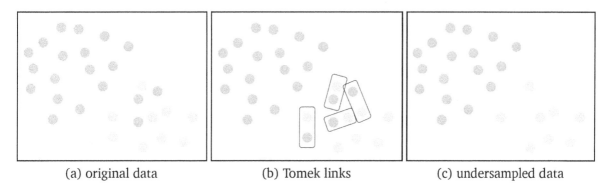

| (a) original data | (b) Tomek links | (c) undersampled data |

Figure 3.17: Undersampling with Tomek links.

selected, no matter how many samples you build.

Historically, nonprobability methods were more manageable for a human to execute manually. Nowadays this advantage is not significant. Data analysts use computers and software that greatly simplify sampling, even from big data. The main drawback of nonprobability sampling methods is that they include non-representative samples and might systematically exclude important examples. These drawbacks outweigh the possible advantages of nonprobability sampling methods. Therefore, in this book I will only present probability sampling methods.

3.10.1   Simple Random Sampling

Simple random sampling is the most straightforward method, and the one I refer to when I say "sample randomly." Here, each example from the entire dataset is chosen purely by chance; each example has an equal chance of being selected.

One way of obtaining a simple random sample is to assign a number to each example, and then use a random number generator to decide which examples to select. For example, if your entire dataset contains 1000 examples, tagged from 0 to 999, use groups of three digits from the random number generator to select an example. So, if the first three numbers from the random number generator were 0, 5, and 7, choose the example numbered 57, and so on.

Simplicity is the great advantage of this sampling method, and it can be easily implemented as any programming language can serve as a random number generator. A disadvantage of simple random sampling is that you may not select enough examples that would have a particular property of interest. Consider the situation where you extract a sample from a large imbalanced dataset. In so doing, you accidentally fail to capture a sufficient number of examples from the minority class - or any at all.

3.10.2 Systematic Sampling

To implement **systematic sampling** (also known as **interval sampling**), you create a list containing all examples. From that list, you randomly select the first example $\mathbf{x}_{start}$ from the first k elements on the list. Then, you select every k^{th} item on the list starting from $\mathbf{x}_{start}$. You choose such a value of k that will give you a sample of the desired size.

An advantage of the systematic sampling over the simple random sampling is that it draws examples from the whole range of values. However, systematic sampling is inappropriate if the list of examples has periodicity or repetitive patterns. In the latter case, the obtained sample can exhibit a bias. However, if the list of examples is randomized, then systematic sampling often results in a better sample than simple random sampling.

3.10.3 Stratified Sampling

If you know about the existence of several groups (e.g., gender, location, or age) in your data, you should have examples from each of those groups in your sample. In **stratified sampling**, you first divide your dataset into groups (called strata) and then randomly select examples from each stratum, like in simple random sampling. The number of examples to select from each stratum is proportional to the size of the stratum.

Stratified sampling often improves the representativeness of the sample by reducing its bias; in the worst of cases, the resulting sample is of no less quality than the results of simple random sampling. However, to define strata, the analyst has to understand the properties of the dataset. Furthermore, it can be difficult to decide which attributes will define the strata.

If you don't know how to best define the strata, you can use **clustering**. The only decision you have to make is how many clusters you need. This technique is also useful to choose the unlabeled examples to send for labeling to a human labeler. It often happens that we have millions of unlabeled examples, and few resources available for labeling. Choose examples carefully, so that each stratum or cluster is represented in our labeled data.

Stratified sampling is the slowest of the three methods due to the additional overhead of working with several independent strata. However, its potential benefit of producing a less biased sample typically outweighs its drawbacks.

3.11 Storing Data

Keeping data safe is insurance for your organization's business: if you lose a business-critical model for any reason, such as a disaster or human mistake (the file with the model was accidentally erased or overwritten), having the data will allow you to rebuild that model easily.

When sensitive data or personally identifiable information (PII) is provided by customers or business partners, it must be stored in not just a safe but also a secure location. Jointly with the DBA or DevOps engineers, access to sensitive data can be restricted by username and, if needed, IP address. Access to a relational database might also be limited on the per row and per column basis.

It's also recommended to limit access to read-only and add-only operations, by restricting write and erase operations to specific users.

If the data is collected on mobile devices, it might be necessary to store it on the mobile device until the owner connects to wifi. This data might need to be encrypted so that other applications cannot access it. Once the user is connected to wifi, the data has to be synchronized with a secure server by using cryptographic protocols, such as Transport Layer Security (TLS). Each data element on the mobile device has to be marked with a timestamp to allow its proper synchronization with the data on the server.

3.11.1   Data Formats

Data for machine learning can be stored in various formats. Data used indirectly, such as dictionaries or gazetteers, may be stored as a table in a relational database, a collection in a key-value store, or a structured text file.

The tidy data is usually stored as comma-separated values (CSV) or tab-separated values (TSV) files. In this case, all examples are stored in one file. Alternatively, collection of XML (Extensible Markup Language) files or JSON (JavaScript Object Notation) files can contain one example per file.

In addition to general-purpose formats, certain popular machine learning packages use proprietary data formats to store tidy data. Other machine learning packages often provide application programming interfaces (APIs) to one or several such proprietary data formats. The most frequently supported formats are **ARFF** (Attribute-Relation File Format used in the Weka machine learning package) and the **LIBSVM** (Library for Support Vector Machines) format, which is the default format used by the LIBSVM and **LIBLINEAR** (Library for Large Linear Classification) machine learning libraries.

The data in the LIBSVM format consists of one file containing all examples. Each line of that file represents a labeled feature vector using the following format:

```
label index1:value1 index2:value2 ...
```

where index$X$:value$Y$ specifies the value Y of the feature at position (dimension) X. If the value at some position is zero, it can be omitted. This data format is especially convenient for **sparse data** consisting of examples in which the values of most features are zero.

Furthermore, different programming languages come with **data serialization** capabilities. The data for a specific machine learning package can be persisted on the hard drive using a serialization object or function provided by the programming language or library. When needed, the data can be deserialized in its original form. For example, in Python, a popular general-purpose serialization module is **Pickle**; R has built-in `saveRDS` and `readRDS` functions. Different data analysis packages can also offer their own serialization/deserialization tools.

In Java, any object that implements the `java.io.Serializable` interface can be serialized into a file and then deserialized when needed.

3.11.2   Data Storage Levels

Before deciding how and where to store the data, it's essential to choose the appropriate **storage level**. Storage can be organized in different levels of abstraction: from the lowest level, the filesystem, to the highest level, such as data lake.

Filesystem is the foundational level of storage. The fundamental unit of data on that level is a **file**. A file can be text or binary, is not versioned, and can be easily erased or overwritten.

A filesystem can be local or networked. A networked filesystem can be simple or distributed.

A **local filesystem** can be as simple as a locally mounted disk containing all the files needed for your machine learning project.

A **distributed filesystem**, such as **NFS** (Network File System), **CephFS** (Ceph File System) or **HDFS**, can be accessed over the network by multiple physical or virtual machines. Files in a distributed filesystem are stored and accessed over multiple machines in the network.

Despite its simplicity, filesystem-level storage is appropriate for a many use cases, including:

File sharing
> The simplicity of filesystem-level storage and support for standard protocols allows you to store and share data with a small group of colleagues with minimal effort.

Local archiving
> Filesystem-level storage is a cost-effective option for archiving data, thanks to the availability and accessibility of scale-out NAS solutions.

Data protection
> Filesystem-level storage is a viable data protection solution thanks to built-in redundancy and replication.

Parallel access to the data on the filesystem level is fast for retrieval access but slow for storage, so it's an appropriate storage level for smaller teams and data.

Object storage is an application programming interface (API) defined over a filesystem. Using an API, you can programmatically execute such operations on files as GET, PUT, or DELETE without worrying where the files are actually stored. The API is typically provided by an **API service** available on the network and accessible by **HTTP** or, more generally, **TCP/IP** or a different communication protocol suite.

The fundamental unit of data in an object storage level is an **object**. Objects are usually binary: images, sound, or video files, and other data elements having a particular format.

Such features as versioning and redundancy can be built into the API service. The access to the data stored on the object storage level can often be done in parallel, but the access is not as fast as on the filesystem level.

Canonical examples of object storage are **Amazon S3** and **Google Cloud Storage** (GCS). Alternatively, **Ceph** is a storage platform that implements object storage on a single distributed computer cluster and provides interfaces for both object- and filesystem-level storage. It's often used as an alternative to S3 and GCS in on-premises computing systems.

The **database** level of data storage allows persistent, fast, and scalable storage of **structured data** with fast parallel access for both storage and retrieval.

A modern database management system (**DBMS**) stores data in random-access memory (**RAM**), but software ensures that data is persisted (and operations on data are logged) to disk and never lost.

The fundamental unit of data at this level is a **row**. A row has a unique ID and contains values in columns. In a relational database, rows are organized in **tables**. Rows can have references to other rows in the same or different tables.

Databases are not exceptionally well suited for storing binary data, though rather small binary objects can sometimes be stored in a column in the form of a **blob** (for Binary Large OBject). Blob is a collection of binary data stored as a single entity. More often, though, a row stores references to binary objects stored elsewhere — in a filesystem or object storage.

The four most frequently used DBMS in the industry are Oracle, MySQL, Microsoft SQL Server, and PostgresSQL. They all support SQL (Structured Query Language), an interface for accessing and modifying data stored in the databases, as well as creating, modifying, and erasing databases.[10]

A **data lake** is a repository of data stored in its natural or raw format, usually in the form of object blobs or files. A data lake is typically an unstructured aggregation of data from multiple sources, including databases, logs, or intermediary data obtained as a result of expensive transformations of the original data.

The data is saved in the data lake in its raw format, including the structured data. To read data from a data lake, the analyst needs to write the programming code that reads and parses the data stored in a file or a blob. Writing a script to parse the data file or a blob is an approach called **schema on read**, as opposed to the **schema on write** in DBMS. In a DBMS, the schema of data is defined beforehand, and, at each write, the DBMS makes sure that the data corresponds to the schema.

---

[10]The SQL Server uses its proprietary Transact SQL (T-SQL) while Oracle uses Procedural Language SQL (PL/SQL).

3.11.3   Data Versioning

If data is held and updated in multiple places, you might need to keep track of versions. Versioning the data is also needed if you frequently update the model by collecting more data, especially in an automated way. This happens when you work on automated driving, spam detection, or personalized recommendations, for example. The new data comes from a human driving a car, or the user cleaning up their electronic mail, or recent video streaming. Sometimes, after an update of the data, the new model performs worse, and you would like to investigate why by switching from one version of the data to another.

Data versioning is also critical in supervised learning when the labeling is done by multiple labelers. Some labelers might assign very different labels to similar examples, which typically hurts the performance of the model. You would like to keep the examples annotated by different labelers separately and only merge them when you build the model. Careful analysis of the model performance may show that labelers didn't provide quality or consistent labels. Exclude such data from the training data, or relabel it, and data versioning will allow this with minimal effort.

Data versioning can be implemented in several levels of complexity, from the most basic to the most elaborate.

Level 0: data is unversioned.
> At this level, data may reside on a local filesystem, object storage, or in a database. The advantage of having unversioned data is the speed and simplicity of dealing with the data. Still, that advantage is outweighed by potential problems you might encounter when working on your model. Most likely, your first problem will be the inability to make versioned deployments. As we will discuss in Chapter 8, model deployments must be versioned. A deployed machine learning model is a mix of code and data. If the code is versioned, the data must be too. Otherwise, the deployment will be unversioned.
>
> If you don't version deployments, you will not be able to get back to the previous level of performance in case of any problem with the model. Therefore, unversioned data is not recommended.

Level 1: data is versioned as a snapshot at training time.
> At this level, data is versioned by storing, at training time, a snapshot of everything needed to train a model. Such an approach allows you to version deployed models and get back to past performance. You should keep track of each version in some document, typically an Excel spreadsheet. That document should describe the location of the snapshot of both code and data, hyperparameter values, and other metadata needed to reproduce the experiment if needed. If you don't have many models and don't update them too frequently, this level of versioning could be a viable strategy. Otherwise, it's not recommended.

Level 2: both data and code are versioned as one asset.
> At this level of versioning, small data assets, such as dictionaries, gazetteers, and small

datasets, are stored jointly with the code in a version control system, such as **Git** or **Mercurial**. Large files are stored in object storage, such as **S3** or **GCS**, with unique IDs. The training data is stored as JSON, XML, or another standard format, and includes relevant metadata such as labels, the identity of the labeler, time of labeling, the tool used to label the data, and so on.

Tools like **Git Large File Storage** (LFS) automatically replace large files such as audio samples, videos, large datasets, and graphics with text pointers, inside Git, while storing the file contents on a remote server.

The version of the dataset is defined by the **git signatures** of the code and the data file. It can also be helpful to add a timestamp to identify a needed version easily.

Level 3: using or building a specialized data versioning solution.
Data versioning software such as **DVC** and **Pachyderm** provide additional tools for data versioning. They typically interoperate with code versioning software, such as Git.

Level 2 of versioning is a recommended way of implementing versioning for most projects. If you feel like Level 2 is not sufficient for your needs, explore Level 3 solutions, or consider building your own. Otherwise, that approach is not recommended, as it adds complexity to what is already a complex engineering project.

3.11.4 Documentation and Metadata

While you are actively working on a machine learning project, you are often capable of remembering important details about the data. However, once the project goes to production and you switch to another project, this information will eventually become less detailed.

Before you switch to another project, you should make sure that others can understand your data and use it properly.

If the data is self-explanatory, then you might leave it undocumented. However, it's rather rare that someone who didn't create a dataset can easily understand it and know how to use it just by looking at it.

Documentation has to accompany any data asset that was used to train a model. This documentation has to contain the following details:

- what that data means,
- how it was collected, or methods used to create it (instructions to labelers and methods for quality control),
- the details of train-validation-test splits,
- details of all pre-processing steps,
- an explanation of any data that were excluded,
- what format is used to store the data,
- types of attributes or features (which values are allowed for each attribute or feature),

- number of examples,
- possible values for labels or the allowable range for a numerical target.

3.11.5   Data Lifecycle

Some data can be stored indefinitely. However, in some business contexts, you might be allowed to store some data for a specific time, and then you might have to erase it. If such restrictions apply to the data you work with, you have to make sure that a reliable alerting system is in place. That alerting system has to contact the person responsible for the data erasure and have a backup plan in case that person is not available. Don't forget that the consequences for not erasing data can sometimes be very serious for the organization.

For every sensitive data asset, a **data lifecycle document** has to describe the asset, the circle of persons who have access to that data asset, both during and after the project development. The document has to describe how long the data asset will be stored and whether it has to be explicitly destroyed.

3.12   Data Manipulation Best Practices

To conclude this chapter, we consider two remaining best practices: reproducibility and "data first, algorithm second."

3.12.1   Reproducibility

Reproducibility should be an important concern in everything you do, including data collection and preparation. You should avoid transforming data manually, or using powerful tools included in text editors or command line shells, such as regular expressions, "quick and dirty" ad hoc awk or sed commands, and piped expressions.

Usually, the data collection and transformation activities consist of multiple stages. These include downloading data from web APIs or databases, replacing multiword expressions by unique tokens, removing stop-words and noise, cropping and unblurring images, imputation of missing values, and so on. Each step in this multistage process has to be implemented as a software script, such as Python or R script with their inputs and outputs. If you are organized like that in your work, it will allow you to keep track of all changes in the data. If during any stage something wrong happens to the data, you can always fix the script and run the entire data processing pipeline from scratch.

On the other hand, manual interventions can be hard to reproduce. These are difficult to apply to updated data, or scale for much more data (once you can afford getting more data or a different dataset).

3.12.2 Data First, Algorithm Second

Remember that in the industry, contrary to academia, "data first, algorithm second," so focus most of your effort and time on getting more data of wide variety and high quality, instead of trying to squeeze the maximum out of a learning algorithm.

Data augmentation, when implemented well, will most likely contribute more to the quality of the model than the search for the best hyperparameter values or model architecture.

3.13 Summary

Before you start collecting the data, there are five questions to answer: is the data you will work with accessible, sizeable, useable, understandable, and reliable.

Common problems with data are high cost, bias, low predictive power, outdated examples, outliers, and leakage.

Good data contains enough information that can be used for modeling, has good coverage of what you want to do with the model, and reflects real inputs that the model will see in production. It is as unbiased as possible and not a result of the model itself, has consistent labels, and is big enough to allow generalization.

Good interaction data contains information on three aspects: context of interaction, action of the user in that context, and outcome of the interaction.

To obtain a good partition of your entire dataset into training, validation and test sets, the process of partitioning has to satisfy several conditions: 1) data was randomized before the split, 2) split was applied to raw data, 3) validation and test sets follow the same distribution, and 4) leakage was avoided.

Data imputation techniques can be used to deal with missing attributes in the data.

Data augmentation techniques are often used to get more labeled examples without additional manual labeling. The techniques usually apply to image data, but could also be applied to text and other types of perceptive data.

Class imbalance can significantly affect the performance of the model. Learning algorithms perform suboptimally when the training data suffers from class imbalance. Such techniques as over- and undersampling can help to overcome the class imbalance problem.

When you work with big data, it's not always practical and necessary to work with the entire data asset. Instead, draw a smaller sample of data that contains enough information for learning. Different data sampling strategies can be used for that, in particular simple random sampling, systematic sampling, stratified sampling, and cluster sampling.

Data can be stored in different data formats and on several data storage levels. Data versioning is a critical element in supervised learning when the labeling is done by multiple labelers.

Different labelers may provide labels of varying quality, so it's important to keep track of who created which labeled example. Data versioning can be implemented with several levels of complexity, from the most basic to the most elaborate: unversioned (level 0), versioned as a snapshot at training time (level 1), versioned as one asset containing both data and code (level 2), and versioned by using or building a specialized data versioning solution (level 3).

Level 2 is recommended for most projects.

Documentation has to accompany any data asset that was used to train a model. That documentation has to contain the following details: what that data means, how it was collected, or methods used to create it (instructions to labelers and methods for quality control), the details of train-validation-test splits and of all pre-processing steps. It must also contain an explanation of any data that were excluded, what format is used to store the data, types of attributes or features, number of examples, and possible values for labels or the allowable range for a numerical target.

For every sensitive data asset, a data lifecycle document has to describe the asset, the circle of persons who have access to that data asset both during and after the project development.

Chapter 4

Feature Engineering

After data collection and preparation, feature engineering is the second most important activity in machine learning. It's also the third stage in the machine learning project life cycle:

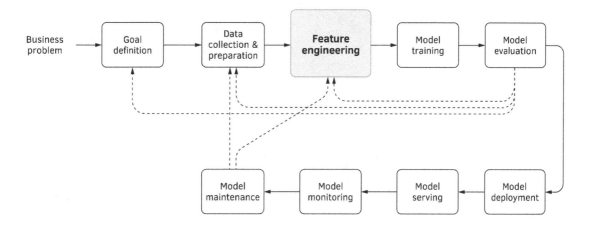

Figure 4.1: Machine learning project life cycle.

Feature engineering is a process of first conceptually and then programmatically transforming a raw example into a feature vector. It consists of conceptualizing a feature and then writing the programming code that would transform the entire raw example, with potentially the help of some indirect data, into a feature.

4.1 Why Engineer Features

To be more specific, consider the problem of recognizing movie titles in tweets. Say you have a vast collection of movie titles; this is data to use **indirectly**. You also have a collection of tweets; this data will be used **directly** to create examples. First, build an index of movie titles for fast string matching.[1] Then find all movie title matches in your tweets. Now stipulate that your examples are matches, and your machine learning problem is that of binary classification: whether a match is a movie, or is not a movie.

Consider the following tweet:

Figure 4.2: A tweet from Kyle.

Our movie title matching index would help us find the following matches: "avatar," "the terminator," "It," and "her". That gives us four unlabeled examples. You can label those four examples: {(avatar, False), (the terminator, True), (It, False), (her, False)}. However, a machine learning algorithm cannot learn anything from the movie title alone (neither can a human): it needs a context. You might decide that the five words preceding the match and the five words following it are a sufficiently informative context. In machine learning jargon, we call such a context a "ten-word window" around a match. You can tune the width of the window as a hyperparameter.

Now, your examples are labeled matches in their context. However, a learning algorithm cannot be applied to such data. Machine learning algorithms can only apply to feature vectors. This is why you resort to feature engineering.

---

[1]To build an index for fast string matching, you can, for example, use the **Aho–Corasick algorithm**.

4.2 How to Engineer Features

Feature engineering is a creative process where the analyst applies their imagination, intuition, and domain expertise. In our illustrative problem of movie title recognition in tweets, we used our intuition to fix the width of the window around the match to ten. Now, we need to be even more creative to transform string sequences into numerical vectors.

4.2.1 Feature Engineering for Text

When it comes to text, scientists and engineers often use simple feature engineering tricks. Two such tricks are one-hot encoding and bag-of-words.

Generally speaking, **one-hot encoding** transforms a categorical attribute into several binary ones. Let's say your dataset has an attribute "Color" with possible values "red," "yellow," and "green." We transform each value into a three-dimensional binary vector, as shown below:

$$\text{red} = [1, 0, 0]$$
$$\text{yellow} = [0, 1, 0]$$
$$\text{green} = [0, 0, 1].$$

In a spreadsheet, instead of one column headed with the attribute "Color," you will use three synthetic columns, with the values 1 or 0. The advantage is you now have a vast range of machine learning algorithms at your disposal, for only a handful of learning algorithms support categorical attributes.

Bag-of-words is a generalization of applying the one-hot encoding technique to text data. Instead of representing one attribute as a binary vector, you use this technique to represent an entire text document as a binary vector. Let's see how it works.

Imagine that you have a collection of six text documents, as shown below:

Document 1	Love, love is a verb
Document 2	Love is a doing word
Document 3	Feathers on my breath
Document 4	Gentle impulsion
Document 5	Shakes me, makes me lighter
Document 6	Feathers on my breath

Figure 4.3: A collection of six documents.

Let your problem be to build a text classifier by topic. A classification learning algorithm expects inputs to be labeled feature vectors, so you have to transform the text document collection into a feature vector collection. Bag-of-words allows you to do just that.

First, tokenize the texts. **Tokenization** is a procedure of splitting a text into pieces called "tokens." A **tokenizer** is software that takes a string as input, and returns a sequence of tokens extracted from that string. Typically, tokens are words, but it's not strictly necessary. It can be a punctuation mark, a word, or, in some cases, a combination of words, such as a company (e.g., McDonald's) or a place (e.g., Red Square). Let's use a simple tokenizer that extracts words and ignores everything else. We obtain the following collection:

Document 1	[Love, love, is a verb]
Document 2	[Love, is, a, doing, word]
Document 3	[Feathers, on, my, breath]
Document 4	[Gentle, impulsion]
Document 5	[Shakes, me, makes, me lighter]
Document 6	[Feathers, on, my, breath]

Figure 4.4: The collection of tokenized documents.

The next step is to build a vocabulary. It contains 16 tokens:[2]

a	breath	doing	feathers
gentle	impulsion	is	lighter
love	makes	me	my
on	shakes	verb	word

Now order your vocabulary in some way and assign a unique index to each token. I ordered the tokens alphabetically:

a	breath	doing	feathers	gentle	impulsion	is	lighter	love	makes	me	my	on	shakes	verb	word
1	2	3	4	5	6	7	8	9	10	11	12	13	14	15	16

Figure 4.5: Ordered and indexed tokens.

[2]I decided to ignore capitalization, but you, as an analyst, might choose to treat the two tokens "Love" and "love" as two separate vocabulary entities.

Each token in the vocabulary has a unique index, from 1 to 16. We transform our collection into a collection of binary feature vectors, as shown below:

	a							...								word
	1	2	3	4	5	6	7	8	9	10	11	12	13	14	15	16
Document 1	1	0	0	0	0	0	1	0	1	0	0	0	0	0	1	0
Document 2	1	0	1	0	0	0	1	0	1	0	0	0	0	0	0	1
Document 3	0	1	0	1	0	0	0	0	0	0	0	1	1	0	0	0
Document 4	0	0	0	0	1	1	0	0	0	0	0	0	0	0	0	0
Document 5	0	0	0	0	0	0	0	1	0	1	1	0	0	1	0	0
Document 6	0	1	0	1	0	0	0	0	0	0	0	1	1	0	0	0

Figure 4.6: Feature vectors.

The 1 is in a specific position if the corresponding token is present in the text. Otherwise, the feature at that position has a 0.

For instance, document 1 "Love, love is a verb" is represented by the following feature vector:

$$[1, 0, 0, 0, 0, 0, 1, 0, 1, 0, 0, 0, 0, 0, 1, 0]$$

Use the corresponding labeled feature vectors as the training data, which any classification learning algorithm can work with.

There are several bag-of-words "flavors." The above binary-value model often works well. Alternatives to binary values include 1) counts of tokens, 2) frequencies of tokens, or 3) **TF-IDF** (term frequency-inverse document frequency). If you use the counts of words, then the feature value for "love" in Document 1 "Love, love is a verb" would be 2, representing the number of times the word "love" appears in the document. If applying frequencies of tokens, the value for "love" would be $2/5 = 0.4$, assuming that the tokenizer extracted two "love" tokens, and five total tokens from Document 1. The TF–IDF value increases proportionally to the frequency of a word in the document and is offset by the number of documents in the corpus that contain that word. This adjusts for some words, such as prepositions and pronouns, appearing more frequently in general. I will not go into further detail on TF-IDF, but would recommend the interested reader to learn more about it online.

A straightforward extension of the bag-of-words technique is **bag-of-n-grams**. An **n-gram** is a sequence of n words taken from the corpus. If $n = 2$, and you ignore the punctuation, then all two-grams (usually called **bigrams**) that can be found in the text "No, I am your father." are as follows: ["No I," "I am," "am your," "your father"]. The three-grams are ["No I am," "I am your," "am your father"]. By mixing all n-grams, up to a certain n, with tokens in one dictionary, we obtain a bag of n-grams that we can tokenize the same way as we deal with a bag-of-words model.

Because sequences of words are often less common than individual words, using n-grams creates a more **sparse** feature vector. At the same time, n-grams allow the machine learning algorithm to learn a more nuanced model. For example, the expressions "this movie was not good and boring" and "this movie was good and not boring" have opposite meaning, but would result in the same bag-of-words vectors, based solely on words. If we consider bigrams of words, then bag-of-words vectors of bigrams for those two expressions would be different.

4.2.2 Why Bag-of-Words Works

Feature vectors only work when certain rules are followed. One rule is that a feature at position j in a feature vector must represent the same property in all examples in the dataset. If that feature represents the height in cm of a certain person in a dataset, where each example represents a different person, then that must hold true in all other examples. The feature at position j must always represent the height in cm, and nothing else.

The bag-of-words technique works the same way. Each feature represents the same property of a document: whether a specific token is present or absent in a document.

Another rule is that similar feature vectors must represent similar entities in the dataset. This property is also respected when using the bag-of-words technique. Two identical documents will have identical feature vectors. Likewise, two texts regarding the same topic will have higher chances to have similar feature vectors, because they will share more words than those of two different topics.

4.2.3 Converting Categorical Features to Numbers

One-hot encoding is not the only way to convert categorical features to numbers, and it's not always the best way.

Mean encoding, also known as **bin counting** or **feature calibration**, is another technique. First, the **sample mean** of the label is calculated using all examples where the feature has value z. Each value z of the categorical feature is then replaced by that sample mean value. The advantage of this technique is that the data dimensionality doesn't increase, and by design, the numerical value contains some information about the label.

If you work on a binary classification problem, in addition to sample mean, you can use other useful quantities: the raw counts of the positive class for a given value of z, the **odds** ratio, and the **log-odds ratio**. The odds ratio (OR) is usually defined between two random variables. In a general sense, OR is a statistic that quantifies the strength of the association between two events A and B. Two events are considered independent if the OR equals 1, that is, the odds of one event are the same in either the presence or absence of the other event.

In application to quantifying a categorical feature, we can calculate the odds ratio between the value z of a categorical feature (event A) and the positive label (event B). Let's illustrate that with an example. Let our problem be to predict whether an email message is spam or not spam. Let's assume that we have a labeled dataset of email messages, and we engineered a feature that contains the most frequent word in each email message. Let us find the numerical value that would replace the categorical value "infected" of this feature. We first build the **contingency table** for "infected" and "spam":

	Spam	Not Spam	Total
contains "infected"	145	8	153
doesn't contain "infected"	346	2909	3255
Total	491	2917	3408

Figure 4.7: Contingency table for "infected" and "spam."

The odds-ratio of "infected" and "spam" is given by:

$$\text{odds ratio(infected, spam)} = \frac{145/8}{346/2909} = 152.4.$$

As you can see, the odds ratio, depending on the values in the contingency table, can be extremely low (near zero) or extremely high (an arbitrarily high positive value). To avoid numerical overflow issues, analysts often use the log-odds ratio:

$$\text{log odds ratio(infected, spam)} = \log(145/8) - \log(346/2909)$$
$$= \log(145) - \log(8) - \log(346) + \log(2909) = 2.2.$$

Now you can replace the value "infected" in the above categorical feature with the value of 2.2. You can proceed the same way for other values of that categorical feature and convert all of them into log-odds ratio values.

Sometimes, categorical features are ordered, but not cyclical. Examples include school marks (from "A" to "E") and seniority levels ("junior," "mid-level," "senior"). Instead of using one-hot encoding, it's convenient to represent them with meaningful numbers. Use uniform numbers in the $[0, 1]$ range, like $1/3$ for "junior", $2/3$ for "mid-level" and 1 for "senior." If some values should be farther apart, you can reflect that with different ratios. If "senior" should be farther from "mid-level" than "mid-level" from "junior," you might use $1/5$, $2/5$, 1 for "junior," "mid-level," and "senior," respectively. This is why domain knowledge is important.

When categorical features are cyclical, integer encoding does not work well. For example, try converting Monday through Sunday to the integers 1 through 7. The difference between Sunday and Saturday is 1, while the difference between Monday and Sunday is -6. However, our reasoning suggests the same difference of 1, because Monday is just one day past Sunday.

Instead, use the **sine-cosine transformation**. It converts a cyclical feature into two synthetic features. Let p denote the integer value of our cyclical feature. Replace the value p of the cyclical feature with the following two values:

$$p_{sin} = \sin\left(\frac{2 \times \pi \times p}{\max(p)}\right), p_{cos} = \cos\left(\frac{2 \times \pi \times p}{\max(p)}\right).$$

The table below contains the values of p_{sin} and p_{cos} for the seven days of the week:

p	p_{sin}	p_{cos}
1	0.78	0.62
2	0.97	-0.22
3	0.43	-0.9
4	-0.43	-0.9
5	-0.97	-0.22
6	-0.78	0.62
7	0	1

Figure 4.8 contains the scatter plot built using the above table. You can see the cyclical nature of the two new features.

Now, in your tidy data, replace "Monday" with two values $[0.78, 0.62]$, "Tuesday" with $[0.97, -0.22]$, and so on. The dataset has added another dimension, but the model's predictive quality is significantly better, compared to integer encoding.

4.2.4 Feature Hashing

Feature hashing, or **hashing trick**, converts text data, or categorical attributes with many values, into a feature vector of arbitrary dimensionality. One-hot encoding and bag-of-words have a drawback: many unique values will create high-dimensional feature vectors. For example, if there are one million unique tokens in a collection of text documents, bag-of-words will produce feature vectors that each have a dimensionality of one million. Working with such high-dimensional data might be very computationally expensive.

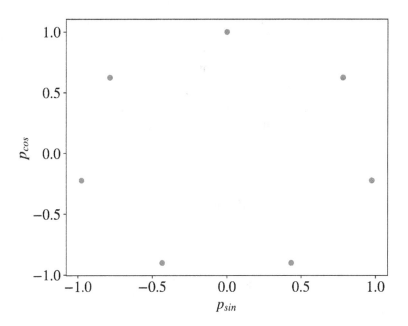

Figure 4.8: The sine-cosine transformed feature that represents the days of the week.

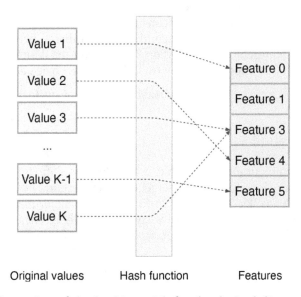

Original values   Hash function   Features

Figure 4.9: An illustration of the hashing trick for the desired dimensionality of 5 for the original cardinality K of values of an attribute.

To keep your data manageable, you can use the hashing trick that works as follows. First you decide on the desired dimensionality of your feature vectors. Then, using a **hash function**, you first convert all values of your categorical attribute (or all tokens in your collection of documents) into a number, and then you convert this number into an index of your feature vector. The process is illustrated in Figure 4.9.

Let's illustrate how it would work for converting a text "Love is a doing word" into a feature vector. Let us have a hash function h that takes a string as input and outputs a non-negative integer, and let the desired dimensionality be 5. By applying the hash function to each word and applying the modulo of 5 to obtain the index of the word, we get:

$$h(love) \bmod 5 = 0$$
$$h(is) \bmod 5 = 3$$
$$h(a) \bmod 5 = 1$$
$$h(doing) \bmod 5 = 3$$
$$h(word) \bmod 5 = 4.$$

Then we build the feature vector as,

$$[1, 1, 0, 2, 1].$$

Indeed, $h(love) \bmod 5 = 0$ means that we have one word in dimension 0 of the feature vector; $h(is) \bmod 5 = 3$ and $h(doing) \bmod 5 = 3$ means that we have two words in dimension 3 of the feature vector, and so on. As you can see, there is a **collision** between words "is" and "doing": they both are represented by dimension 3. The lower the desired dimensionality, the higher are the chances of collision. This is the trade-off between speed and quality of learning.

Commonly used hash functions are **MurmurHash3**, **Jenkins**, **CityHash**, and **MD5**.

4.2.5   Topic Modeling

Topic modeling is a family of techniques that uses unlabeled data, typically in the form of natural language text documents. The model learns to represent a document as a vector of topics. For example, in a collection of news articles, the five major topics could be "sports," "politics," "entertainment," "finance," and "technology". Then, each document could be represented as a five-dimensional feature vector, one dimension per topic:

$$[0.04, 0.5, 0.1, 0.3, 0.06]$$

The above feature vector represents a document that mixes two major topics: politics (with a weight of 0.5) and finance (with a weight of 0.3). Topic modeling algorithms, such as

Latent Semantic Analysis (LSA) and **Latent Dirichlet Allocation** (LDA), learn by analyzing the unlabeled documents. These two algorithms produce similar outputs, but are based on different mathematical models. LSA uses **singular value decomposition** (SVD) of the word-to-document matrix (constructed using a binary **bag-of-words** or **TF-IDF**). LDA uses a hierarchical **Bayesian model**, in which each document is a **mixture** of several topics, and each word's presence is attributable to one of the topics.

Let us illustrate how it works in Python and R. Below is a Python code for LSA:

```python
from sklearn.feature_extraction.text import TfidfVectorizer
from sklearn.decomposition import TruncatedSVD

class LSA():
    def __init__(self, docs):
        # Convert documents to TF-IDF vectors
        self.TF_IDF = TfidfVectorizer()
        self.TF_IDF.fit(docs)
        vectors = self.TF_IDF.transform(docs)

        # Build the LSA topic model
        self.LSA_model = TruncatedSVD(n_components=50)
        self.LSA_model.fit(vectors)
        return

    def get_features(self, new_docs):
        # Get topic-based features for new documents
        new_vectors = self.TF_IDF.transform(new_docs)
        return self.LSA_model.transform(new_vectors)

# Later, in production, instantiate LSA model
docs = ["This is a text.", "This another one."]
LSA_featurizer = LSA(docs)

# Get topic-based features for new_docs
new_docs = ["This is a third text.", "This is a fourth one."]
LSA_features = LSA_featurizer.get_features(new_docs)
```

The corresponding code[3] in R is shown below:

```r
library(tm)
library(lsa)

```

---

[3]The R code for LSA and LDA is courtesy of Julian Amon.

```
4   get_features <- function(LSA_model, new_docs){
5       # new_docs can be passed as a tm::Corpus object or as a vector
6       # holding character strings representing documents:
7       if(!inherits(new_docs, "Corpus")) new_docs <- VCorpus(VectorSource(new_docs))
8       tdm_test <- TermDocumentMatrix(
9           new_docs,
10          control = list(
11              dictionary = rownames(LSA_model$tk),
12              weighting = weightTfIdf
13          )
14      )
15      txt_mat <- as.textmatrix(as.matrix(tdm_test))
16      crossprod(t(crossprod(txt_mat, LSA_model$tk)), diag(1/LSA_model$sk))
17  }
18
19  # Train LSA model using docs
20  docs <- c("This is a text.", "This another one.")
21  corpus <- VCorpus(VectorSource(docs))
22  tdm_train <- TermDocumentMatrix(
23  corpus, control = list(weighting = weightTfIdf))
24  txt_mat <- as.textmatrix(as.matrix(tdm_train))
25  LSA_fit <- lsa(txt_mat, dims = 2)
26
27  # Later, in production, get topic-based features for new_docs
28  new_docs <- c("This is a third text.", "This is a fourth one.")
29  LSA_features <- get_features(LSA_fit, new_docs)
```

Below is a Python code for LDA:

```
1   from sklearn.feature_extraction.text import CountVectorizer
2   from sklearn.decomposition import LatentDirichletAllocation
3
4   class LDA():
5       def __init__(self, docs):
6           # Convert documents to TF-IDF vectors
7           self.TF = CountVectorizer()
8           self.TF.fit(docs)
9           vectors = self.TF.transform(docs)
10          # Build the LDA topic model
11          self.LDA_model = LatentDirichletAllocation(n_components=50)
12          self.LDA_model.fit(vectors)
13          return
14      def get_features(self, new_docs):
```

```
15      # Get topic-based features for new documents
16      new_vectors = self.TF.transform(new_docs)
17      return self.LDA_model.transform(new_vectors)
18
19  # Later, in production, instantiate LDA model
20  docs = ["This is a text.", "This another one."]
21  LDA_featurizer = LDA(docs)
22
23  # Get topic-based features for new_docs
24  new_docs = ["This is a third text.", "This is a fourth one."]
25  LDA_features = LDA_featurizer.get_features(new_docs)
```

And here is the corresponding code in R:

```
1   library(tm)
2   library(topicmodels)
3
4   # Generate feature for new_docs by using LDA_model
5   get_features <- function(LDA_mode, new_docs){
6     # new_docs can be passed as tm::Corpus object or as a vector
7     # holding character strings representing documents:
8     if(!inherits(new_docs, "Corpus")) new_docs <- VCorpus(VectorSource(new_docs))
9     new_dtm <- DocumentTermMatrix(new_docs, control = list(weighting = weightTf))
10    posterior(LDA_mode, newdata = new_dtm)$topics
11  }
12
13  # train LDA model using docs
14  docs <- c("This is a text.", "This another one.")
15  corpus <- VCorpus(VectorSource(docs))
16  dtm <- DocumentTermMatrix(corpus, control = list(weighting = weightTf))
17  LDA_fit <- LDA(dtm, k = 5)
18
19  # later, in production, get topic-based features for new_docs
20  new_docs <- c("This is a third text.", "This is a fourth one.")
21  LDA_features <- get_features(LDA_fit, new_docs)
```

In the above listings, docs is a collection of text documents. It can, for example, be a list of strings, where each string is a document.

4.2.6   Features for Time-Series

Time-series data is different from the traditional supervised learning data, which has a form of unordered collections of independent observations. A time series is an ordered sequence of observations, and each is marked with a time-related attribute, such as timestamp, date, month-year, year, and so on. An example of a time-series data is given in Figure 4.10.

Date	Stock Price	S&P 500	Dow Jones
2020-01-11	...	...	...
2020-01-12	14.5	3,345	28,583
2020-01-12	14.7	3,352	28,611
2020-01-12	15.9	3,347	29,001
2020-01-13	17.9	3,298	28,312
2016-01-13	16.8	3,521	28,127
2020-01-14	17.9	3,687	28,564
2016-01-15	16.8	3,540	27,998
2016-01-16	...	...	...

Figure 4.10: An example of time-series data in the form of an event stream.

Date	Stock Price	S&P 500	Dow Jones
2020-01-11	...	...	...
2020-01-12	15.0	3,348	28,732
2020-01-13	17.4	3,410	28,220
2020-01-14	17.9	3,687	28,564
2016-01-15	16.8	3,540	27,998
2016-01-16	...	...	...

Figure 4.11: Classical time series obtained by aggregating the event stream from Figure 4.10.

In Figure 4.10, each row corresponds to the cost of a certain stock at a moment in time, as well as the values of two indices: S&P 500 and Dow Jones. The observations were made

example i			
$t-2$	15.0	3,348	28,732
$t-1$	17.4	3,410	28,220

example $i+1$			
$t-2$	17.4	3,410	28,220
$t-1$	17.9	3,687	28,564

example $i+2$			
$t-2$	17.9	3,687	28,564
$t-1$	16.8	3,540	27,998

Figure 4.12: Time-series chunked into segments of length $w = 2$.

irregularly: on 2020-01-12, three observations were made. On 2020-01-13, there were two observations. In the **classical time-series data**, observations are evenly spaced over time, such as one observation per second, per minute, per day, and so on. If observations are irregular, such time-series data is called a **point process** or an **event stream**.

It's usually possible to convert an event stream into the classical time-series data by aggregating observations. Examples of aggregation operators are COUNT and AVERAGE. By applying the AVERAGE operator to the event stream data in Figure 4.10, we obtain the classical time-series data shown in Figure 4.11.

While it's possible to directly work with event streams, bringing time series to the classical form makes it simpler to apply further aggregations and generate features for machine learning.

Analysts typically use time-series data to solve two kinds of prediction problems. Given a sequence of recent observations:

- predict something about the next observation (for example, given the stock price and the value of stock indices for the last seven days, predict the stock price for tomorrow), or
- predict something about the phenomenon that generated that sequence (for example, given a user's connection log to a software system, predict whether they are likely to cancel their subscription during the current quarter).

Before neural networks reached their modern learning capacity, analysts worked with time-series data using the **shallow machine learning** toolkit. To transform a time-series into training data in the form of feature vectors, two decisions must be made:

- how many of the consecutive observations are needed to make an accurate prediction (so-called prediction window), and
- how to convert a sequence of observations into a fixed-dimensionality feature vector.

There's no simple way to answer either question. Usually decisions are made based on the subject-matter expert's knowledge, or by using a **hyperparameter tuning** technique. However, some recipes work for many time-series data. Below is one such recipe:

1) chunk the entire time series into segments of length w,
2) create a training example e from each segment s,
3) for each e, calculate various statistics on the observations in s.

We take Figure 4.11's data and chunk it into segments of length $w = 2$, where w the length of the prediction window. Figure 4.12 shows that each segment is now a separate example.

In practice, w is usually larger than 2. Let's say our prediction window has a length of seven. The statistics calculated at step (3) of the above recipe could be:

- average (e.g., the **mean** or **median** of the stock price during the last seven days),
- spread (e.g., **standard deviation**, **median absolute deviation**, or **interquartile range** of the values of the S&P 500 index during the last seven days),
- outliers (e.g., the fraction of observations, in which the values of the Dow Jones index was atypically low; for example, more than two standard deviations from the mean),
- growth (e.g., whether the values of the S&P 500 index have grown between the day $t - 6$ and t, days $t - 3$ and t, and between $t - 1$ and t.
- visual (e.g., how different the curve of the stock price values is from a known visual image, such as a hat, or head and shoulders).

Now you see why converting a time series into a classical form is recommended: the above statistics are only meaningful when calculated on the comparable values.

It should be noted that in the modern neural-network era, analysts most often prefer to train deep neural networks. **Long short-term memory** (LSTM), **convolutional neural network** (CNN), and **Transformer** are popular choices of architecture for a time-series model. These can read arbitrary length time-series as input, and generate a prediction based on the entire sequence. Similarly, neural networks are often applied to texts by reading them word-by-word, or character-by-character. Words and characters are usually represented as **embedding vectors**; the latter are learned from large corpora of text documents. We will talk about embeddings in Section 4.7.1.

4.2.7 Use Your Creativity

As I mentioned at the beginning of this section, feature engineering is a creative process. As an analyst, you are in the best position to determine what are good features for your prediction model. Put yourself "in the shoes" of a learning algorithm and imagine what you would look at in your data to decide which label to assign.

Say you are classifying emails as important or unimportant. You might notice that a significant number of important messages come from the government revenue agency on the first Monday of each month. Create a feature "government first monday." Let it equal 1 when the email came from the government revenue agency on the first Monday of a month, and 0 otherwise. Alternatively, you might notice that an email with more than one smiley is rarely important. Create a feature "contains smileys." Let it equal 1 when an email contains more than one smiley, and 0 otherwise.

4.3 Stacking Features

Back to our problem of movie title classification in tweets. Each example has three parts:

1) five words[4] that precede the extracted potential movie title (the left context),
2) the extracted potential movie title (the extraction),
3) five words that follow the extracted movie title (the right context).

To represent such multi-part examples, we first transform each part into a feature vector, and then stack the three feature vectors next to one another to obtain the feature vector for the entire example.

4.3.1 Stacking Feature Vectors

In our movie title classification problem, we first collect all the left contexts. We then apply bag-of-words to transform each left context into a binary feature vector. Next, collect all extractions and, using bag-of-words, transform each extraction into a binary feature vector. Then we collect all the right contexts and apply bag-of-words to transform each right context into a binary feature vector. Finally, we concatenate each example, joining the feature vectors of the left context, the extraction, and the right context. We obtain the final feature vector that represents the entire example, as shown in Figure 4.13.

Note that the three feature vectors (one from each part of the example) are created independently of one another. This means that the vocabulary of tokens is different for each part and, therefore, the feature vector dimensionality of each part may also be different.

The order in which you concatenate feature vectors doesn't matter. The left context features can be placed in the middle or right side of the final feature vector. However, you must keep the same concatenation order in all examples. This ensures each feature represents the same property from one example to another.

4.3.2 Stacking Individual Features

Until now, we engineered features in bulk. One-hot encoding and bag-of-words often generate thousands of features. This is a very time-efficient way of engineering features, but some problems require more to obtain feature vectors with high enough **predictive power**. We consider the predictive power of a feature in the next section.

Imagine that you already have a classifier m_A that takes an entire tweet as input and predicts its topic. Let one of the topics be cinema. You might want to enrich the feature vectors in

---

[4]In practice, the context to the left or the right of the potential movie title can for some examples be shorter than five words, because it's either the beginning or the end of the tweet.

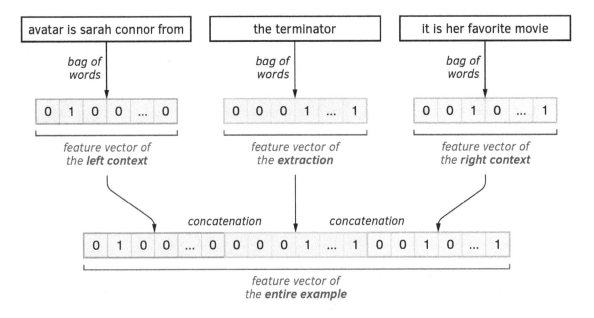

Figure 4.13: Creating and stacking feature vectors.

your movie title classification problem with this additional information available from the classifier m_A. In this case, you will engineer one feature that can be described as "whether the topic of the tweet is cinema" and that feature will also be binary: 1 if the topic predicted by m_A for the entire tweet is cinema, and 0 otherwise. Again, we concatenate the three partial feature vectors, as shown in Figure 4.14.

You might come up with many more useful features for title classification in tweets. Examples of such features are:

- the average IMDB score of the movie,
- the number of votes for the movie on IMDB,
- the Rotten Tomato score of the movie,
- whether the movie is recent (or the number that represents the release year),
- whether the tweet text contains other movie titles, and
- whether the tweet text includes the names of actors or directors.

All these additional features, as long as they are numerical, can be concatenated to the feature vector. The only condition is that they are concatenated in the same order in all examples.

	B-o-w 1	B-o-w 2														B-o-w M-1	B-o-w M	Is cinema?
Example 1	0	1	0	0	...	0	0	0	0	1	...	1	0	0	1	0	...	1	1
Example 2	0	0	1	1	...	1	0	1	0	1	...	0	1	1	1	0	...	0	0
⋮	...	...	...	...	...	...	...	...	...	...	...	...	...	...	...	...	...	...	...
Example N	0	0	1	1	...	0	1	1	0	1	...	1	1	0	1	1	...	1	1

Figure 4.14: Single feature stacking.

4.4 Properties of Good Features

Not all features are created equal. In this section, we consider the properties of a good feature.

4.4.1 High Predictive Power

First of all, a good feature has high **predictive power**. In Chapter 3, you read about predictive power as a property of data. However, a feature can also have high or low predictive power. Let's say you want to predict whether a patient has cancer. Among other features, you know the make of the person's car and whether the person is married. These two features are not good predictors for cancer, so our machine learning algorithm will not learn a meaningful relationship between these features and the label. Predictive power is a property of the feature with respect to the problem. The make of the person's car and whether the person is married could have high predictive power if the problem were different.

4.4.2 Fast Computability

Good features can be computed fast. Let's say you want to predict the topic of a tweet. A tweet is short, and a bag-of-words-based feature vector will be sparse. A **sparse vector** is a vector whose values in most dimensions are zero. If your dataset is small and the texts are short, the learning algorithm will have a hard time seeing patterns in sparse vectors because they contain little information compared to their size. The information in one sparse vector is rarely contained in the same dimensions as the information in another sparse vector, even if they represent similar concepts.

To reduce sparsity, you might want to augment your sparse feature vectors with additional non-zero values. To do that, you might send the tweet text to Wikipedia as a search query, and then extract other words from the search results. Wikipedia's API doesn't give any guarantee for the speed of response, so it could take several seconds to get a response. For real-time systems, feature extraction must be fast: a less informative feature computed in a fraction of a millisecond is often preferred to a feature with a high predictive power that takes seconds to compute. If your application must be fast, the features obtained from Wikipedia might not be appropriate for your task.

4.4.3   Reliability

A good feature must also be reliable. Again, in our Wikipedia example, we cannot have a guarantee that the website will respond at all: it can be down, on planned maintenance, or the API may be temporarily overused and is rejecting requests. Therefore, we cannot trust that Wikipedia-based features will always be available and complete. Thus, we cannot call such features reliable. One unreliable feature can reduce the quality of predictions made by your model. Furthermore, some predictions can become entirely wrong if the value of an important feature is missing.

4.4.4   Uncorrelatedness

Correlation of two features means their values are related. If the growth of one feature implies the growth of the other, and the inverse is also true, then the two features are correlated.

Once the model is in production, its performance may change because the input data's properties may change over time. When many of your features are highly correlated, even a minor change in the input data's properties may result in significant changes in the model's behavior.

Sometimes the model was built under strict time constraints, so the developer used all possible sources of features. With time, maintaining those sources can become costly. It's generally recommended to eliminate redundant or highly correlated features. Feature selection techniques help reduce such features.

4.4.5   Other Properties

An essential property of a good feature is that the distribution of its values in the training set is similar to the distribution it will receive in production. For example, a tweet's date might be necessary for some predictions about it. However, if you apply the model built on historical tweets to predict something about current tweets, the date of your production examples will always be out of the training distribution, which can result in a significant error.[5]

Finally, features that you design should be unitary, easy to understand, and maintain. Unitary means the feature represents a certain simple-to-understand and -explain quantity. For

---

[5]The date information often is relevant for machine learning and can still be included in the training data. For instance, you could consider engineering **cyclical features** like "hour of the day," "day of the week," "month of the year." For the prediction problems in which time seasonality has predictive power, having such features can be useful.

example, when classifying a car's type given its characteristics, you may use such unitary features as weight, length, width, and color. A feature like "length divided by weight" is not unitary, as it's composed of two unitary features.

Some learning algorithms may benefit from combining features. However, it's preferable to do this in a dedicated stage in the model training pipeline. We will consider feature combination and generation of synthetic features later in this chapter.

4.5 Feature Selection

Not all features will be equally important for your problem. For instance, in the problem of detecting movies in tweets, the length of the movie might not be a very important feature. At the same time, when you use bag-of-words, the vocabulary can be very large, while most tokens will appear in the collection of texts only once. If the learning algorithm "sees" that some feature has a non-zero value only in a couple of training examples, it is doubtful the algorithm will learn any useful pattern from that feature. However, if the feature vector is very wide (contains thousands or millions of features), the training time can become prohibitively long. Furthermore, the overall size of the training data can become too large to fit in the RAM of a conventional server.

If we could estimate the importance of features, we would keep only the most important ones. That would allow us to save time, fit more examples in memory, and improve the model's quality. Below, we consider some feature selection techniques.

4.5.1 Cutting the Long Tail

Typically, if a feature contains information (e.g., a non-zero value) only for a handful of examples, such a feature could be removed from the feature vector. In **bag-of-words**, you can build a graph with the distribution of token counts, and then cut off the so-called long tail, as shown in Figure 4.15.

A **long tail** of a distribution is such a part of that distribution that contains elements with substantially lower counts compared to a smaller group of elements with the highest counts. This smaller group is called the head of the distribution, and their aggregated counts make for at least half of all the counts.

The decision on a threshold for defining the long tail is somewhat subjective. You can set it as a hyperparameter for your problem and discover the optimal value experimentally. On the other hand, the decision can be made by looking at the distribution of counts, as shown in Figure 4.15a. As you can see, I cut off the long tail at a point where the distribution of the elements in the tail has become visually flat (Figure 4.15b).

Whether to cut the long tail, and where to do it, is debatable. In classification problems with many classes, the difference between some classes can be very subtle. Even features whose

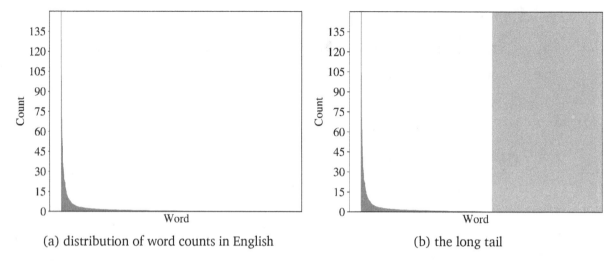

(a) distribution of word counts in English   (b) the long tail

Figure 4.15: The distribution of word counts in a collection of texts in English (a) and the long tail (b, zone in blue). The highest count corresponds to "the" (a count of 615); the lowest count corresponds to "zambia" (a count of 1).

values are rarely non-zero may become important. However, removing long-tail features often results in faster learning and a better model.

4.5.2   Boruta

Cutting the long tail is not the only way to select important features and remove less important ones. One popular tool used in **Kaggle** competitions is **Boruta**. Boruta iteratively trains **random forest** models and runs **statistical tests** to identify features as important and unimportant. The tool exists both in the form of an R package and a Python module.

Boruta works as a wrapper around the random forest learning algorithm, hence its name — Boruta is a spirit of the forests in Slavic mythology. To understand the Boruta algorithm, let's first recall how the random forest learning algorithm works.

Random forest is based on the idea of **bagging**. It makes many random samples of the training set and then trains a different statistical model on each sample. The prediction is then made by taking the majority vote (for classification) or an average (for regression) of all models. The only substantial difference of random forest from the vanilla bagging algorithm is that in the former, the trained statistical models are decision trees. At each split of the decision tree, a random subset of all features is considered.

One useful feature of the random forest is its built-in capability to estimate the importance of each feature. Below, I will explain how this estimation works for the case of classification.

The algorithm works in two stages. First, it classifies all training examples from the original training set. Each decision tree in the random forest model votes only on the classification of examples that weren't used to build that tree. After a tree is tested, the number of correct predictions is recorded for that tree.

At the second stage, the values of a certain feature are randomly permuted across examples, and the tests are repeated. The number of correct predictions is once again recorded for each tree. The importance of the feature for a single tree is then computed as the difference between the number of correct classifications between the original and permuted setting, divided by the number of examples. To obtain the feature importance score, the feature importance measures for individual trees are averaged. While not strictly necessary, it's convenient to use **z-scores** instead of the raw importance scores.

To obtain a z-score for a feature, we first find the average value and the standard deviation of individual feature scores for individual trees. The feature's z-score is obtained by subtracting the average value from the score, and then dividing it by the standard deviation.

You might stop here and use the z-scores of each feature as the criterion to keep it (the higher, the better). However, in practice, the importance score alone often doesn't reflect meaningful correlations between features and the target. Therefore, we need a different tool to distinguish the truly important features from the non-important ones, and, as you could guess, Boruta provides that tool.

The underlying idea of Boruta is simple: we first extend the list of features by adding a randomized copy of each original feature, and then build a classifier based on this extended dataset. To assess the importance of an original feature, we compare it to all randomized features. Only features for which the importance is higher than that of the randomized features — and statistically significant — are considered truly important.

Below, I outline the main steps of the Boruta algorithm in the way it was described by its authors[6] with adaptations for consistency and clarity:

The Boruta Algorithm

- Build extended training feature vectors, where each original feature is replicated. Randomly permute the values of the replicated features across the training examples to remove any correlation between the replicated variables and the target.
- Perform several random forest learning runs. The replicated features are randomized before each run by applying the same random feature value permutation process as in the previous step.
- For each run, compute the importance (z-score) of all original and replicated features.
  - A feature is deemed important for a single run if its importance is higher than the maximal importance among all replicated features.

---

[6]Miron B. Kursa, Aleksander Jankowski, Witold R. Rudnicki, "Boruta - A System for Feature Selection," published in Fundamenta Informaticae 101 in 2010, pages 271–285.

- Perform a **statistical test** for all original features.
  - The **null hypothesis** is that the feature's importance is equal to the maximal importance of the replicated features (MIRA).
  - The statistical test is a **two-sided equality test** - the hypothesis may be rejected either when the importance of the feature is significantly higher or significantly lower than MIRA.
  - For each original feature, we count and record the number of hits.
  - The number of hits for a feature is the number of runs in which the importance of that feature was higher than MIRA.
  - The expected number of hits for R runs is $E(R) = 0.5R$ with standard deviation $S = \sqrt{0.25R}$ (**binomial distribution** with $p = q = 0.5$).
  - An original feature is deemed important (accepted) when the number of hits is significantly higher than the expected number of hits and is deemed unimportant (rejected) when the number of hits is significantly lower than the expected. (It is possible to compute limits for accepting and rejecting feature for any number of runs for the desired confidence level.)
- Remove the features which are deemed unimportant from the feature vectors (both original and replicated).
- Perform the same procedure for a predefined number of iterations, or until all features are either rejected or conclusively deemed important, whichever comes first.

Boruta worked well for many Kaggle competitions; therefore, you can consider it a universally applicable tool for feature selection. One thing worth noting, though, before using Boruta in production: Boruta is a heuristic. There are no theoretical guarantees for its performance. If you want to be sure that Boruta doesn't harm, run it multiple times and make sure that the feature selection is stable (i.e., consistent across multiple Boruta applications to your data). If the feature selection is not stable, make sure that the number of trees in the random forest is large enough to generate stable results.

Though Boruta is an effective method of feature selection, it's not the only one used by practitioners. You will find the description of several other methods in the book's companion wiki in an extended version of this chapter.

4.5.3 L1-Regularization

Regularization is an umbrella term for a range of techniques that improve the **generalization** of the model. Generalization, in turn, is the model's ability to correctly predict the label for unseen examples.

While regularization doesn't let you identify important features, some regularization techniques, such as L1, allow the machine learning algorithm to learn to ignore some features.

Depending on the kind of model you train, L1 may apply differently, but the main principle remains the same: L1 penalizes the model for being too complex.

In practice, L1 regularization produces a **sparse model**, which is a model that has most of its parameters equal to zero. Therefore, L1 implicitly performs feature selection by deciding which features are essential for prediction, and which ones are not. We will talk about regularization in more detail in the next chapter.

4.5.4 Task-Specific Feature Selection

Feature selection can also be task-specific. For example, we can remove some features from bag-of-words vectors representing natural language texts by excluding the dimensions corresponding to **stop words**. Stop words are the words that are too generic or common for the problem we are trying to solve. Frequent examples of stop words are articles, prepositions, and pronouns. Dictionaries of stop words for most languages are available online.

To further reduce the feature vector dimensionality obtained from the text data, sometimes it's practical to preprocess the text by replacing infrequent words (e.g., those whose count in the corpus is below three) with the same synthetic token, for example RARE_WORD.

4.6 Synthesizing Features

The learning algorithms implemented in the most popular machine learning package for Python, **scikit-learn**, only work with numerical features. But it can still be useful to convert numerical features into categorical ones.

4.6.1 Feature Discretization

The reasons to discretize a real-valued numerical feature can be numerous. For example, some feature selection techniques only apply to categorical features. A successful discretization adds useful information to the learning algorithm when the training dataset is relatively small. Numerous studies show that discretization can lead to improved predictive accuracy. It is also simpler for a human to interpret a model's prediction if it is based on discrete groups of values, such as age groups or salary ranges.

Binning, also known as **bucketing**, is a popular technique that allows transforming a numerical feature into a categorical one by replacing numerical values in a specific range by a constant categorical value.

There are three typical approaches to binning:

- uniform binning,
- k-means-based binning, and

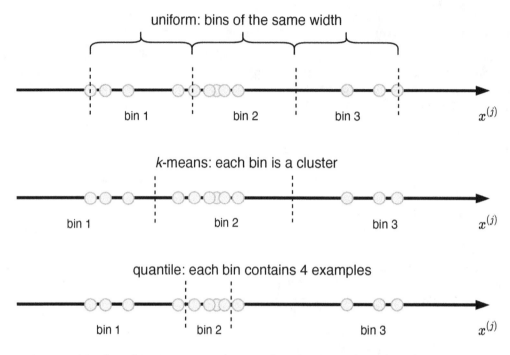

Figure 4.16: Three binning approaches: uniform, k-means-based, and quantile-based.

- quantile-based binning.

In all three cases, you should decide how many bins you want to have. Consider an illustration in Figure 4.16. Here, we have a numerical feature j and 12 values of this feature, one for each of the 12 examples in our dataset. Let's say we decided to have three bins. In uniform binning, all bins for a feature have identical widths, as illustrated in Figure 4.16 on the top.

In k-means-based binning, values in each bin belong to the nearest one-dimensional k-means cluster, as shown in Figure 4.16 in the middle.

In quantile-based binning, all bins have the same number of examples, as shown in Figure 4.16 at the bottom.

In uniform binning, once the model is deployed in production, if the value of the feature in the input feature vector is below or above the range of any bin, then the closest bin is assigned, which is either the leftmost or the rightmost bin.

Remember, most modern machine learning algorithm implementations require numerical features. The bins must be transformed back to numerical values by using a technique like **one-hot encoding**.

User

User ID	Gender	Age	...	Date Subscribed
1	M	18	...	2016-01-12
2	F	25	...	2017-08-23
3	F	28	...	2019-12-19
4	M	19	...	2019-12-18
5	F	21	...	2016-11-30

Order

Order ID	User ID	Amount	...	Order Date
1	2	23	...	2017-09-13
2	4	18	...	2018-11-23
3	2	7.5	...	2019-12-19
4	2	8.3	...	2016-11-30

Call

Call ID	User ID	Call Duration	...	Call Date
1	4	55	...	2016-01-12
2	2	235	...	2016-01-13
3	3	476	...	2016-12-17
4	4	334	...	2019-12-19
5	4	14	...	2016-11-30

Figure 4.17: Relational data for churn analysis.

User features

User ID	Gender	Age	Mean Order Amount	Std Dev Order Amount	Mean Call Duration	Std Dev Call Duration
2	F	25	12.9	7.1	235	0
4	M	19	18	0	134.3	142.7

Figure 4.18: Synthetic features based on sample mean and standard deviation.

4.6.2 Synthesizing Features from Relational Data

Data analysts often work with data in a **relational database**. For example, a mobile phone operator wants to know whether a customer will soon abandon the subscription. This problem is known as **churn analysis**. We have to represent each customer as a vector of features.

Let's say the data on the users is contained in three relational tables: User, Order, and Call, as shown in Figure 4.17.

The table User already contains two potentially useful features: Gender and Age. We can also create synthetic features using the data from tables Order and Call. As you can see, user 2 has three rows in table Order, while user 4 has one row in table Order, but three rows in table Calls. In order to create a feature that represents one user, we have to reduce those several records into one value. A typical approach is to compute various statistics from the data coming from multiple rows and use the value of each statistic as a feature. The most commonly used statistics are **sample mean** and **standard deviation**. (Standard deviation is the square root of **sample variance**.)

To give a concrete example, I have calculated the values of four features for users 2 and 4. You can find them in Figure 4.18.

Sometimes, a relational database can have a deeper structure. For example, a user can have orders, while each order can have ordered items. In such a case, we can compute a statistic of a statistic. For example, one feature can be created by first calculating the standard deviation of item prices in each order, and then by taking the average of those standard deviations for a specific user. You can combine the statistics in arbitrary ways: the mean of the mean, the standard deviation of the mean, the standard deviation of the standard deviation, and so on. The same principle applies to the database whose table structure is deeper than two levels.

Once you have generated features based on all possible combinations of statistics, you can select the most useful ones by using one of the feature selection methods.

If you want to increase the predictive power of your feature vectors, or when your training set is rather small, you can synthesize additional features that would help in predictions. There are two typical ways to synthesize additional features: from the data, or from other features.

4.6.3 Synthesizing Features from the Data

One technique commonly used to synthesize one or more additional features is **clustering**. Let us use the **k-means clustering**. Choose a value for k. If your ultimate goal is to build a classification model, a common way to assign a value for k is to use the number C of classes. In regression, use your intuition or apply any technique allowing to determine the right value of clusters in your data, such as **prediction strength** or the **elbow method**. Apply k-means clustering to the feature vectors in your training data. Then add k additional features to your feature vectors. The additional feature $D + j$, where $j = 1, \ldots, k$, will be binary and equal to 1 if the corresponding feature vector belongs to cluster j.

You can synthesize even more features by applying different clustering algorithms, or by restarting k-means multiple times from randomly chosen starting points.

4.6.4 Synthesizing Features from Other Features

Neural networks are notorious for their ability to learn complex features by combining simple features in unordinary ways. They combine simple features by letting their values undergo several levels of nested nonlinear transformations. If you have data in abundance, you can train a deep **multilayer perceptron** model that will learn to cleverly combine the basic unitary features it receives as input.

If you don't have an infinite supply of training examples (often the case in practice), very deep neural networks lose their appeal.[7] In the case of smaller to moderately large datasets (the number of training examples varies between a thousand and a hundred thousand), you might prefer to use a shallow learning algorithm and "help" your learning algorithm learn by providing a richer set of features.

In practice, the most common way to obtain new features from the existing features is to apply a simple transformation to one or a pair of existing features. Three typical simple transformations that apply to a numerical feature j in example i are 1) **discretization** of the feature, 2) squaring the feature, and 3) computing the sample mean and the standard deviation of feature j from k-nearest neighbors of the example i found by using some metric like Euclidean distance or cosine similarity.

Transformations that apply to a pair of numerical features are simple arithmetic operators: $+$, $-$, $\times$, and $\div$ (a technique also known as **feature-crossing**). For example, you can obtain the value of a new feature q in example i, where $q > D$, by combining the values of features 2 and 6 in the following way: $x_i^{(q)} \overset{\text{def}}{=} x_i^{(2)} \div x_i^{(6)}$. I selected features 2 and 6, as well as the transformation $\div$ arbitrarily. If the number D of original features is not too large, you can generate all possible transformations (by considering all pairs of features and all arithmetic operators). Then, by using one of the feature selection methods, select those that increase the quality of the model.

---

[7]Unless you use deep pre-trained models in **transfer learning**, as we will discuss in the next chapter.

4.7 Learning Features from Data

Sometimes, useful features can be learned from data. Learning features from data is especially effective when we can get access to large collections of relevant labeled or unlabeled data, such as text corpora or collections of images from the Web.

4.7.1 Word Embeddings

In Chapter 3, we used word embeddings for data augmentation. **Word embeddings** are feature vectors that represent words. Similar words have similar feature vectors, where similarity is given by a certain measure, such as **cosine similarity**. Word embeddings are learned from large corpora of text documents. A **shallow neural network** with one hidden layer (called the **embedding layer**) is trained to predict a word, given its surrounding words, or to predict the surrounding words, given the word in the middle. Once the neural network is trained, the parameters of the embedding layer are used as word embeddings. There are many algorithms to learn word embeddings from data. The most widely used algorithm, invented at Google, with the code available in open source, is **word2vec**. Pre-trained word2vec embeddings for many languages are available for download.

Once you have a collection of word embeddings for some language, you can use them to represent individual words in sentences or documents written in that language, instead of using **one-hot encoding**.

Let's see how word embeddings are trained by one version of the word2vec algorithm called **skip-gram**. In word embedding learning, our goal is to build a model that we can use to convert a one-hot encoding of a word into a word embedding. Let our dictionary contain 10,000 words. The one-hot vector for each word is a 10,000-dimensional vector of all zeros, except for one dimension that contains a 1. Different words have a 1 in different dimensions.

Consider a sentence: "I am attentively reading the book on machine learning engineering." Now, take the same sentence, but remove one word, say "book." Our sentence becomes: "I am attentively reading the · on machine learning engineering." Now let's only keep the three words before the · and the three words after it: "attentively reading the · on machine learning." Looking at this six-word window around the ·, if I ask you to guess what · stands for, you would probably say: "book," "article," or "paper." That's how the context words let you predict the word they surround. It's also how the machine can learn that words "book," "paper," and "article" have a similar meaning. They share similar contexts in multiple texts.

It turns out that it works the other way around too: a word can predict the context surrounding it. The piece "attentively reading the · on machine learning" is called a skip-gram, with window size 6 (3 + 3). By using the documents available on the Web, we can easily create hundreds of millions of skip-grams.

Let's denote a skip-gram in the following way: $[\mathbf{x}_{-3}, \mathbf{x}_{-2}, \mathbf{x}_{-1}, \mathbf{x}, \mathbf{x}_{+1}, \mathbf{x}_{+2}, \mathbf{x}_{+3}]$. In our sentence, $\mathbf{x}_{-3}$ is the one-hot vector for "attentively," $\mathbf{x}_{-2}$ corresponds to "reading," $\mathbf{x}$ is the skipped word $(\cdot)$, $\mathbf{x}_{+1}$ is "on," and so on.

A skip-gram with window size 4 will look like this: $[\mathbf{x}_{-2}, \mathbf{x}_{-1}, \mathbf{x}, \mathbf{x}_{+1}, \mathbf{x}_{+2}]$. It can also be schematically depicted, as shown in Figure 4.19. It is a **fully-connected network**, like the **multilayer perceptron**. The input word is denoted as $\cdot$ in the skip-gram. The neural network has to learn to predict the context words of the skip-gram, given the input's central word.

The **activation function** used in the output layer is **softmax**. The **cost function** is the **negative log-likelihood**. The embedding for a word is given by the parameters of the embedding layer that apply when a one-hot encoded word is given as the input to the model.

One problem with word embeddings trained using word2vec is that the set of word embeddings is fixed, and you cannot use the model for out-of-vocabulary words, that is, the words that weren't present in the corpus used to train word embeddings. There are other architectures of neural networks that allow obtaining embeddings for any word, including out-of-vocabulary words. One such architecture, often used in practice, is **fastText**. It was invented at Facebook, and the code is available in open source.

The key difference between word2vec and fastText is that word2vec treats each word in the corpus as a unitary entity, and learns a vector for each word. Alternatively, fastText treats each word as an average of embedding vectors representing character n-grams that word is composed of. For example, the embedding for the word "mouse" is an average of the embedding vectors of the n-grams "<mo," "mou," "<mou," "mous," "<mous," "mouse," "<mouse," "mouse>," "ous," "ouse," "ouse>," "use," "use>," "se>" (assuming that the sizes of the smallest and the largest n-gram are, respectively, 3 and 6).

Word embeddings are an effective way of representing natural language texts for use in such neural network architectures as **recurrent neural networks** (RNN) and convolutional neural networks (CNN) adapted for working with sequences. However, if you want to use word embeddings for representing variable-length texts for **shallow learning** algorithms (which require the input feature vectors of fixed dimensions), you would have to apply some aggregation operation to word vectors, such as weighted sum or average. The representation of a text document obtained as an average of the words composing that document turns out to be not very useful in practice.

4.7.2 Document Embeddings

A popular way of obtaining an embedding for a sentence or an entire document is to use the **doc2vec** neural network architecture, also invented at Google and available in open source. The architecture of doc2vec is very similar to word2vec. The only major difference is that now there are two embedding vectors, one for the document ID and one for the word. The prediction of the surrounding words for an input word is made by, first, averaging the two embedding vectors (the document embedding vector and the word embedding vector), and then predicting the surrounding words from that average. To average the two vectors, they must be of the same dimensionality. Interestingly, this makes it possible to compare not just

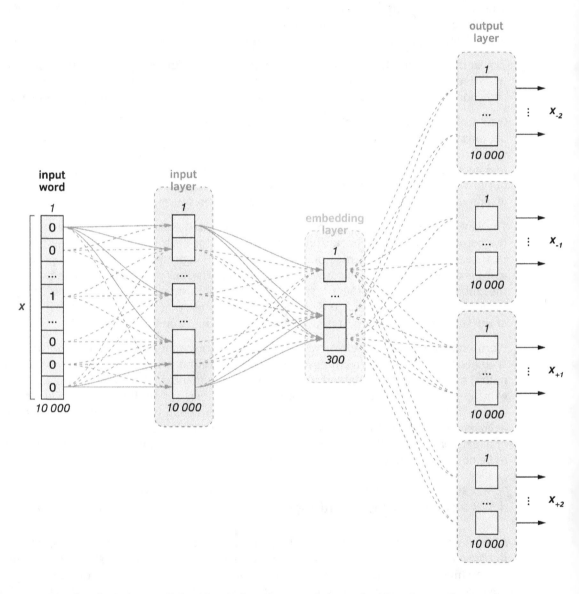

Figure 4.19: The skip-gram model with window size 4 and the embedding layer of 300 units.

document vectors (by finding the cosine similarity), but also a document and a word vector. The word vectors trained that way are very similar to those trained using word2vec.

To obtain an embedding for a new document, not belonging to the corpus of documents used to train document embeddings, this new document is first added to the corpus. It gets a new document ID assigned to it. Then the existing model is additionally trained for several epochs with all trained parameters being frozen but the new ones, corresponding to the new document ID. The input document ID is provided as a one-hot encoding.

4.7.3 Embeddings of Anything

The following technique is commonly used to obtain embedding vectors for any object (and not just words or documents). First, we formulate a supervised learning problem that takes our objects as input and outputs a prediction. Then we build a labeled dataset and train a neural network model that solves our supervised learning problem. Then we use the outputs of one of the fully connected layers near the output layer of the neural network model (before non-linearity) as embeddings of the input object.

For example, the ImageNet labeled dataset of images and a deep **convolutional neural network** (CNN) architecture, similar to **AlexNet**, is often used to train embeddings for images. An illustration of the embedding layers for images is shown in Figure 4.20. In this illustration, we have a deep CNN with two **fully connected layers** near the output. The neural network was trained to predict the object depicted in the image. To obtain an embedding of an image not used for training the model, we send that image (usually represented as three matrices of pixels, one per channel R, G, and B) to the input of the neural network, and then use the output of one of the fully connected layers before non-linearity. Which of the fully connected layers is better depends on the task you want to solve, and must be decided experimentally.

By following the above approach, we can train embeddings of any type. The data analyst only needs to figure out three things:

- what supervised learning problem to solve (for images, usually object classification),
- how to represent the input for the neural network (for images, matrices of pixels, one per channel), and
- what will be the architecture of the neural network before the fully connected layers (for images, usually a deep CNN).

4.7.4 Choosing Embedding Dimensionality

The embedding dimensionality is usually determined experimentally or from experience. For example, Google, in its TensorFlow documentation, recommends the following rule of thumb:

$$d = \sqrt[4]{D},$$

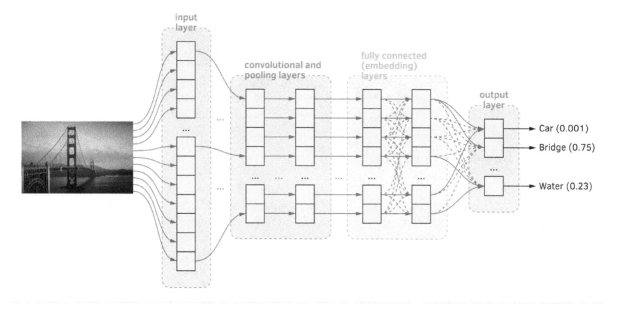

Figure 4.20: A neural network architecture for training image embeddings. The embedding layers are shown in green.

where d is the embedding dimensionality and D is the "number of categories." The number of categories for word embeddings is the number of unique words in the corpus. For arbitrary embeddings, it's the dimensionality of the original input. For example, if the number of the unique words in the corpus is $D = 5000000$ then the embedding dimensionality $d = \sqrt[4]{5000000} = 47$. In practice, values between 50 and 600 are often used.

A more principled approach to choose the embedding dimensionality is to treat it as a hyperparameter tuned on a downstream task. For example, if you have a labeled corpus of documents, then you can optimize the embedding dimensionality by minimizing the number of prediction errors made by the classifier trained on that labeled data, where the words in the documents are represented by the embeddings.

4.8 Dimensionality Reduction

Sometimes, it might be necessary to reduce the dimensionality of examples. This is different from the problem of feature selection. In the latter, we analyze the properties of all existing features and remove those that, in our opinion, do not contribute much to the quality of the model. When we apply a **dimensionality reduction** technique to a dataset, we replace all features in the original feature vector with a new vector, of lower dimensionality, and of synthetic features.

Dimensionality reduction often results in increased learning speed and better generalization. In addition, it improves visualization of datasets: humans can only see in three dimensions.

There are several ways to reduce dimensionality. And depending on why we want to do that, some are more popular than others. The dimensionality reduction techniques are well described in the machine learning theory books, so I will only discuss when a data analyst should prefer one technique over the others.

4.8.1 Fast Dimensionality Reduction with PCA

Principal Component Analysis (PCA) is the oldest of the techniques. It is also, by far, the fastest option. Performance comparison tests show a very weak dependence of the speed of the PCA algorithm on the size of the dataset. Therefore, you can effectively use PCA as a step preceding your model training, and find the optimal value of the reduced dimensionality experimentally as part of the hyperparameter tuning process.

PCA's most significant drawback is that the data must fit in memory entirely for the algorithm to work. There's an out-of-core version of PCA, called **Incremental PCA** that allows running the algorithm on batches of the dataset, loading in memory one batch at a time. Still, Incremental PCA is an order of magnitude slower than PCA. PCA is also less practical for visualization purposes as compared to the other two techniques considered below.

4.8.2 Dimensionality Reduction for Visualization

If visualization is your goal, then you would prefer Uniform Manifold Approximation and Projection (**UMAP**) algorithm, or an **autoencoder**. Both can be specifically programmed to produce 2D or 3D feature vectors, while in PCA, the algorithm produces D so-called **principal components** (where D is the dimensionality of your data), and the analyst must pick the first two or three principal components as features for visualization. UMAP is generally much faster than autoencoder, but the two techniques produce very different looking visualizations, so you would prefer one over the other based on the properties of the specific dataset. Furthermore, like PCA, UMAP requires all data to be in memory, while autoencoder can be trained in batches.

Dimensionality reduction can also be task-specific. For example, we can reduce the dimensionality of pictures by using an image editor. Similarly, we can reduce the bit rate and the number of channels of the sound sequences.

4.9 Scaling Features

Once all your features are numerical, you are almost ready to start working on your model. The only remaining step that might be helpful is scaling your features.

Feature scaling is bringing all your features to the same, or very similar, ranges of values or distributions. Multiple experiments demonstrated that a learning algorithm applied to scaled features might produce a better model. While there's no guarantee that scaling will have a positive impact on the quality of your model, it's considered a best practice. Scaling can also increase the training speed of deep neural networks. It also assures that no individual feature dominates, especially in the initial iterations of gradient descent or other iterative optimization algorithms. Finally, scaling reduces the risk of **numerical overflow**, the problem that computers have when working with very small or very big numbers.

4.9.1 Normalization

Normalization is the process of converting an actual range of values, which a numerical feature can take, into a predefined and artificial range of values, typically in the interval $[-1, 1]$ or $[0, 1]$.

For example, let the natural range of a feature be 350 to 1450. By subtracting 350 from every value of the feature, and dividing the result by 1100, we normalize those values to the range $[0, 1]$. More generally, the normalization formula looks like this:

$$\bar{x}^{(j)} \leftarrow \frac{x^{(j)} - \min^{(j)}}{\max^{(j)} - \min^{(j)}},$$

where $x^{(j)}$ is an original value of feature j in some example; $\min^{(j)}$ and $\max^{(j)}$ are, respectively, the minimum and the maximum value of the feature j in the training data.

If you prefer the range of $[-1, 1]$ then the normalization formula would look like this:

$$\bar{x}^{(j)} \leftarrow \frac{2 \times x^{(j)} - \max^{(j)} - \min^{(j)}}{\max^{(j)} - \min^{(j)}},$$

A drawback of normalization is that the values $\max^{(j)}$ and $\min^{(j)}$ are usually outliers, so normalization will "squeeze" the normal feature values into a very small range. One solution to this problem is to apply **clipping**, that is to pick "reasonable" values for $\max^{(j)}$ and $\min^{(j)}$ instead of using extreme values from the training data. Let a reasonable range for a feature be estimated as $[a, b]$. Before calculating the scaled value by using one of the above two formulas, the value $x^{(j)}$ of the feature is set ("clipped") to a if $x^{(j)}$ is below a, or to b if it's above b. A frequent way to estimate the values for a and b is **winsorization**. The technique is named after the engineer and biostatistician Charles Winsor (1895—1951). Winsorization consists of setting all outliers to a specified percentile of the data; for example, a 90% winsorization would see all data below the 5th percentile set to the 5th percentile, and data above the 95th percentile set to the 95th percentile. In Python, winsorization could be applied to a list of numbers as follows:

```
1  from scipy.stats.mstats import winsorize
2  winsorize(list_of_numbers, limits=[0.05, 0.05])
```

The output of the `winsorize` function will be a list of numbers of the same length as the input, with the values of outliers "clipped." A corresponding code in R is shown below:

```
1  library(DescTools)
2  DescTools::Winsorize(vector_of_numbers, probs = c(0.05, 0.95))
```

Sometimes, the **mean normalization** is used:

$$\bar{x}^{(j)} \leftarrow \frac{x^{(j)} - \mu^{(j)}}{\max^{(j)} - \min^{(j)}},$$

where $\mu^{(j)}$ is the sample mean of the values of feature j.

4.9.2 Standardization

Standardization (or **z-score normalization**) is the procedure during which the feature values are rescaled so that they have the properties of a **standard normal distribution**, with $\mu = 0$ and $\sigma = 1$, where μ is the **sample mean** (the average value of the feature, averaged over all examples in the training data) and σ is the standard deviation from the sample mean.

Standard scores (or **z-scores**) of features are calculated as follows:

$$\hat{x}^{(j)} \leftarrow \frac{x^{(j)} - \mu^{(j)}}{\sigma^{(j)}},$$

where $\mu^{(j)}$ is the sample mean of the values of feature j, and $\sigma^{(j)}$ is the **standard deviation** of the values of feature j from the sample mean.

In addition, sometimes it's helpful to apply simple mathematical transformations to the feature values prior to applying the scaling techniques described above. Such transformations include taking the logarithm of the feature, squaring it, or extracting the square root of the feature. The idea is to obtain a distribution as close to a normal distribution as possible.

You may wonder when you should use normalization, or when to use standardization. There's no definitive answer to this question. In theory, normalization would work better for uniformly distributed data, while standardization tends to work best for normally distributed data. However, in practice, data is rarely distributed following a perfect curve. Usually, if your dataset is not too big and you have time, you can try both and see which one performs better for your task. Feature scaling is usually beneficial to most learning algorithms.

4.10   Data Leakage in Feature Engineering

Data leakage during feature engineering can happen in several situations, including feature discretization and scaling.

4.10.1   Possible Problems

Imagine that you use your entire dataset to calculate the ranges of each bin or the feature scaling factors. Then you split the dataset into training, validation, and test sets. If you proceed like that, the values of features in the training data will, in part, be obtained by using the examples that belong to the holdout sets. When your dataset is small enough, it might result in an overly optimistic performance of your model on the holdout data.

Now imagine you are working with text, and that you use **bag-of-words** to create features with the entire dataset. After building the vocabulary, you split your data into the three sets. In this situation, the learning algorithm will be exposed to features based on tokens only present in the holdout sets. Again, the model will display artificially better performance than had you divided your data before feature engineering.

4.10.2   Solution

A solution, as you might have guessed, is first to split the entire dataset into training and holdout sets, and only do feature engineering on the training data. This also applies when you use **mean encoding** to transform a categorical feature to a number: split the data first and then compute the sample mean of the label, based on the training data only.

4.11   Storing and Documenting Features

Even if you plan to train the model right after you finish engineering features, it's advised to design a **schema file** that provides a description of the features' expected properties.

4.11.1   Schema File

A schema file is a document that describes features. This file is machine-readable, versioned, and updated each time someone makes significant updates to features. Here are several examples of the properties that can be encoded in the schema:

- names of features;
- for each feature:
    - its type (categorical, numerical),
    - the fraction of examples that are expected to have that feature present,
    - minimum and maximum values,
    - sample mean and variance,
    - whether it allows zeros,
    - whether it allows undefined values.

An example of a schema file for a four-dimensional dataset is shown below:

```
1   feature {
2       name : "height"
3       type : float
4       min : 50.0
5       max : 300.0
6       mean : 160.0
7       variance : 17.0
8       zeroes : false
9       undefined : false
10      popularity : 1.0
11  }
12
13  feature {
14      name : "color_red"
15      type : binary
16      zeroes : true
17      undefined : false
18      popularity : 0.76
19  }
20
21  feature {
22      name : "color_green"
23      type : binary
24      zeroes : true
25      undefined : false
26      popularity : 0.65
27  }
```

```
28
29   feature {
30       name : "color_blue"
31       type : binary
32       zeroes : true
33       undefined : false
34       popularity : 0.81
35   }
```

4.11.2   Feature Store

Large and distributed organizations may use a **feature store** that allows keeping, document-
ing, reusing, and sharing features across multiple data science teams and projects. The ways
features are maintained and served can differ significantly across projects and teams. This
introduces infrastructure complexity and often results in duplicated work. Large distributed
organizations face some of these challenges:

Features not being reused
> Features representing the same attribute of an entity are being implemented several
> times by different engineers and teams, when existing work from other teams and
> existing machine learning pipelines could have been reused.

Feature definitions vary
> Different teams define features differently, and it's not always possible to access the
> documentation of a feature.

Computationally intensive features
> Some real-time machine learning models aren't based on informative but computation-
> ally intensive features. Having those features available in a fast store would allow using
> such features in real-time, and not only in batch mode.

Inconsistency between training and serving
> The model is usually trained using the historical data, but when served, is exposed
> to the real-time online data. The values of some features might depend on the entire
> historical dataset unavailable at the service time. For the model to work correctly, each
> feature must have the same value for the same input data entity, both in the offline
> (development) and online (production) mode.

Feature expiration is unknown
> When a new input example comes into the production environment, there is no way to
> know exactly which features need to be recomputed; rather the entire pipeline needs to
> be run to compute the values of all features needed for prediction.

A feature store is a central vault for storing documented, curated, and access-controlled features within an organization. Each feature is described by four elements: 1) name, 2) description, 3) metadata, and 4) definition.

The feature name is a string that uniquely identifies the feature, for example: "average_session_length" or "document_length."

The feature description is a natural language textual description of the object's property it represents, for example, "The average length of the session for a user." or "The number of words in the document."

In addition to those attributes in the schema file, the feature metadata may supply: why the feature was added to the model, how it contributes to generalization, the person's name in the organization responsible for maintaining the feature's data source,[8] the input type (e.g., numerical, string, image), the output type (e.g., numerical scalar, categorical, numerical vector), whether the feature store must cache the value of the feature, and if yes, for how long. A feature can also be marked as available online and offline, or just for offline processing. Features available for online processing must be implemented in such a way that their value can be either: 1) read fast from a cache or a value store or 2) computed in real-time. Features that can be computed in real-time include, for example, squaring the input number, determining the shape of the word, or doing a search in the organization's intranet.

The definition of the feature is the versioned code, such as Python or Java. It will be executed in a runtime environment and applied to the input to compute the feature value.

A feature store allows data engineers to insert features. In turn, data analysts and machine learning engineers use an API to get feature values which they deem relevant. A feature store can provide features for a single online input. Or, the analyst working on a model offline may want to convert the training data into a collection of feature vectors, and will send to the feature store a batch of inputs.

For **reproducibility**, feature values in a feature store are versioned. With feature value versioning, the data analyst is able to rebuild the model with the same feature values as those used to train the previous model version. After the feature value for a given input is updated, the previous value is not erased. Rather, it is saved with a timestamp indicating when that value was generated. Furthermore, a feature j used by model m_B can itself be the output of some model m_A. Once model m_A changes, it is important to keep its older versions: model m_B still might expect as input the outputs generated by an older version of m_A.

The feature store is located in the overall machine learning pipeline as shown in Figure 4.21. The architecture was inspired by Uber's Michelangelo machine learning platform. It contains two feature stores, online and offline, whose data is in sync. At Uber, the online feature store is updated frequently, in near real-time, by using the real-time data. In contrast, the offline feature store is updated in batch-mode by using values of some features computed online, as well as with historical data from logs and offline databases. An example of a feature computed online is "restaurant's average meal preparation time over the last hour."

---

[8]If the person responsible for the feature leaves the company, the product owner must be alerted automatically.

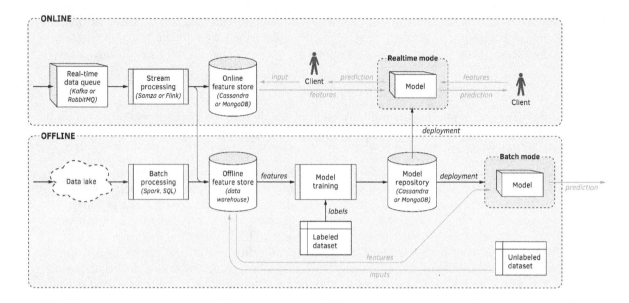

Figure 4.21: The place of the feature store in the overall machine learning pipeline.

An example of a feature computed offline is "restaurant's average meal preparation time over the last seven days." At Uber, the features from the offline store are synced to the online store once or several times a day.

4.12 Feature Engineering Best Practices

Throughout the years, analysts and engineers have invented, experimented with, and validated various best practices. Today, they are recommended for nearly every machine learning project. Using those best practices might not significantly improve each project, but they will definitely not hurt. One best practice already considered in this chapter is to normalize or standardize the features.

4.12.1 Generate Many Simple Features

At the beginning of the modeling process, try to engineer as many "simple" features as possible. A feature is simple when it doesn't take significant time to code. For example, the bag-of-words approach in document classification generates thousands of features with just a couple lines of code. As long as your hardware has the capacity, use anything measurable as a feature. You cannot know in advance whether some quantity, in combination with other quantities, will be useful for prediction.

4.12.2 Reuse Legacy Systems

When replacing an old, non-machine-learning-based algorithm with a statistical model, use the output of the old algorithm as a feature for the new model. Make sure that the old algorithm doesn't change anymore; otherwise, your model's performance might be negatively affected over time. If the old algorithm is too slow to be a feature, use the old algorithm's inputs as features for the new model.

Use an external system as a feature source only if you control the external system's behavior. Otherwise, there's a chance that the external system evolves with time, unbeknownst to you. Furthermore, an external system's owner might decide to use the output of your model as the input for their model. This creates the **hidden feedback loop**, a situation where you influence the phenomenon from which you learn.

4.12.3 Use IDs as Features when Needed. . .

Use IDs as features when needed. This might seem counter-intuitive because unique IDs don't contribute to generalization. However, the use of IDs allows creating one model that has one behavior in a general case, and different behaviors in other cases.

For example, you want to make predictions about some location (city or village), and you have some properties of the location as features. By using location ID as a feature, you can add the training examples for one general location, and train the model to behave differently in other specific locations.

However, avoid using example ID as a feature.

4.12.4 . . . But Reduce the Cardinality When Possible

Use categorical features with many values (more than a dozen) only when you want the model to have different "modes" of behavior that depend on that categorical feature. Typical examples of this are zip code (postal code) or country. You might consider using the categorical feature "Country" if you want the model to behave differently in Russia versus the United States, for otherwise similar inputs.[9]

If you have a categorical feature with many values, but you do not need a model that has several modes depending on that feature, try to reduce the cardinality (i.e., the number of distinct values) of that feature. There are several ways to do that. We already considered one of them, **feature hashing**, in Section 4.2.4. Other techniques are briefly discussed below:

---

[9]Often, what you want your model to do and what the data dictates are two very different things. Even if you think that the model must make similar predictions independently of the country, in reality, you might get poor model performance because the distribution of labels in the training data is different for different countries.

Group similar values

Try to group some values into the same category. For example, if you think it's unlikely that, within one region, different locations might need different predictions, then group all postal codes from the same state into one state code. Group states into regions.

Group the long tail

Likewise, try to group the long tail of infrequent values under the name "Other," or merge them with similar frequent values.

Remove the feature

If all, or almost all, values of a categorical feature are unique, or one value dominates all other values, consider removing the feature entirely.

The reduction of a feature's granularity should be made with care. Categorical features often have functional dependencies with other categorical features, and their predictive power often comes from their combinations. Take state and city as an example. If we decide to group or remove some values in the state feature, we might inadvertently destroy the information that would allow the model to distinguish one "Springfield" from another.

4.12.5   Use Counts with Caution

Use features based on counts with caution. Some counts remain roughly in the same bounds over time. For example, in bag-of-words, if you use the count of each token instead of the binary value, then it's not a problem, as long as the input document length doesn't grow or shrink with time. But, if you have a feature like "Number of calls since subscription" for a customer of a growing mobile phone provider, some oldtimers can have a very high number of calls, compared to the newer customer base. On the other hand, the training data could have been built when the company was still young and didn't have any oldtimers.

The same caution must be applied when you group feature values in bins based on how common those values are in the dataset. Infrequent values today may become more frequent over time, as more data is added. It is considered a best practice to re-evaluate the model and the features from time to time.

4.12.6   Make Feature Selection When Necessary

Make feature selection when it's necessary. The reasons could be:

- the need to have an explainable model (so you keep the most significant predictors),
- strict hardware requirements, such as RAM, hard drive space, or
- short time available to experiment and/or rebuild the model in production,
- you expect a significant **distribution shift** between two model trainings.

If you decide to do feature selection, start with Boruta.

4.12.7 Test the Code Carefully

The feature engineering code must be carefully tested. Unit tests should cover each feature extractor. Check that each feature is generated correctly using as many inputs as possible. For each boolean feature, check that it is true when it should be true and is false when it should be false. Check numerical features for a reasonable value range. Check for NaNs (Not-a-Number values), nulls, zeros, and empty values. A broken extractor for one feature can result in arbitrarily poor performance of the model. Feature extractors are the first place to look for a problem if the model's behavior is strange.

Each feature has to be tested for speed, memory consumption, and compatibility with the production environment. What works reasonably well in your local environment may perform poorly when deployed in production.

Once the model is deployed in the production environment, and each time it is loaded, you must rerun feature extractor tests. If a feature consumes some external resources like a database or an API, these resources might be unavailable on a specific production runtime instance. The feature extractor has to throw an exception and die if any resource during feature extraction is unavailable. Avoid silent failures that may remain unnoticed for a long time with model performance degrading or becoming completely wrong.

It is also recommended to perform regular runs of feature extractors on a fixed test data to make sure that the feature value distribution remains the same.

4.12.8 Keep Code, Model, and Data in Sync

The version of the feature extraction code must be in sync with the model's version and the data used to build it. The three have to be deployed or rolled back at the same time. Each time the model is loaded in production, it's useful to check that the three elements are in sync (that is, their versions are the same).

4.12.9 Isolate Feature Extraction Code

The feature extraction code must be independent of the remaining code that supports the model. It should be possible to update the code responsible for each feature without affecting other features, the data processing pipeline, or the way the model is called. The only exception is when many features are generated in bulk, like in one-hot encoding and bag-of-words.

4.12.10 Serialize Together Model and Feature Extractor

When possible, jointly serialize (pickle in Python, RDS in R) the model and the feature extractor object that was used when the model was built. In the production environment, deserialize both and use them. When possible, avoid having several versions of the feature extraction code.

If your production environment doesn't let you deserialize both the model and the feature extraction code, use the same feature extraction code when you train the model and serve it. Even a tiny difference between the code a data scientist used to train the model, and the optimized code the IT team might have written for the production environment, may result in significant prediction error.

Once the production code for feature extraction is ready, use it to retrain the model. Always completely retrain the model after any change in the feature extraction code.

4.12.11   Log the Values of Features

Log the feature values extracted in production for a random sample of online examples. When you work on a new version of the model, these values will be useful to control the quality of the training data. They will allow you to compare and ensure that the feature values logged in the production environment are the same as those you observed in the training data.

4.13   Summary

Features are values extracted from the data entities your model is designed to work with. Each feature represents a specific property of a data entity. Features are organized in feature vectors, and the model learns to perform mathematical operations on those feature vectors to generate the desired output.

For text, features can be generated in bulk by using techniques like bag-of-words. Numbers in the bag-of-words feature vectors mean the presence or absence of specific vocabulary words in the text document. Those numbers can be binary or contain more information, such as the frequency of each word in the document, or a TF-IDF value.

Most machine learning algorithms and libraries require that all features are numerical. To convert categorical features to numbers, techniques such as one-hot encoding and mean encoding are used. If the categorical feature's values are cyclical, like days of the week or hours in a day, a better alternative is to convert that cyclical feature into two features, using the sine-cosine transformation.

Feature hashing is a way to convert text data, or categorical attributes with many values, into a feature vector of an arbitrary dimensionality. That can be useful when one-hot encoding or bag-of-words generate feature vectors with impractical dimensions.

Topic modeling is a family of algorithmic techniques, such as LDA and LSA, that allow us to learn a model that converts any document into a vector of topics of a required dimensionality.

A time series is an ordered sequence of observations. Each observation is marked with a time-related attribute, such as timestamp, date, year, and so on. Before neural networks reached their modern capacity to learn, analysts worked with time-series data using the shallow machine learning toolkit. The time-series had to be converted into "flat" feature vectors. Nowadays, analysts use neural network architectures adapted to work with sequences, such as LSTM, CNN, and Transformer.

Good features have high predictive power, can be computed fast, are reliable and uncorrelated.

It is important that the distribution of feature values in the training set is similar to the distribution of values the production model will receive. Furthermore, good features are unitary, easy to understand and maintain. The property of being unitary means that the feature represents a simple-to-understand and -explain quantity.

To increase the predictive power of the data, additional features can be synthesized by discretizing an existing numerical feature, clustering training examples, or applying simple transformations to existing features or combining pairs of features.

For text, features can be learned from unlabeled data in the form of word and document embeddings. More generally, embeddings can be trained for any type of data if we manage to formulate an appropriate prediction problem and train a deep model. Embedding vectors are then extracted from several rightmost (i.e., closest to the output) fully-connected layers.

Wise use of feature selection techniques remove features that don't contribute to a model's quality. Two common techniques are cutting the long tail and Boruta. L1 regularization also works as a features selection technique.

Dimensionality reduction can improve visualization of high-dimensional datasets. It can also improve the model's predictive quality. Presently, such techniques as PCA, UMAP, and autoencoders are used for dimensionality reduction. PCA is very fast, but UMAP and autoencoders produce better visualizations.

It is considered best practices to scale features before training the model, store and document features in schema files or feature stores, and keep code, model, and training data in sync.

Feature extraction code is one of the most important parts of a machine learning system. It must be extensively and systematically tested.

Chapter 5

Supervised Model Training (Part 1)

Model training (or modeling) is the fourth stage in the machine learning project life cycle:

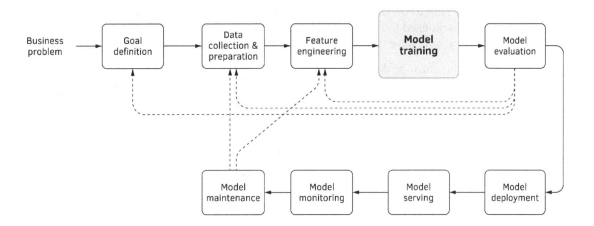

Figure 5.1: Machine learning project life cycle.

It's clear that without training, no model will be built. However, model training is one of the most overrated activities in machine learning. On average, a machine learning engineer spends only $5 - 10\%$ of their time on modeling, if at all. Successful data collection, preparation, and feature engineering are more important. Usually, modeling is simply applying an algorithm from scikit-learn or R to your data, and randomly trying several combinations of hyperparameters. So, if you skipped the preceding two chapters and jumped directly into modeling, please go back and read those chapters, they are important.

As indicated by this chapter's title, I have divided supervised model training into two parts. In this first part, we will consider learning preparation, choosing the learning algorithm, a shallow learning strategy, assessing model performance, bias-variance tradeoff, regularization, the concept of the machine learning pipeline, and hyperparameter tuning.

5.1 Before You Start Working on the Model

Before working on the model, you should validate schema conformity, define an achievable level of performance, choose a performance metric, and make several other decisions.

5.1.1 Validate Schema Conformity

First, ensure the data conforms to the schema, as defined by the **schema file**. Even if you initially prepared the data, it's likely the original data and the current data are not the same. This difference can be explained by various factors, most probably:

- the method used to persist the data, to hard drive or to database, contains an error;
- the method you used to read the data, from where it was persisted, contains an error;
- someone else may have changed the data, or the schema, without informing you.

These schema errors must be detected, identified, and corrected just as when a programming code error is detected. If needed, the entire data collection and preparation pipeline should be run from scratch, as we discussed at the end of Chapter 3 when talked about **reproducibility**.

5.1.2 Define an Achievable Performance Level

Defining an achievable performance level is a crucial step. It gives you an idea of when to stop trying to improve the model. Here are some guidelines:

- if a human can label examples without too much effort, math, or complex logic derivations, then you can hope to achieve human-level performance with your model;
- if the information needed to make a labeling decision is fully contained in the features, you can expect to have near-zero error;
- if the input feature vector has a high number of signals (such as pixels in an image, or words in a document), you can expect to come close to near-zero error;
- if you have a computer program solving the same classification or regression problem, you can expect your model to perform at least as well. Often the machine learning model performance can improve as more labeled data comes in; and,
- if you observe a similar, but different system, you can expect to get a similar, but different machine learning model performance.

5.1.3 Choose a Performance Metric

We will talk about assessing the model performance later. For now, there are several ways — metrics — to estimate the level of model performance (its quality). There's no single best metric you can use for every project. You will choose based on your data and the problem.

It is recommended to choose one, and only one, **performance metric** before you start working on the model. Then, compare different models and track the overall progress by using this one metric.

In Section 5.5, you will read about the most popular and handy model performance metrics, and about the approaches allowing us to combine multiple metrics to obtain a single number.

5.1.4 Choose the Right Baseline

Before you start working on a predictive model, it is important to establish baseline performance on your problem. A **baseline** is a model or an algorithm that provides a reference point for comparison.

Having a baseline gives an analyst confidence that the machine-learning-based solution works. If the value of the performance metric for the machine learning model is better than the value obtained using the baseline, then machine learning provides value.

Comparing your current model's performance to a baseline can orient the work in different directions. Let's say we know that human-level performance is achievable on our problem. We then take human performance as a baseline, as shown in Figure 5.2. In Figure 5.2a, the model looks good, so we can decide to regularize it or add more training examples. On the other hand, in Figure 5.2b, the model isn't performing well, so we should add more features, or increase the **model complexity**.

The baseline is a model or an algorithm that gets an input, and outputs a prediction. The baseline's prediction output must be of the same nature as the model's prediction. Otherwise, you cannot compare them.

A baseline doesn't have to be the result of any learning algorithm. It can be a rule-based or heuristic algorithm, a simple statistic applied to the training data, or something else.

The two most commonly used baseline algorithms are:

- random prediction, and
- zero rule.

The **random prediction algorithm** makes a prediction by randomly choosing a label from the collection of labels assigned to the training examples. In the classification problem, it corresponds to randomly picking one class from all classes in the problem. In the regression problem it means selecting from all unique target values in the training data.

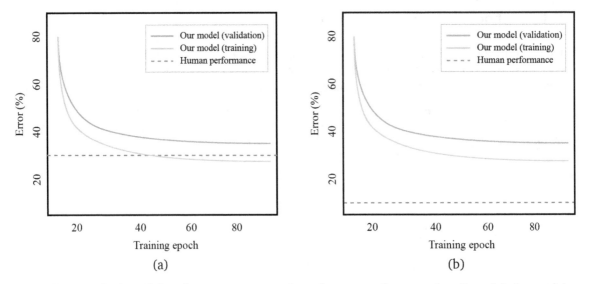

Figure 5.2: A model performance compared to a human-performance baseline: (a) the model looks good, so we can decide to regularize it or add more training examples; (b) the model isn't performing well, so we need to add more features, or increase the model complexity.

The **zero rule algorithm** yields a tighter baseline than the random prediction algorithm. This means that it usually improves the value of the metric as compared to random prediction. To make predictions, the zero rule algorithm uses more information about the problem.

In classification, the zero rule algorithm strategy is to always predict the class most common in the training set, independently of the input value. It can look ineffective, but consider the following problem. Let the training data for your classification problem contain 800 examples of the positive class, and 200 examples of the negative class. The zero rule algorithm will predict the positive class all the time, and the **accuracy** (one of the popular performance metrics that we will consider in Section 5.5.2) of the baseline will be $800/1000 = 0.8$ or 80%, which is not bad for such a simple classifier. Now you know that your statistical model, independently of how close it is to the optimum, must have an accuracy of at least 80%.

Now, let's consider the zero rule algorithm for regression. According to the zero rule algorithm, the strategy for regression is to predict the sample average of the target values observed in the training data. This strategy will likely have a lower error rate than random prediction.

If you work on a standard, so-called classical, prediction problem, you can use a state-of-the-art algorithm found in a popular library such as Python's scikit-learn. For text classification, for example, represent the text as **bag-of-words**, and then train a **support vector machine** model with a **linear kernel**. Then try to beat that result with your own more advanced approach. This approach would also work well with image classification, machine translation, and other well-studies, so-called benchmark problems.

For a general numerical dataset, a linear model such as linear or logistic regression, or **k-nearest neighbors**, for $k = 5$, would be a decent baseline. For image classification, a simple **convolutional neural network** (CNN), with three convolutional layers ($32 - 64 - 32$ units per layer, each convolutional layer followed by a max pooling layer and a dropout layer) and two fully connected layers at the end (one with 128 units, and one with the number of units corresponding to the number of desired outputs) would be a good baseline.

You could also use an existing rule-based system, or build your own simple rule-based system. For example, if the problem is to build a model that predicts whether a given website visitor will like a recommended article, a simple rule-based system could work as follows. Take all articles liked by the user, find the top ten words in those articles according to their **TF-IDF** score, and then predict that the user will like an article if at least five of those ten can be found in the recommended article. Additionally, multiple specialized machine learning libraries and APIs are available online. If they can be used directly, or repurposed to solve your problem, you should definitely consider them as a baseline.

Finding a good human baseline is not always simple. You might use Amazon **Mechanical Turk** service. Mechanical Turk (MT) is a web-platform where people solve simple tasks for a reward. MT provides an API that you can call to get human predictions. The quality of such predictions can vary from very low to relatively high, depending on the task and the reward. MT is relatively inexpensive, so you can get predictions fast and in large numbers.

To increase the quality of the predictions provided by turkers (this is how MT human workers are called), some analysts use an **ensemble of turkers**. You can ask three or five turkers to label the same example, and then pick the majority class among the labels (or average labels for regression). A more expensive alternative is to ask domain experts (or an ensemble, for even better quality) to label your data.

5.1.5   Split Data Into Three Sets

Recall that three sets are generally needed to build a solid model. The first, the **training set**, is used to train the model. It is the data the machine learning algorithm "sees." The second and third are the holdout sets. The **validation set** is not seen by the machine learning algorithm. The data analyst uses it to estimate the performance of different machine learning algorithms (or the same algorithm configured with different values of hyperparameters) or models when applied to new data. The remaining **test set**, which is also not seen by the learning algorithm, is used at the end of the project to evaluate and report the performance of the model the best performing on the validation data.

The process of splitting the entire dataset into three sets is described in Section 3.6 of Chapter 3. Here, I only reiterate the two most important properties of that process:

1. Validation and test sets must come from the same statistical distribution. That is, their properties have to be maximally similar, but the examples belonging to the two sets must be, obviously and ideally, different and obtained independently of one another.

2. Draw validation and test data from a distribution that looks much like the data you expect to observe once the model is deployed in production. It can be different from the distribution of the training data.

A couple of words about the latter point. Most of the time, the analyst simply shuffles the entire dataset, and then randomly fills the three sets from this shuffled data. In practice, however, it's common to have many examples that do not look like the production data. Sometimes, these examples are abundant and/or inexpensive. Using this data in the project may result in **distribution shift**, and the analyst may or may not be aware of it.

If you are aware of distribution shift, you will place all those easily available examples into your training set, but will avoid using them in the validation and test sets. This way, you evaluate the models against the data that is similar to that in your production setting. Doing otherwise might result in achieving overly optimistic values of the performance metric during model testing, and selecting for production a suboptimal model.

The distribution shift can be a hard problem to tackle. Using a different data distribution for training could be a conscious choice because of the data availability. However, the analyst may be unaware that the statistical properties of the training and development data are different. This often happens when the model is frequently updated after production deployment, and new examples are added to the training set. The properties of the data used to train the model, and that of the data used to validate and test it, can diverge over time. Section 6.3 in the next chapter provides guidance on how to handle that problem.

5.1.6 Preconditions for Supervised Learning

Before you start working on your model, make sure the following conditions are satisfied:

1. You have a labeled dataset.
2. You have split the dataset into three subsets: training, validation, and test.
3. Examples in the validation and test sets are statistically similar.
4. You engineered features and filled missed values using only the training data.
5. You converted all examples into numerical feature vectors.[1]
6. You have selected a performance metric that returns a single number (see Section 5.5).
7. You have a baseline.

5.2 Representing Labels for Machine Learning

In the classical formulation of classification, labels look like values of a categorical feature. For example, in image classification, the labels could be "cat," "dog," "car," "building," and so on.

---

[1]As mentioned in the previous chapter, most modern machine learning libraries and packages expect numerical feature vectors. However, some algorithms, like decision tree learning, can naturally work with categorical features.

Some machine learning algorithms, like those you find in scikit-learn, accept labels in their natural form: strings. The library take care of transforming strings to numbers that are accepted by a specific learning algorithm.

Some implementations, however, like those in neural networks, require the analyst to transform the labels to numbers.

5.2.1 Multiclass Classification

In the case of **multiclass classification** (that is, when the model predicts only one label given an input feature vector), **one-hot encoding** is typically used to convert labels to binary vectors. For example, let your classes be {dog, cat, other}, and you have the following data:

Image	Label
image_1.jpg	dog
image_2.jpg	dog
image_3.jpg	cat
image_4.jpg	other
image_5.jpg	cat

One-hot encoding would generate the following binary vectors for your classes:

$$\text{dog} = [1, 0, 0],$$
$$\text{cat} = [0, 1, 0],$$
$$\text{other} = [0, 0, 1].$$

After you convert categorical labels into binary vectors, your data becomes:

Image	Label
image_1.jpg	[1,0,0]
image_2.jpg	[1,0,0]
image_3.jpg	[0,1,0]
image_4.jpg	[0,0,1]
image_5.jpg	[0,1,0]

5.2.2 Multi-label Classification

In **multi-label classification**, the model may predict several labels for one input at the same time (for example, an image can contain both a dog and a cat). In this case, you can use

133

bag-of-words to represent the labels assigned to each example. Let your data be as follows:

Image	Labels
image_1.jpg	dog, cat
image_2.jpg	dog
image_3.jpg	cat, other
image_4.jpg	other
image_5.jpg	cat, dog

After you convert labels into binary vectors, your data becomes:

Image	Labels
image_1.jpg	[1,1,0]
image_2.jpg	[1,0,0]
image_3.jpg	[0,1,1]
image_4.jpg	[0,0,1]
image_5.jpg	[1,1,0]

Read the documentation of the specific implementation of a learning algorithm to know the format of the input expected by the learning algorithm.

5.3   Selecting the Learning Algorithm

Choosing a machine learning algorithm can be a difficult task. If you had a lot of time, you could try all of them. However, usually, the time to solve a problem is limited. To make an informed choice, you can ask yourself several questions before starting to work on the problem. Depending on your answers, you can shortlist some algorithms and try them on your data.

5.3.1   Main Properties of a Learning Algorithm

Below are several questions and answers which may guide you in choosing a machine learning algorithm or model.

Explainability

Do the model predictions require explanation for a non-technical audience? The most accurate machine learning algorithms and models are so-called "black boxes." They make very few prediction errors, but it may be difficult to understand, and even harder to explain, why a model or an algorithm made a specific prediction. Examples of such models are **deep neural networks** and **ensemble models**.

In contrast, **kNN**, **linear regression**, and **decision tree learning** algorithms are not always the most accurate. However, their predictions are easy to interpret by a non-expert.

In-memory vs. out-of-memory

Can your dataset be fully loaded into the RAM of your laptop or server? If yes, then you can choose from a wide variety of algorithms. Otherwise, you would prefer **incremental learning algorithms** that can improve the model by reading data gradually. Examples of such algorithms are **Naïve Bayes** and the algorithms for training neural networks.

Number of features and examples

How many training examples do you have in your dataset? How many features does each example have? Some algorithms, including those used for training **neural networks** and **random forests**, can handle a huge number of examples and millions of features. Others, like the algorithms for training **support vector machines** (SVM), can be relatively modest in their capacity.

Nonlinearity of the data

Is your data linearly separable? Can it be modeled using a linear model? If yes, SVM with the linear kernel, linear and logistic regression can be good choices. Otherwise, deep neural networks or ensemble models might work better.

Training speed

How much time is a learning algorithm allowed to use to build a model, and how often you will need to retrain the model on updated data? If training takes two days, and you need to retrain your model every 4 hours, then your model will never be up to date. Neural networks are slow to train. Simple algorithms like linear and logistic regression, or decision trees, are much faster.

Specialized libraries contain very efficient implementations of some algorithms. You may prefer to do research online to find such libraries. Some algorithms, such as random forest learning, benefit from multiple CPU cores, so their training time can be significantly reduced on a machine with dozens of cores. Some machine learning libraries leverage GPU (graphics processing unit) to speed up training.

Prediction speed

How fast must the model be when generating predictions? Will your model be used in a production environment where very high throughput is required? Models like SVMs and linear and logistic regression models, and not-very-deep feedforward neural networks, are extremely fast at prediction time. Others, like kNN, ensemble algorithms, and very deep or recurrent neural networks, are slower.

If you don't want to guess the best algorithm for your data, a popular way to choose one is by testing several candidate algorithms on the **validation set** as a hyperparameter. We talk about hyperparameter tuning in Section 5.6.

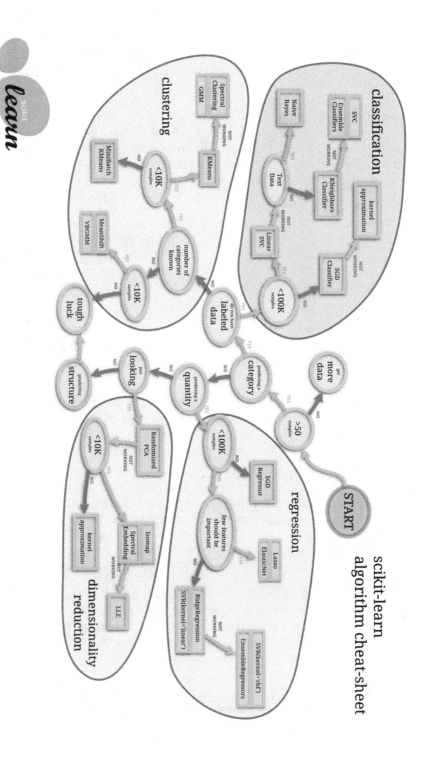

Figure 5.3: Machine learning algorithm selection diagram for scikit-learn. Source: scikit-learn.org

5.3.2 Algorithm Spot-Checking

Shortlisting candidate learning algorithms for a given problem is sometimes called **algorithm spot-checking**. For the most effective spot-checking, it is recommended to:

- select algorithms based on different principles (sometimes called orthogonal), such as instance-based algorithms, kernel-based, shallow learning, deep learning, ensembles;
- try each algorithm with $3 - 5$ different values of the most sensitive hyperparameters (such as the number of neighbors k in k-nearest neighbors, penalty C in support vector machines, or decision threshold in logistic regression);
- use the same training/validation split for all experiments,
- if the learning algorithm is not deterministic (such as the learning algorithms for neural networks and random forests), run several experiments, and then average the results;
- once the project is over, note which algorithms performed the best, and use this information when working on a similar problem in the future.

While you don't know your problem well, try to solve it using as many orthogonal approaches as possible, rather than spending a lot of time on the most promising approach. It is generally a better idea to spend time experimenting with new algorithms and libraries, rather than trying to squeeze the maximum from the one with which you have the most experience.

If you don't have time to carefully spot-check algorithms, one simple "hack" is to find an efficient implementation of a learning algorithm or a model that most modern papers claim to beat, when applied to a problem similar to yours, and use it for solving your problem.

If you use scikit-learn, you could try their algorithm selection diagram shown in Figure 5.3.

5.4 Building a Pipeline

Many modern machine learning packages and frameworks support the notion of a **pipeline**. A pipeline is a sequence of transformations the training data goes through, before it becomes a model. An example of a pipeline used to train a document classification model out of a collection of labeled text documents is shown below:

Figure 5.4: A pipeline used to produce a model starting with raw data.

Every stage of a pipeline receives the output of the previous stage, except for the first stage, whose input is the training dataset.

Below is a Python code fragment that constructs a simple **scikit-learn** pipeline. It consists of two steps: 1) dimensionality reduction using **Principal Component Analysis** (PCA), and 2) training a **support vector machine** (SVM) classifier:

```python
from sklearn.pipeline import Pipeline
from sklearn.svm import SVC
from sklearn.decomposition import PCA

# Define a pipeline
pipe = Pipeline([('dim_reduction', PCA()), ('model_training', SVC())])

# Train parameters of both PCA and SVC
pipe.fit(X, y)

# Make a prediction
pipe.predict(new_example)
```

When the command `pipe.predict(new_example)` is executed, the input example is first transformed into a reduced dimensionality vector using the PCA model. That reduced dimensionality vector is used as input to the SVM model. PCA and SVM models were trained, one after the other, when the command `pipe.fit(X, y)` were executed.

Unfortunately, defining and training pipelines in R is not as straightforward as in Python, so we don't put the code in the book.

The pipeline can be saved to a file similar to saving a model. It will be deployed to production and used to generate predictions. In other words, during the **scoring**, the input example passes through the entire pipeline and "becomes" an output.

As you can see, the notion of a pipeline is a generalization of the notion of a model. From this point forward, unless stated otherwise, when I refer to model training, saving, deployment, serving, monitoring, or post-production maintenance, I mean the entire pipeline.

Before we consider the challenge of training a model, we need to decide how to measure the model quality. Often, we have a choice between several competing models, so-called model candidates, but only one will be deployed in production.

5.5   Assessing Model Performance

Remember, the **holdout data** consists of examples the learning algorithm didn't see during training. If our model performs well on a holdout set, we can say our model **generalizes well** and is of good quality or, simply, that it's good. The most common way to get a good model is to compare different models by calculating a **performance metric** on the holdout data.

5.5.1 Performance Metrics for Regression

Regression and classification models are assessed using different metrics. Let's first consider performance metrics for regression: mean squared error (MSE), median absolute error (MAE), and almost correct predictions error rate (ACPER).

The metric most often used to quantify the performance of a regression model is the same as the **cost function**: **mean squared error** (MSE), defined as,

$$\text{MSE}(f) \overset{\text{def}}{=} \frac{1}{N} \sum_{i=1...N} (f(\mathbf{x}_i) - y_i)^2, \tag{5.1}$$

where f is the model that takes a feature vector $\mathbf{x}$ as input and outputs a prediction, and i, ranging from 1 to N, denotes the index of an example from a dataset.

A **well-fitting** regression model predicts values close to the observed data values. The **mean model**, which always predicts the average of the training data labels, generally would be used if there were no informative features. Therefore, the regression model should fit better than that of the mean model. Thus, the mean model acts as a **baseline**. If the regression model MSE is greater than the baseline MSE, then we have a problem in our regression model. It may be **overfitting** or **underfitting** (we consider these in Section 5.8). It could also be that the problem was defined with an error, or the programming code contains a bug.

If the data contains outliers, the examples very far from the "true" regression line, they can significantly affect the value of MSE. By definition, the squared error for such outlying examples will be high. In such situations, it is better to apply a different metric, the **median absolute error**, MdAE:

$$\text{MdAE} \overset{\text{def}}{=} \text{median}\left(\{|f(\mathbf{x}_i) - y_i|\}_{i=1}^{N} \right),$$

where $\{|f(\mathbf{x}_i) - y_i|\}_{i=1}^{N}$ denotes the set of absolute error values for all examples, from $i = 1$ to N, on which the evaluation of the model is performed.

The **almost correct predictions error rate** (ACPER) is the percentage of predictions that is within p percentage of the true value. To calculate ACPER, proceed as follows:

1. Define a threshold percentage error that you consider acceptable (let's say 2%).
2. For each true value of the target y_i, the desired prediction should be between $y_i + 0.02 y_i$ and $y_i - 0.02 y_i$.
3. By using all examples $i = 1, \ldots, N$, calculate the percentage of predicted values fulfilling the above rule. This will give the value of the ACPER metric for your model.

5.5.2 Performance Metrics for Classification

For classification, things are a little more complicated. The most widely used metrics to assess a classification model are:

- precision-recall,
- accuracy,
- cost-sensitive accuracy, and
- area under the ROC curve (AUC).

To simplify, I will illustrate with a binary classification problem. Where necessary, I show how to extend the approach to the multiclass case.

First, we need to understand the confusion matrix.

A **confusion matrix** is a table that summarizes how successful the classification model is at predicting examples belonging to various classes. One axis of the confusion matrix is the class that the model predicted; the other axis is the actual label. Let's say, our model predicts classes "spam" and "not_spam":

	spam (predicted)	not_spam (predicted)
spam (actual)	23 (TP)	1 (FN)
not_spam (actual)	12 (FP)	556 (TN)

The above matrix shows that out of 24 actual spam examples, the model correctly classified 23. In this case, we say that we have 23 **true positives** or TP = 23. The model incorrectly classified 1 spam example as not_spam. In this case, we have 1 **false negative**, or FN = 1. Similarly, out of 568 actual not_spam examples, the model classified correctly 556 and incorrectly 12 examples (556 **true negatives**, TN = 556, and 12 **false positives**, FP = 12).

The confusion matrix for multiclass classification has as many rows and columns as there are different classes. It can help you to determine mistake patterns. For example, a confusion matrix could reveal that a model trained to recognize different species of animals tends to mistakenly predict "cat" instead of "panther," or "mouse" instead of "rat." In this case, you can add more labeled examples of these species to help the learning algorithm "see" the difference between those animals. Alternatively, you might add features that would help the learning algorithm do better at distinguishing between those pairs of species.

The confusion matrix is used to calculate three performance metrics: precision, recall, and accuracy. Precision and recall are most frequently used to assess a binary model.

Precision is the ratio of true positive predictions to the overall number of positive predictions:

$$\text{precision} \overset{\text{def}}{=} \frac{\text{TP}}{\text{TP} + \text{FP}}.$$

Recall is the ratio of true positive predictions to the overall number of positive examples:

$$\text{recall} \overset{\text{def}}{=} \frac{\text{TP}}{\text{TP} + \text{FN}}.$$

To understand the meaning and the importance of precision and recall for model assessment, it's useful to think about the prediction problem as the problem of research of documents in a database using a query. The precision is the proportion of relevant documents actually found in the list of all returned documents. The recall is the ratio of the relevant documents returned by the search engine, compared to the total number of relevant documents that should have been returned.

In spam detection, we want to have high precision, to avoid wrongly placing a legitimate message in our spam folder. We are willing to tolerate lower recall, since we can deal with some spam messages in our inbox.

In practice, we choose between high precision or high recall. It's practically impossible to have both. This is called the **precision-recall tradeoff**. We can achieve either by various means:

- by assigning a higher weigh to the examples of a specific class. For example, SVM in scikit-learn accepts weights of classes as input;
- by tuning hyperparameters to maximize either precision or recall on the validation set;
- by varying the decision threshold for algorithms that return prediction scores. Let's say we have a logistic regression model or a decision tree. To increase precision (at the cost of a lower recall), we can decide that the prediction will be positive only if the score returned by the model is higher than 0.9 (instead of the default value of 0.5).

Even if precision and recall are defined for binary classification, you can also use them to assess a **multiclass classification** model. First select a class for which you want to assess these metrics. Then you consider all examples of the selected class as positives and all examples of the remaining classes as negatives.

In practice, to compare the performance of two models, you would prefer to have only one number that represents the performance of each model. For example, you would like to avoid situations where the first model has a higher precision, when the second model has a higher recall: if it's the case, which model is better?

One way to compare models based on one number is to threshold the minimum acceptable value for one metric, say recall, and then only compare models based on the value of another metric. For example, say you will accept any model whose recall is above 90%. Then you will give preference to the model whose precision is the highest (assuming that its recall is above 90%). This technique is known as **optimizing and satisficing technique**.

Some practitioners use a combination of precision and recall called **F-measure**, also known as **F-score**. The traditional F-measure, or F_1-score, is the harmonic mean of precision and recall:

$$F_1 = \left(\frac{2}{\text{recall}^{-1} + \text{precision}^{-1}} \right) = 2 \times \frac{\text{precision} \times \text{recall}}{\text{precision} + \text{recall}}$$

More generally, F-measure is parametrized with a positive real β, chosen such that recall is considered β times as important as precision:

$$F_\beta = (1 + \beta^2) \times \frac{\text{precision} \times \text{recall}}{(\beta^2 \times \text{precision}) + \text{recall}}$$

Two commonly used values for β are 2, which weighs recall twice as high as precision, and 0.5, which weighs recall twice as low as precision.

You should find a way to combine the two metrics that works best for your problem. Besides F-score, there are other ways to obtain a single number by combining multiple metrics:

- simple average, or weighted average of metrics;
- threshold $n - 1$ metrics and optimize the nth (a generalization of the above optimizing and satisficing technique);
- invent your own domain-specific "recipe."

Accuracy is given by the number of correctly classified examples, divided by the total number of classified examples. In terms of the confusion matrix, it is given by:

$$\text{accuracy} \overset{\text{def}}{=} \frac{\text{TP} + \text{TN}}{\text{TP} + \text{TN} + \text{FP} + \text{FN}} \tag{5.2}$$

Accuracy is a useful metric when errors in predicting all classes are judged to be equally important. It's the case, for example, for object recognition for a domestic robot: a chair is no more important than a table. In the case of the spam/not spam prediction, this probably would not be so. Likely, you would tolerate false negatives more than false positives. Remember, a false positive is when your friend sends you an email, but the model places it in the spam folder and you don't see it. A false negative, a situation in which a spam message gets to the inbox, is less of a problem.

For dealing with the situations in which different classes have different importance, a useful metric is **cost-sensitive accuracy**. First, assign a cost (a positive number) to both types of mistakes: FP and FN. Then compute the counts TP, TN, FP, FN as usual, and multiply the counts for FP and FN by their corresponding costs before calculating the accuracy using Equation 5.2, above.

Accuracy measures the performance of the model for all classes at once, and it conveniently returns a single number. However, accuracy is not a good performance metric when the data is imbalanced. In an **imbalanced dataset**, examples belonging to some class or a few classes constitute the vast majority, while other classes include very few examples. Imbalanced training data can significantly and adversely affect the model. We will talk more about dealing with the imbalanced data in Section 6.4 of Chapter 6.

For imbalanced data, a better metric is **per-class accuracy**. First, calculate the accuracy of prediction for each class $\{1, \ldots, C\}$, and then take an average of C individual accuracy measures. For the above confusion matrix of the spam detection problem, the accuracy for the class "spam" is $23/(23+1) = 0.96$, the accuracy for the class "not_spam" is $556/(12+556) = 0.98$. The per-class accuracy is then $(0.96+0.98)/2 = 0.97$.

Per-class accuracy will not be an appropriate model quality measure for a multiclass classification problem where many classes have very few examples (roughly, less than a dozen examples per class). In that case, the accuracy values obtained for the binary classification problems corresponding to these minority classes will not be statistically reliable.

Cohen's kappa statistic is a performance metric that applies to both multiclass and imbalanced learning problems. The advantage of this metric over accuracy is that Cohen's kappa tells you how much better your classification model is performing, compared to a classifier that randomly guesses a class according to the frequency of each class.

Cohen's kappa is defined as:

$$\kappa \stackrel{\text{def}}{=} \frac{p_o - p_e}{1 - p_e},$$

where p_o is called the observed agreement, and p_e is the expected agreement.

Let's look once again at a confusion matrix:

	class1 (predicted)	class2 (predicted)
class1 (actual)	a	b
class2 (actual)	c	d

The observed agreement p_o is obtained from the confusion matrix as,

$$p_o \stackrel{\text{def}}{=} \frac{a+d}{a+b+c+d}.$$

The expected agreement p_e, in turn, is obtained as $p_e \stackrel{\text{def}}{=} p_{\text{class1}} + p_{\text{class2}}$, where,

$$p_{\text{class1}} \stackrel{\text{def}}{=} \frac{a+b}{a+b+c+d} \times \frac{a+c}{a+b+c+d},$$

and

$$p_{\text{class2}} \stackrel{\text{def}}{=} \frac{c+d}{a+b+c+d} \times \frac{b+d}{a+b+c+d}$$

The value of Cohen's kappa is always less than or equal to 1. Values of 0 or less indicate that the model has a problem. While there is no universally accepted way to interpret the values of Cohen's kappa, it's usually considered that values between 0.61 and 0.80 indicate that the model is good, and values 0.81 or higher suggest that the model is very good.

The **ROC curve** (stands for "receiver operating characteristic;" the term comes from radar engineering) is a commonly-used method of assessing classification models. ROC curves use a combination of the **true positive rate** (defined exactly as **recall**) and **false positive rate** (the proportion of negative examples predicted incorrectly) to build up a summary picture of the classification performance.

The true positive rate (TPR) and the false positive rate (FPR) are respectively defined as,

$$\text{TPR} \stackrel{\text{def}}{=} \frac{\text{TP}}{\text{TP}+\text{FN}} \quad \text{and} \quad \text{FPR} \stackrel{\text{def}}{=} \frac{\text{FP}}{\text{FP}+\text{TN}}$$

ROC curves can only be used to assess classifiers that return a score (or a probability) of prediction. For example, logistic regression, neural networks, and decision trees (and ensemble models based on decision trees) can be assessed using ROC curves.

To draw a ROC curve, you first discretize the range of the score. For instance, you can discretize the range $[0, 1]$ like this: $[0, 0.1, 0.2, 0.3, 0.4, 0.5, 0.6, 0.7, 0.8, 0.9, 1]$. Then, use each discrete value as the prediction threshold for your model. For example, if you want to calculate TPR and FPR for the threshold equal to 0.7, you apply the model to each example and get the score. If the score is greater than or equal to 0.7, you predict the positive class. Otherwise, you predict the negative class.

Look at the illustration in Figure 5.5. It's easy to see that if the threshold equals 0, all our predictions will be positive, so both TPR and FPR will equal 1 (the upper right corner). On the other hand, if the threshold equals 1, then no positive prediction will be possible. Both TPR and FPR will equal 0, which corresponds to the lower-left corner.

The greater the **area under the ROC curve** (AUC), the better the classifier. A classifier with an AUC greater than 0.5 is better than a model that classifies at random. If AUC is lower than 0.5, then something is wrong, most likely a bug in the code or wrong labels in the data. A perfect classifier would have an AUC of 1. In practice, you obtain a good classifier by selecting the value of the threshold that gives TPR close to 1 while keeping FPR near 0.

ROC curves are popular because they are relatively simple to understand. They capture more than one aspect of the classification, by taking both false positives and false negatives into account. They allow the analyst to easily and visually compare different model performances.

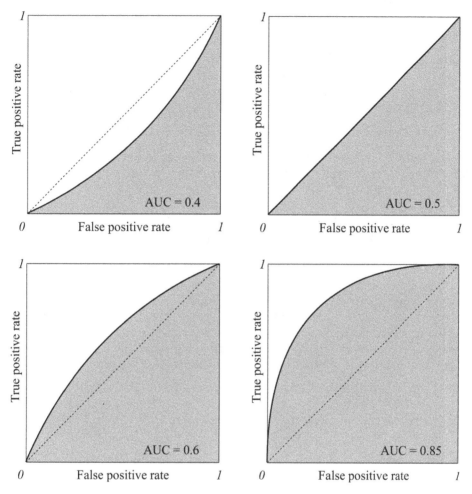

Figure 5.5: The area under the ROC curve (shown in grey).

5.5.3 Performance Metrics for Ranking

Precision and recall can be naturally applied to the ranking problem. Recall that it's convenient to think of these two metrics as measuring the quality of document search results. Precision is the proportion of relevant documents actually found in the list of all returned documents. The recall is the ratio of the relevant documents returned by the search engine, compared to the total number of the relevant documents that should have been returned.

The drawback of measuring the quality of ranking models with precision and recall is that these metrics treat all retrieved documents equally. A relevant document listed at position k is worth just as much as a relevant document at the top of the list. This is usually not what we want in document retrieval. When a human looks at search results, the few top-most results matter more than the results shown at the bottom of the list.

Discounted cumulative gain (DCG) is a popular measure of ranking quality in search engines. DCG measures the usefulness, or gain, of a document based on its position in the result list. The gain is accumulated from the top of the result list to the bottom, with the gain of each result discounted at lower positions.

To understand discounted cumulative gain, we introduce a measure called cumulative gain.

Cumulative gain (CG) is the sum of the graded relevance values of all results in a search result list. The CG at a particular rank position p is defined as:

$$\text{CG}_p \stackrel{\text{def}}{=} \sum_{i=1}^{p} rel_i,$$

where rel_i is the graded relevance of the result at position i. Generally, graded relevance reflects the relevance of a document to a query on a scale using numbers, letters, or descriptions (such as "not relevant," "somewhat relevant," "relevant," or "very relevant"). To use it in the above formula, rel_i must be numeric, for example, ranging from 0 (the document at position i is entirely irrelevant to the query) to 1 (the document at position i is maximally relevant to the query). Alternatively, rel_i can be binary: 0 when the document is not relevant to the query, and 1 when relevant. Notice that CG_p is independent of the position each document holds in the ranked result list. It only characterizes the documents ranked up to position p as relevant or irrelevant to the query.

Discounted cumulative gain is based on two assumptions:

1. Highly relevant documents are more useful when appearing earlier in the result list.
2. Highly relevant documents are more useful than marginally relevant documents, while the latter, in turn, are more useful than non-relevant documents.

For a given search result, DCG accumulated at a particular rank position p is often defined as:

$$\text{DCG}_p \stackrel{\text{def}}{=} \sum_{i=1}^{p} \frac{rel_i}{\log_2(i+1)} = rel_1 + \sum_{i=2}^{p} \frac{rel_i}{\log_2(i+1)}.$$

An alternative formulation of DCG, commonly used in industry and data science competitions such as Kaggle, places a stronger emphasis on retrieving relevant documents:

$$\text{DCG}_p \stackrel{\text{def}}{=} \sum_{i=1}^{p} \frac{2^{rel_i} - 1}{\log_2(i+1)}.$$

For a query, the **normalized discounted cumulative gain** (nDCG), is defined as:

$$\text{nDCG}_p \stackrel{\text{def}}{=} \frac{\text{DCG}_p}{\text{IDCG}_p},$$

where IDCG is the ideal discounted cumulative gain,

$$\text{IDCG}_p \stackrel{\text{def}}{=} \sum_{i=1}^{|\text{REL}_p|} \frac{2^{rel_i} - 1}{\log_2(i+1)},$$

and REL_p represents the list of the documents relevant to the query in the corpus up to position p (ordered by their relevance). So, REL_p is the ideal ranking, up to position p, that the search engine ranking algorithm (or model) should have returned for the query. The nDCG values for all queries are usually averaged to obtain a performance measure for a search engine ranking algorithm or model.

Let's consider the following example. Let a search engine return a list of documents in response to a search query. We ask a ranker (a human) to judge each document's relevance. The ranker must assign a score from 0 to 3, where 0 means not relevant, 3 means highly relevant, while 1 and 2 mean "somewhere in between." Say the documents appeared in this order:

$$D_1, D_2, D_3, D_4, D_5.$$

Our ranker provides the following relevance scores:

$$3, 1, 0, 3, 2.$$

This means that document D_1 has a relevance of 3, D_2 has a relevance of 1, D_3 has a relevance of 0, and so on. The cumulative gain of this search result, up to position $p = 5$, is,

$$\text{CG}_5 = \sum_{i=1}^{5} rel_i = 3 + 1 + 0 + 3 + 2 = 9.$$

You can see that changing the order of any documents will not affect the value of cumulative gain. Now we will calculate the discounted cumulative gain designed, with the presence of the logarithmic discounting, to have a higher value if highly relevant documents appear early in the result list. To calculate DCG_5, let's calculate the value of the expression $\frac{rel_i}{\log_2(i+1)}$ for each i:

i	rel_i	$\log_2(i+1)$	$\frac{rel_i}{\log_2(i+1)}$
1	3	1.00	3.00
2	1	1.58	0.63
3	0	2.00	0.00
4	3	2.32	1.29
5	2	2.58	0.77

So DCG_5 of this ranking is given by $3.00 + 0.63 + 0.00 + 1.29 + 0.77 = 5.70$.

Now, if we switch the positions of D_1 and D_2, the value of DCG_5 will become lower. This is because a less relevant document is now placed higher in the ranking, while a more relevant document is discounted more by being placed in a lower position.

To calculate the normalized discounted cumulative gain, nDCG_5, we first need to find the value of the discounted cumulative gain of the ideal ordering, IDCG_5. The ideal ordering, according to the relevance scores, is $3, 3, 2, 1, 0$. The value of IDCG_5 is then equal to $3.00 + 1.89 + 1.00 + 0.43 + 0.0 = 6.32$. Finally, nDCG_5 is given by,

$$\text{nDCG}_5 = \frac{\text{DCG}_5}{\text{IDCG}_5} = \frac{5.70}{6.32} = 0.90.$$

To obtain nDCG for a collection of test queries and the corresponding lists of search results, we average the values of nDCG_p obtained for each individual query. The advantage of using the normalized discounted cumulative gain over other measures is that the values of nDCG_p obtained for different values of p are comparable. This property is useful when the number p of relevance scores, provided by the rankers, is different for different queries.

Now that we have a performance metric, we can use it to compare models in the process known as hyperparameter tuning.

5.6 Hyperparameter Tuning

Hyperparameters play an important role in the model training process. Some hyperparameters influence the speed of training, but the most important hyperparameters control the two tradeoffs: bias-variance and precision-recall.

Hyperparameters aren't optimized by the learning algorithm itself. The data analyst "tunes" hyperparameters by experimenting with combinations of values, one per hyperparameter. Each machine learning model and each learning algorithm have a unique set of hyperparameters. Furthermore, every step in your entire machine learning pipeline, data pre-processing, feature extraction, model training, and making predictions, can have its own hyperparameters.

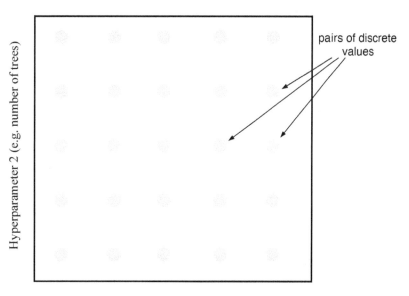

Figure 5.6: Grid search for two hyperparameters: each green circle represents a pair of hyperparameter values.

For example, in data pre-processing, the hyperparameters could specify whether to use data-augmentation or using which technique to fill missing values. In feature engineering, a hyperparameter could define which feature selection technique to apply. When making predictions with a model that returns a score, a hyperparameter could specify the decision threshold for each class.

Below, we consider several popular **hyperparameter tuning techniques**.

5.6.1 Grid Search

Grid search is the simplest hyperparameter tuning technique. It's used when the number of hyperparameters and their range is not too large.

We explain it for the problem of tuning two numerical hyperparameters. The technique consists of discretizing each of the two hyperparameters, and then evaluating each pair of discrete values, as shown in Figure 5.6.

Each evaluation consists of:

1) configuring a pipeline with a pair of hyperparameter values,
2) applying the pipeline to the training data and training a model, and

3) computing the performance metric for the model on the validation data.

The pair of hyperparameter values that results in the best performing model is then selected for training the final model.

The Python code below uses grid search with cross-validation.[2] It shows how to optimize the hyperparameters of the simple two-stage scikit-learn pipeline considered above:

```python
from sklearn.pipeline import Pipeline
from sklearn.svm import SVC
from sklearn.decomposition import PCA
from sklearn.model_selection import GridSearchCV

# Define a pipeline
pipe = Pipeline([('dim_reduction', PCA()), ('model_training', SVC())])

# Define hyperparamer values to try
param_grid = dict(dim_reduction__n_components=[2, 5, 10], \
model_training__C=[0.1, 10, 100])

grid_search = GridSearchCV(pipe, param_grid=param_grid)

# Make a prediction
pipe.predict(new_example)
```

In the above example, we use grid search to try the values $[2, 5, 10]$ of the hyperparameter n_components of PCA, and the values $[0.1, 10, 100]$ of the hyperparameter C of SVM.

Trying multiple combinations of hyperparameters could be time-consuming for large datasets. There are more efficient techniques, such as random search, coarse-to-fine search, and Bayesian hyperparameter optimization.

5.6.2   Random Search

Random search differs from grid search in that you do not provide a discrete set of values to explore for each hyperparameter. Instead, you provide a statistical distribution for each hyperparameter from which values are randomly sampled. Then set the total number of combinations you want to evaluate, as shown in Figure 5.7.

---

[2]We talk about cross-validation in Subsection 5.6.5.

Figure 5.7: Random search for two hyperparameters and 16 pairs to test.

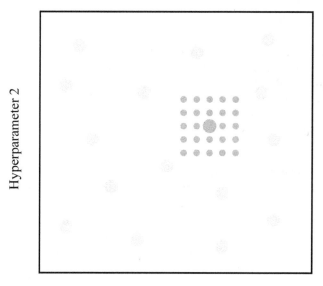

Figure 5.8: Coarse-to-fine search for two hyperparameters: 16 coarse random search pairs to test and one grid search in the region of the highest value found using the random search.

5.6.3 Coarse-to-Fine Search

In practice, analysts often use a combination of grid search and random search called **coarse-to-fine search**. This technique uses a coarse random search to first find the regions of high potential. Then, using a fine grid search in these regions, one finds the best values for hyperparameters, as shown in Figure 5.8.

You can decide to only explore one high-potential region or several such regions, depending on the available time and computational resources.

5.6.4 Other Techniques

Bayesian techniques differ from random and grid searches in that they use past evaluation results to choose the next values to evaluate. In practice, this allows Bayesian hyperparameter optimization techniques to find better values of hyperparameters in less time.

There are also gradient-based techniques, evolutionary optimization techniques, and other algorithmic hyperparameter tuning methods. Most modern machine learning libraries implement one or more such techniques. There are also hyperparameter tuning libraries that can be used to tune hyperparameters of virtually any learning algorithm, including the algorithms you programmed yourself.

5.6.5 Cross-Validation

Grid search and other techniques of hyperparameter tuning discussed above are used when you have a good-sized validation set.[3] When you don't, a common technique of model evaluation is **cross-validation**. Indeed, when you have few training examples, it could be prohibitive to have both validation and test sets. You would prefer to use more data to train the model. In such a case, you should only split your data in two: a training and a test set. Then use cross-validation on the training set to simulate a validation set.

Cross-validation works as follows. First, you fix the values of the hyperparameters to evaluate. Then you split your training set into several subsets of the same size. Each subset is called a fold. Typically, **five-fold cross-validation** is used, and you randomly split your training data into five folds: $\{F_1, F_2, \ldots, F_5\}$. Each F_k, $k = 1, \ldots, 5$, contains 20% of your training data. Then you train five models in a specific manner. To train the first model, f_1, you use all examples from folds F_2, F_3, F_4, and F_5 as the training set, and the examples from F_1 as the validation set. To train the second model, f_2, you use the examples from folds F_1, F_3, F_4, and F_5 to train, and the examples from F_2 to validate. You continue training models f_k iteratively[4] for all remaining folds, and compute the value of the metric of interest on each

---

[3]A decent validation set contains at least a hundred examples, and each class in the set is represented by at least a couple of dozen examples.

[4]The process of cross-validation is easier to illustrate as an iterative process; though, one can, of course, build all five models F_1 to F_5 in parallel.

validation set, from F_1 to F_5. Then you average the five values of the metric to get the final value. More generally, in n-fold cross-validation, you train model f_n on all folds, except for the n-th fold F_n.

You can use grid search, random search, or any other such technique with cross-validation to find the best values of hyperparameters. Once you have found those values, you typically use the entire training set to train the final model by using the best values of hyperparameters found via cross-validation. Finally, you assess the final model using the test set.

While finding the best values of hyperparameters is tempting, it might be unrealistic to try all of them. Remember that time is precious, and perfect is often an enemy of good. Deploy a "good enough" model to production, then continue to run the search of the ideal values for hyperparameters (for weeks if it is what it takes).

Now, let's consider the challenge of training a shallow model.

5.7 Shallow Model Training

Shallow models make predictions based directly on the values in the input feature vector. Most popular machine learning algorithms produce shallow models. The only kind of deep models commonly used are deep neural networks. We consider a strategy to train them in Section 6.1 of the next chapter.

5.7.1 Shallow Model Training Strategy

A typical model training strategy for shallow learning algorithms looks as follows:

1. Define a performance metric P.
2. Shortlist learning algorithms.
3. Choose a hyperparameter tuning strategy T.
4. Pick a learning algorithm A.
5. Pick a combination H of hyperparameter values for algorithm A using strategy T.
6. Use the training set and train a model M using algorithm A parametrized with hyperparameter values H.
7. Use the validation set and calculate the value of metric P for model M.
8. Decide:
   a. If there are still untested hyperparameter values, pick another combination H of hyperparameter values using strategy T and go back to step 6.
   b. Otherwise, pick a different learning algorithm A and go back to step 5, or proceed to step 9 if there are no more learning algorithms to try.
9. Return the model for which the value of metric P is maximized.

In the above strategy, step 1, you define the performance metric for your problem. As we have seen in Section 5.5, it is a mathematical function or a subroutine that takes a model and a dataset as input, and produces a numerical value that reflects how well the model works.

In step 2, you choose candidate algorithms and then shortlist some of them (usually, two or three). To do that, you can use the selection criteria considered in Section 5.3.

In step 3, you choose a hyperparameter tuning strategy. It is a sequence of actions that generates the combinations of hyperparameter values to test. We have considered several hyperparameter-tuning strategies in Section 5.6.

5.7.2   Saving and Restoring the Model

Once you trained a model or a pipeline, you must save it to a file so that it can be deployed to production and then used for scoring. Both model and pipeline can be serialized. In Python, **Pickle** is typically used for serialization (saving) and deserialization (restoring) of objects. In R, it's RDS.

Here's how model serialization/deserialization is done in Python:

```
import pickle
from sklearn.svm import SVC
from sklearn import datasets

# Prepare data
X, y = datasets.load_iris(return_X_y=True)

# Instantiate the model
model = SVC()

# Train the model
model.fit(X, y)

# Save the model to file
pickle.dump(model, open("model_file.pkl", "wb"))

# Restore the model from file
restored_model = pickle.load(open("model_file.pkl", "rb"))

# Make a prediction
prediction = restored_model.predict(new_example)
```

A similar code in R would look as follows:

```r
1   library("e1071")
2
3   # Prepare data
4   attach(iris)
5   X <- subset(iris, select=-Species)
6   y <- Species
7
8   # Train the model
9   model <- svm(X,y)
10
11  # Save the model to file
12  saveRDS(model, "./model_file.rds")
13
14  # Restore the model from file
15  restored_model <- readRDS("./model_file.rds")
16
17  # Make a prediction
18  prediction <- predict(restored_model, new_example)
```

Now, let's talk about the particularities of the model training process that analysts must take care of in practice to produce an optimal model.

5.8   Bias-Variance Tradeoff

Developing a model includes both searching for an optimal algorithm, as well as finding the best performing hyperparameters. Tweaking the hyperparameters actually controls two tradeoffs. We already discussed the first one: the precision-recall tradeoff. The second one, equally important, is the **bias-variance tradeoff**.

5.8.1   Underfitting

The model is said to have a **low bias** if it ably predicts the training data labels. If the model makes too many mistakes on the training data, we say that it has a **high bias**, or that the model **underfits** the training data. There could be several reasons for underfitting:

- the model is too simple for the data (for example linear models often underfit);
- the features are not informative enough;
- you regularize too much (we talk about regularization in the next section).

An example of underfitting in regression is shown in Figure 5.9 (left). The regression line doesn't repeat the bends of the line to which the data seemingly belongs. The model oversimplifies the data. The possible solutions to the problem of underfitting include:

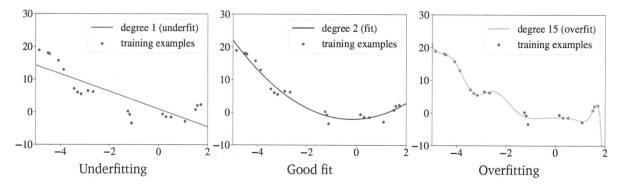

Figure 5.9: Examples of underfitting (linear model), good fit (quadratic model), and overfitting (polynomial of degree 15).

- trying a more complex model,
- engineering features with higher **predictive power**,
- adding more training data, when possible, and
- reducing regularization.

5.8.2   Overfitting

Overfitting is another problem a model can exhibit. The model that overfits usually predicts the training data labels very well, but works poorly on the holdout data.

An example of overfitting in regression is shown in Figure 5.9 (right). The regression line predicts almost perfectly the targets for almost all training examples, but will likely make significant errors on new data if you decide to use it for predictions.

You will find another name for overfitting in the literature: **high variance**. The model is unduly sensitive to small fluctuations in the training set. If you sampled the training data differently, the result would be a significantly different model. These overfitting models perform poorly on the holdout data, since holdout and training data are sampled from the dataset independently of one another. So, the small fluctuations in the training and holdout data are likely to be different.

Several reasons can lead to overfitting:

- the model is too complex for the data. Very tall decision trees or a very deep neural network often overfit;
- there are too many features and few training examples; and
- you don't regularize enough.

Several solutions to overfitting are possible:

- use a simpler model. Try linear instead of polynomial regression, or SVM with a linear kernel instead of **radial basis function** (RBF), or a neural network with fewer layers/units;[5]
- reduce the dimensionality of examples in the dataset;
- add more training data, if possible; and,
- regularize the model.

5.8.3 The Tradeoff

In practice, by trying to reduce variance, you increase bias, and vice versa. In other words, reducing overfitting leads to underfitting, and the other way around. This is called the **bias-variance tradeoff**: by trying too hard to build a model that performs perfectly on the training data, you end up with a model that performs poorly on the holdout data.

While many factors determine whether the model performs well on the training data, the most important factor is the complexity of the model. A sufficiently complex model will learn to memorize all training examples and their labels and, thus, will not make prediction errors when applied to the training data. It will have low bias. However, a model relying on memorization will not be able to correctly predict labels of previously unseen data. It will have high variance.

As the model complexity grows, the typical evolution of the average prediction error of a model when applied to the training and holdout data is shown in Figure 5.10.

The zone you would like to be in is the "zone of solutions," the light-blue rectangle where both bias and variance are low. Once in this zone, you can fine-tune the hyperparameters to reach the needed precision-recall ratio, or optimize another model performance metric appropriate for your problem.

To reach the zone of solutions, you can either,

- move to the right by increasing the complexity of the model, and, by so doing, reducing its bias, or
- move to the left by regularizing the model to reduce variance by making the model simpler (we talk about regularization in the next section).

If you work with shallow models, like linear regression, you can increase the complexity by switching to higher-order polynomial regression. Similarly, you can increase the depth of the decision tree, or use polynomial or RBF kernels, in support vector machine (SVM) instead of the linear kernel. Ensemble learning algorithms, based on the idea of boosting, allow bias reduction by combining several (usually, hundreds of) high-bias "weak" models.

---

[5]While reducing the number of model parameters is generally recommended to reduce overfitting and improve the generalization of the model, the phenomenon of **deep double descent** sometimes proves otherwise. The phenomenon was observed in various architectures, including **CNN** and **transformers**: validation performance first improves, then gets worse, and then improves again with increasing model size. As of July 2020, we don't yet fully understand why it happens.

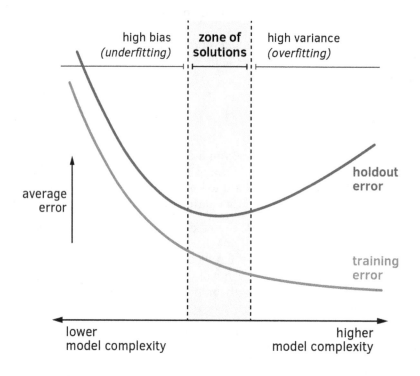

Figure 5.10: Bias-variance tradeoff.

If you work with neural networks, you can increase the model's complexity by increasing its size: the number of units per layer, and the number of layers. Training a neural network model longer (i.e., for more epochs) also usually results in lower bias. The advantage of using neural networks, with respect to the bias-variance tradeoff, is that you can slightly increase the size of the network and observe a slight decrease in bias. Most popular shallow models and the associated learning algorithms cannot provide you such flexibility.

If, by increasing the complexity of your model, you find yourself in the right-hand side of the graph in Figure 5.10, you have to reduce the variance of the model. The most common way to do that is to apply regularization.

5.9 Regularization

Regularization is an umbrella term for methods that force a learning algorithm to train a less complex model. In practice, it leads to higher bias, but significantly reduces the variance.

The two most widely used types of regularization are **L1** and **L2 regularization**. The idea is quite simple. To create a regularized model, we modify the objective function. This is the expression optimized by the learning algorithm when training the model. Regularization adds a penalizing term whose value is higher when the model is more complex.

For simplicity, we will illustrate regularization using linear regression, but same principle can be applied to a wide variety of models.

Let $\mathbf{x}$ be a two-dimensional feature vector $\left[x^{(1)}, x^{(2)}\right]$. Recall the linear regression objective:

$$\min_{w^{(1)},w^{(2)},b} \left[\frac{1}{N} \times \sum_{i=1}^{N} (f_i - y_i)^2 \right],\tag{5.3}$$

In the above equation, $f_i \overset{\text{def}}{=} f(\mathbf{x}_i)$, and f is the equation of the regression line. The equation of the linear regression line f will have the form $f = w^{(1)}x^{(1)} + w^{(2)}x^{(2)} + b$. The learning algorithm will deduce the values of parameters $w^{(1)}$, $w^{(2)}$, and b from the training data by minimizing the objective. A model is considered less complex if some of the parameters $w^{(\cdot)}$ are close to or equal to zero.

5.9.1 L1 and L2 Regularization

An L1-regularized objective in Equation 5.3 looks like this:

$$\min_{w^{(1)},w^{(2)},b} \left[C \times \left(|w^{(1)}| + |w^{(2)}| \right) + \frac{1}{N} \times \sum_{i=1}^{N} (f_i - y_i)^2 \right],\tag{5.4}$$

where C is a **hyperparameter** that controls the importance of regularization. If we set C to zero, the model becomes a standard non-regularized linear regression model. On the other hand, if we set C to a high value, the learning algorithm will try to set most $w^{(\cdot)}$ to a value close or equal to zero to minimize the objective. The model will become very simple, which can lead to underfitting. The role of the data analyst is to find such a value of the hyperparameter C that doesn't increase the bias too much, but reduces the variance to a level reasonable for the problem at hand.

An L2-regularized objective in our two-dimensional setting looks like this:

$$\min_{w^{(1)},w^{(2)},b} \left[C \times \left((w^{(1)})^2 + (w^{(2)})^2 \right) + \frac{1}{N} \times \sum_{i=1}^{N} (f_i - y_i)^2 \right],\tag{5.5}$$

In practice, L1 regularization produces a **sparse model**, assuming the value of hyperparameter C is great enough. This is a model where most of its parameters equal exactly zero. So, as discussed in the previous chapter, L1 implicitly performs **feature selection** by deciding which features are essential for prediction, and which are not. This property of L1 regularization is useful when we want to increase model **explainability**. However, if our goal is to maximize the model performance on the holdout data, then L2 usually gives better results.

In the literature, you will also see the names **lasso** for L1 and **ridge regularization** for L2.

5.9.2 Other Forms of Regularization

L1 and L2 regularization methods can be combined in what's called **elastic net regularization**.

In addition to being widely used with linear models, L1 and L2 are often used with neural networks and many other types of models that directly minimize an objective function.

Neural networks can also benefit from two other regularization techniques: **dropout** and **batch-normalization**. There are also non-mathematical methods that have a regularization effect: **data augmentation** and **early stopping**. We will talk about these techniques in more detail in the next chapter, when we consider training neural networks.

5.10   Summary

Before starting to work on the model, you should make several checks and decisions. First, make sure that the data conforms to the schema, as defined by the schema file. Then, define an achievable level of performance, and choose a performance metric. Ideally, it should represent the model performance as a single number. Furthermore, it is important to establish a baseline that provides a reference point to compare your machine learning models. Finally, split your data into three sets: train, validation, and test.

Most modern implementations of classification learning algorithms require that the training examples have numerical labels, so you typically must transform your labels into numerical vectors. Two popular ways to do that are one-hot encoding (for binary and multiclass problems) and bag-of-words (for multi-label problems).

To choose a machine learning algorithm that would work best for your problem, ask yourself the following questions:

- Do the model's predictions have to be explainable to a non-technical audience? If yes, you would prefer using less accurate, but more explainable algorithms, such as kNN, linear regression, and decision tree learning.
- Can your dataset be fully loaded into the RAM of your laptop or server? If not, you would prefer incremental learning algorithms.
- How many training examples do you have in your dataset, and how many features does each example have? Some algorithms, including those used for training neural networks and random forests, can handle a huge number of examples and millions of features. Others are relatively modest in their capacity.

- Is your data linearly separable, or can it be modeled using a linear model? If yes, SVM with the linear kernel, linear and logistic regression, can be good choices. Otherwise, deep neural networks or ensemble models might work better.
- How much time is a learning algorithm allowed to use to train a model? Neural networks are known to be slow to train. Simple algorithms like linear and logistic regression, or decision trees are much faster.
- How fast must the scoring perform in production? Models like SVM, linear and logistic regression, as well as not very deep feedforward neural networks, are extremely fast at the prediction time. The scoring using deep and recurrent neural networks, as well as gradient boosting models, is slower.

If you don't want to guess the best algorithm for your problem, a recommended approach is to spot-check several algorithms, and then test them on the validation set as a hyperparameter.

A typical way to know how good is the model, is to calculate the value of a performance metric on the holdout data. There are performance metrics defined for classification and regressions models, as well as for ranking models.

Tweaking the values of hyperparameters controls two tradeoffs: precision-recall and bias-variance. By varying the complexity of the model, we can reach the so-called "zone of solutions," a situation in which both bias and variance of the model are relatively low. The solution that optimizes the performance metric is usually found inside that zone.

Regularization is an umbrella term for methods that force the learning algorithm to build a less complex model. In practice, that often leads to slightly higher bias, but significantly reduces the variance. Two popular techniques of regularization are L1 and L2. In addition, neural networks benefit from two other regularization techniques: dropout and batch normalization.

Most modern machine learning packages and frameworks support the notion of a pipeline. A pipeline is a sequence of transformations the training data undergoes before it becomes a model. In a pipeline, each stage applies some transformation to the input it receives. Every stage receives the output of the previous stage, except for the first stage. The first stage receives the training dataset as input. The pipeline can be saved to a file similar to saving a model. It can be deployed to production and used to generate predictions.

Hyperparameters aren't optimized by the learning algorithm itself. A data analyst must "tune" hyperparameters by experimenting with different combinations of values. Grid search is the simplest and the most widely used hyperparameter tuning technique. It consists of discretizing the values of hyperparameters, and trying all combinations of values by 1) training a model for each combination of hyperparameters, and 2) computing the performance metric by applying each trained model to the validation set.

A decent validation set contains at least a hundred examples, and each class in the set is represented by at least a couple of dozen examples. When you don't have a decent validation set to tune your hyperparameters, you can use cross-validation.

Chapter 6

Supervised Model Training (Part 2)

In this second part of our conversation about supervised model training, we consider such topics as training deep models, stacking models, handling imbalanced datasets, distribution shift, model calibration, troubleshooting and error analysis, and other best practices.

Compared to shallow models, the model training strategy for deep neural networks has more moving parts. On the other hand, it's more principled and better amenable to automation.

6.1   Deep Model Training Strategy

Model training starts with shortlisting several network architectures, also known as **network topologies**. If you work with image data and you want to build your model from scratch, then a **convolutional neural network** (CNN) with at least one **convolutional layer**, followed by a **max-pooling layer**, and one **fully connected layer** may be your default topology choice.

If you work with text or other sequence data, such as time series, you have a choice between a CNN, a **gated recurrent neural network** (such as Long Short Term Memory, **LSTM**, or gated recurrent units, **GRU**), or a **Transformer**.

Instead of training your model from scratch, you can also start with a **pre-trained model**. Companies like Google and Microsoft have trained very deep neural networks with architectures optimized for image or natural language processing tasks.

Among the most used pre-trained models for image processing tasks are **VGG16** and **VGG19** (based on the Visual Geometry Group, **VGG**, architecture), **InceptionV3** (based on the **GoogLeNet** architecture), and **ResNet50** (based on the **residual network** architecture).

For natural language text processing, such pre-trained models as Bi-directional Encoder Representations from Transformer, **BERT**, (based on the Transformer architecture) and

Embeddings from Language Models, **ELMo** (based on the **bi-directional LSTM** architecture) often improve the quality of the model, compared to training a model from scratch.

An advantage of using pre-trained models is that these were trained on huge quantities of data available to its creators, but likely unavailable to you. Even if your dataset is smaller and not exactly similar to the one used to pre-train the model, the parameters learned by the pre-trained models may still be useful.

You can use a pre-trained model in two ways:

1) use its learned parameters to initialize your own model, or
2) use the pre-trained model as a feature extractor for your model.

If you use the pre-trained model the former way, it gives you more flexibility. The downside is you end up training a very deep neural network. That requires significant computational resources. In the latter case, you "freeze" the parameters of the pre-trained model and only train the parameters of added layers.

6.1.1   Neural Network Training Strategy

Using an existing model to create a new model is called **transfer learning**. We will talk more on this topic in Section 6.1.10. For the moment, assume you are building a model from scratch, based on the architecture of your choice. A common strategy to build a neural network looks as follows:

1. Define a performance metric P.
2. Define the cost function C.
3. Pick a parameter-initialization strategy W.
4. Pick a cost-function optimization algorithm A.
5. Choose a hyperparameter tuning strategy T.
6. Pick a combination H of hyperparameter values using the tuning strategy T.
7. Train model M, using algorithm A, parametrized with hyperparameters H, to optimize cost function C.
8. If there are still untested hyperparameter values, pick another combination H of hyperparameter values using strategy T, and repeat step 7.
9. Return the model for which the metric P was optimized.

Now let's discuss some of the steps of the above strategy in detail.

6.1.2   Performance Metric and Cost Function

Step 1 is similar to step 1 of the shallow model training strategy (Section 5.7): we define a metric that would allow comparing the performance of two models on the holdout data, and select the better of the two. An example of a performance metric is **F-score** or **Cohen's kappa**.

In step 2, we define what our learning algorithm will optimize in order to train a model. If our neural network is a regression model, then, in most cases, the **cost function** is the **mean squared error** (MSE) defined in Equation 5.1 in the previous chapter. Let's repeat it here:

$$\text{MSE}(f) \stackrel{\text{def}}{=} \frac{1}{N} \sum_{i=1\ldots N} (f(\mathbf{x}_i) - y_i)^2.$$

For classification, a typical choice for the cost function is either **categorical cross-entropy** (for multiclass classification) or **binary cross-entropy** (for binary and multi-label classification).

Recall that when we train a neural network for **multiclass classification**, we should represent labels using the **one-hot encoding**. Let C be the number of classes in our classification problem. Let $\mathbf{y}_i$ be a one-hot encoded label of example i, where i spans from 1 to N. Let $y_{i,j}$ denote the value in position j (where j spans from 1 to C) in example i. The categorical cross-entropy loss for classification of example i is defined as,

$$\text{CCE}_i \stackrel{\text{def}}{=} -\sum_{j=1}^{C} [y_{i,j} \times \log_2(\hat{y}_{i,j})],$$

where $\hat{\mathbf{y}}_i$ is the C-dimensional vector of prediction issued by the neural network for the input $\mathbf{x}_i$. The cost function is typically defined as the sum of losses of individual examples:

$$\text{CCE} \stackrel{\text{def}}{=} \sum_{i=1}^{N} \text{CCE}_i.$$

In **binary classification**, the output of the neural network for the input feature vector $\mathbf{x}_i$, is a single value $\hat{y}_i$, while the label of the example is a single value y_i, just like in logistic regression. The binary cross-entropy loss for classification of example i is defined as,

$$\text{BCE}_i \stackrel{\text{def}}{=} -y_i \times \log_2(\hat{y}_i) - (1 - y_i) \times \log_2(1 - \hat{y}_i).$$

Similarly, the cost function for classification of the training set is typically defined as the sum of losses of individual examples:

$$\text{BCE} \stackrel{\text{def}}{=} \sum_{i=1}^{N} \text{BCE}_i.$$

Binary cross-entropy is also used in **multi-label classification**. The labels are now C-dimensional **bag-of-words** vectors $\mathbf{y}_i$, while the predictions are C-dimensional vectors $\hat{\mathbf{y}}_i$, whose values $\hat{y}_{i,j}$ in each dimension j range between 0 and 1. The loss for the prediction of one label $\hat{\mathbf{y}}_i$ is defined as,

$$\text{BCEM}_i \overset{\text{def}}{=} \sum_{j=1}^{C} \left[-y_{i,j} \times \log_2(\hat{y}_{i,j}) - (1 - y_{i,j}) \times \log_2(1 - \hat{y}_{i,j}) \right].$$

The cost function for the classification of the entire training set is typically defined as the sum of losses of individual examples,

$$\text{BCEM} \overset{\text{def}}{=} \sum_{i=1}^{N} \text{BCEM}_i.$$

Note that the output layers in multiclass and multi-label classification are different. In multiclass classification, one **softmax** unit is used. It generates a C-dimensional vector whose values are bounded by the range $(0, 1)$, and whose sum equals 1. In multi-label classification, the output layer contains C logistic units whose values also lie in the range $(0, 1)$, but their sum lies in the range $(0, C)$.

Neural Network Output

The curious reader may wish to better understand the logic behind choosing a specific loss function. This block will mathematically describe the output of a neural network.

In regression, the output layer contains only one unit. If the output value can be any number, from minus infinity to infinity, then the output unit will not contain non-linearity. On the other hand, if the neural network must predict a positive number, then the **ReLU** (rectified linear unit) non-linearity can be used. Let the output value of the output unit before non-linearity for the input example i be denoted as z_i. Then the output after applying the ReLU non-linearity is given by $\max(0, z_i)$.

In a binary classification, the output layer contains only one logistic unit. Let the output value of the output unit before non-linearity for the input example i be denoted as z_i. The output $\hat{y}_i$ after applying the logistic nonlinearity is given by,

$$\hat{y}_i \overset{\text{def}}{=} \frac{1}{1 + e^{-z_i}},$$

where e is the base of the natural logarithm, also known as **Euler's number**.

Binary and multi-label classification models are defined in a similar way. The only difference is that in multi-label classification, the output layer contains C logistic units, one per class. If $\hat{y}_{i,j}$ denotes the output, after nonlinearity, of the logistic unit for class j, when input example is i, then the sum of $\hat{y}_{i,j}$, for all $j = 1, \ldots, C$, lies between 0 and C.

In the multiclass classification, the output layer also produces C outputs. However, in this case, the output of each unit of the output layer is controlled by the softmax function. Let the output of the output unit j, before nonlinearity, for the input example i, be $z_{i,j}$. Then the output $\hat{y}_{i,j}$ after nonlinearity is given by,

$$\hat{y}_{i,j} \overset{\text{def}}{=} \frac{e^{z_{i,j}}}{\sum_{k=1}^{C} e^{z_{i,k}}}.$$

The sum of $\hat{y}_{i,j}$, for all $j = 1, \ldots C$, equals 1.

6.1.3   Parameter-Initialization Strategies

In step 3, we select a **parameter-initialization strategy**. Before the training starts, the parameter values in all units are unknown. We must initialize them with some values. Training algorithms for neural networks, such as **gradient descent** and its stochastic variants that we consider in a few moments, are iterative in nature and require the analyst to specify some initial point from which to begin the iterations. This initialization might affect the properties of the training model. You will likely choose from one of these strategies:

- **ones** — all parameters are initialized to 1;
- **zeros** — all parameters are initialized to 0;
- **random normal** — parameters are initialized to values sampled from the **normal distribution**, typically with mean of 0 and standard deviation of 0.05;
- **random uniform** — parameters are initialized to values sampled from the **uniform distribution** with the range $[-0.05, 0.05]$;
- **Xavier normal** — parameters are initialized to values sampled from the truncated normal distribution, centered on 0, with standard deviation equal to $\sqrt{2/(\text{in} + \text{out})}$ where "in" is the number of units in the preceding layer to which the current unit is connected (the one whose parameters you initialize); and "out" is the number of units on the subsequent layer to which the current unit is connected; and,
- **Xavier uniform** — parameters are initialized to values sampled from a uniform distribution within $[-\text{limit}, \text{limit}]$, where "limit" is $\sqrt{6/(\text{in} + \text{out})}$, and "in" and "out" are defined as in Xavier normal, above.

There are other initialization strategies. If you work with a neural network training module such as TensorFlow, Keras, or PyTorch, they provide some parameter initializers, and also recommend default choices.

The bias term is usually initialized with a zero.

While we know the parameter initialization affects the model properties, we cannot predict which strategy will provide the best result for your problem. Random and Xavier initializers are the most common. It's recommended to start your experiments with one of those two.

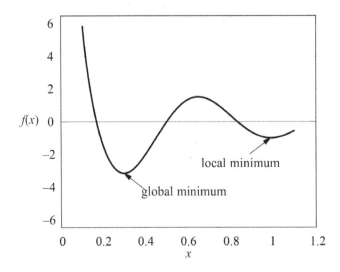

Figure 6.1: A local and a global minima of a function.

6.1.4   Optimization Algorithms

In step 4, we select a cost-function optimization algorithm. When the cost function is differentiable (and it's the case for all cost functions we considered above) **gradient descent** and **stochastic gradient descent** are two most frequently used optimization algorithms.

Gradient descent is an iterative optimization algorithm for finding a **local minimum** of any differentiable function. We say that $f(x)$ has a **local minimum** at $x = c$ if $f(x) \geq f(c)$ for every x in some **open interval** around $x = c$. An **interval** is a set of real numbers with the property that any number that lies between two numbers in the set is also included in the set. An open interval does not include its endpoints and is denoted using parentheses. For example, $(0, 1)$ means "all numbers greater than 0 and less than 1." The minimal value among all the local minima is called the **global minimum**. The difference between a local and a global minimum of a function is shown in Figure 6.1.

Functions and optimization

In this block, for the curious reader, we explain the basics of mathematical function and function optimization. If you only want to know the mechanics of training neural networks, you can safely skip it.

A **function** is a relation that associates each element x of a set $\mathcal{X}$, the **domain** of the function, to a single element y of another set $\mathcal{Y}$, the **codomain** of the function. A function usually has a name. If the function is called f, this relation is denoted $y = f(x)$, read "y equals f of x." The element x is the argument, or input of the function, and y is the value of the function, or the output. The symbol that is used for representing the input is the variable of the function. We often say that f is a function of the variable x.

A **derivative** f' of a function f is a function or a value that describes how fast f increases or decreases. If the derivative is a constant value, like 5 or -3, then the function increases or decreases constantly, at any point x of its domain. If the derivative f' is itself a function, then the function f can grow at a different pace in different regions of its domain. If the derivative f' is positive at some point x, then the function f increases at this point. If the derivative of f is negative at some x, then the function decreases at this point. The derivative of zero at x means that the function neither decreases nor increases at x; the function's slope at x is horizontal.

The process of finding a derivative is called **differentiation**.

Derivatives for basic functions are known. For example if $f(x) = x^2$, then $f'(x) = 2x$; if $f(x) = 2x$ then $f'(x) = 2$; if $f(x) = 2$ then $f'(x) = 0$. The derivative of any function $f(x) = c$, where c is a constant value, is zero.

If the function we want to differentiate is not basic, we can find its derivative using the **chain rule**. For instance if $F(x) = f(g(x))$, where f and g are some functions, then $F'(x) = f'(g(x))g'(x)$. For example if $F(x) = (5x + 1)^2$ then $g(x) = 5x + 1$ and $f(g(x)) = (g(x))^2$. By applying the chain rule, we find $F'(x) = 2(5x + 1)g'(x) = 2(5x + 1)5 = 50x + 10$.

Gradient is the generalization of derivatives for functions that take several inputs, or one input in the form of a vector or some other complex structure. A gradient of a function is a vector of **partial derivatives**. Finding a partial derivative of a function is the process of finding the derivative by focusing on one of the function's inputs and considering all other inputs as constant values.

For example, if our function is defined as $f([x^{(1)}, x^{(2)}]) = ax^{(1)} + bx^{(2)} + c$, then the partial derivative of function f with respect to $x^{(1)}$, denoted as $\frac{\partial f}{\partial x^{(1)}}$, is given by,

$$\frac{\partial f}{\partial x^{(1)}} = a + 0 + 0 = a,$$

where a is the derivative of the function $ax^{(1)}$. The two zeros are respectively derivatives of $bx^{(2)}$ and c, because $x^{(2)}$ is considered constant when we calculate the derivative with respect to $x^{(1)}$, and the derivative of any constant is zero.

Similarly, the partial derivative of function f with respect to $x^{(2)}$, $\frac{\partial f}{\partial x^{(2)}}$, is given by,

$$\frac{\partial f}{\partial x^{(2)}} = 0 + b + 0 = b.$$

The gradient of function f, denoted as ∇f is given by the vector $[\frac{\partial f}{\partial x^{(1)}}, \frac{\partial f}{\partial x^{(2)}}]$.

The chain rule works with partial derivatives too.

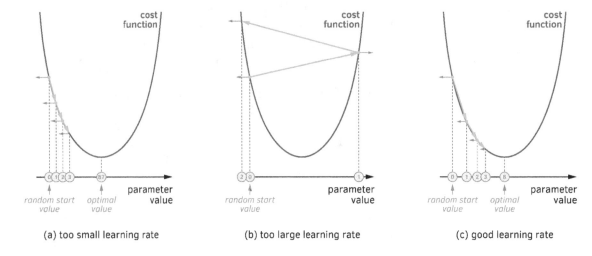

(a) too small learning rate   (b) too large learning rate   (c) good learning rate

Figure 6.2: The influence of the learning rate on the convergence: (a) too small, the convergence will be slow; (b) too large, no convergence; (c) the right value of learning rate.

To find a local minimum of a function using **gradient descent**, we start at some random point in the domain of the function. Then we move proportionally to the negative of the gradient (or approximate gradient) of the function at the current point.

Gradient descent in machine learning proceeds in **epochs**. An epoch consists of using the training set entirely to update each parameter. In the first epoch, we initialize the parameters of our neural network using one of the parameter-initialization strategies discussed above. The **backpropagation** algorithm computes the partial derivatives of each parameter using the chain rule for derivatives of complex functions.[1] At each epoch, gradient descent updates all parameters using partial derivatives. The **learning rate** controls the significance of an update. The process continues until **convergence**, the state when the values of parameters don't change much after each epoch. Then the algorithm stops.

Gradient descent is sensitive to the choice of the learning rate α. Picking the right learning rate for your problem is not easy. If you select a value that is too high, you might not reach convergence at all. On the other hand, too small values of α can slow down the learning to the point of no observable progress. In Figure 6.2, you can see an illustration of gradient descent for one parameter of a neural network and three values of the learning rate. The value of the parameter at each iteration is shown as a blue circle. The number inside the circle indicates the epoch. The red arrows indicate the direction of the gradient along the

---

[1]The explanation of backpropagation is beyond the scope of this book. You should only know that every modern software library for training neural networks contains an implementation of this algorithm. The curious reader can find the explanation of backpropagation in the extended version of The Hundred-Page Machine Learning Book on its companion wiki.

horizontal axis — the direction away from the minimum. The green arrows show the change in the value of the cost function after each epoch.

Therefore, at each epoch, gradient descent moves the parameter value towards the minimum. If the learning rate is too small, the movement towards the minimum will be very slow (Figure 6.2a). If the learning rate is too large, the value of the parameter will oscillate away from the minimum (Figure 6.2b).

Gradient descent is rather slow for large datasets because it uses the entire dataset to compute the gradient of each parameter at each epoch. Fortunately, several significant improvements to this algorithm have been proposed.

Minibatch stochastic gradient descent (minibatch SGD) is a variant of the gradient descent algorithm. It approximates the gradient using small subsets of the training data called **minibatches**. This effectively speeds up the computation. The size of the minibatch is a hyperparameter, and you can tune it. Powers of two, between 32 and a few hundred, are recommended: 32, 64, 128, 256, and so on.

The problem of choosing a value for the learning rate α is still present in the "vanilla" minibatch SGD. Learning can still stagnate at later epochs. Instead of reaching a local minimum, the gradient descent might keep oscillating around it due to too large updates. There are many **learning rate decay schedules** that allow updating the learning rate, as the learning progresses, by reducing it later in the epoch count. The benefits of using a learning rate decay schedule include faster gradient descent convergence (faster learning) and higher model quality. Below, we consider several popular learning rate decay schedules.

6.1.5 Learning Rate Decay Schedules

Learning rate decay consists of gradually reducing the value of the **learning rate** α as the epochs progress. Consequently, the parameter updates become finer. There are several techniques, known as schedules, to control α.

Time-based learning rate decay schedules alter the learning rate depending on the learning rate of the previous epoch. The mathematical formula for the learning rate update, according to a popular time-based learning rate decay schedule, is:

$$\alpha_n \leftarrow \frac{\alpha_{n-1}}{1 + d \times n},$$

where α_n is the new value of the learning rate, α_{n-1} is the value of the learning at the previous epoch $n - 1$, and d is the **decay rate**, a hyperparameter. For example, if the initial value of the learning rate $\alpha_0 = 0.3$, then the values of the learning rate at the first five epochs are shown in the table below:

learning rate	epoch
0.15	1
0.10	2
0.08	3
0.06	4
0.05	5

Step-based learning rate decay schedules change the learning rate according to some predefined drop steps. The mathematical formula for the learning rate update, according to a popular step-based learning rate decay schedule, is:

$$\alpha_n \leftarrow \alpha_0 d^{\text{floor}\left(\frac{1+n}{r}\right)},$$

where α_n is the learning rate at epoch n, α_0 is the initial value of the learning rate, d is the decay rate that reflects how much the learning rate should change at each drop step (0.5 corresponds to halving), and r is the so-called **drop rate** defining the length of drop steps (10 corresponds to a drop every 10 epochs). The floor operator in the above formula equals 0 if the value of its argument is less than 1.

Exponential learning rate decay schedules are similar to step-based. However, instead of drop steps, a decreasing exponential function is used. The mathematical formula for the learning rate update, according to a popular exponential learning rate decay schedule, is:

$$\alpha_n \leftarrow \alpha_0 e^{-d \times n}$$

where d is the decay rate and e is **Euler's number**.

There are several popular upgrades to **minibatch SGD**, such as Momentum, Root Mean Squared Propagation (RMSProp), and Adam. These algorithms update the learning rate automatically based on the performance of the learning process. You don't have to worry about choosing the initial learning rate value, the decay schedule and rate, or other related hyperparameters. These algorithms have demonstrated good performance in practice, and practitioners often use them instead of manually tuning the learning rate.

Momentum helps accelerate minibatch SGD by orienting the gradient descent to the relevant direction, and reducing oscillations. Instead of using only the current gradient's epoch to guide the search, Momentum accumulates the gradient of past epochs to determine the direction to go. Momentum removes the need to manually adjust the learning rate.

More recent advancements in neural network cost function optimization algorithms include **RMSProp** and **Adam**, the latter being the most recent and versatile. It's recommended to start training the model with Adam. Then, if the quality of the model doesn't reach the acceptable level, try a different cost function optimization algorithm.

6.1.6 Regularization

In neural networks, besides **L1** and **L2 regularization**, you can use neural network-specific regularizers: dropout, early stopping, and batch-normalization. The latter is technically not a regularization technique, but it often has a regularization effect on the model.

The concept of **dropout** is very simple. Each time you "run" a training example through the network, you temporarily exclude at random some units from the computation. The higher the percentage of units excluded, the stronger the regularization effect. Popular neural network libraries allow you to add a dropout layer between two successive layers, or you can specify the dropout hyperparameter for a layer. The dropout hyperparameter varies in the range $[0, 1]$ and characterizes the fraction of units to randomly exclude from computation. The value of the hyperparameter has to be found experimentally. While simple, dropout's flexibility and regularizing effect are phenomenal.

Early stopping trains a neural network by saving the preliminary model after every epoch. Models saved after each epoch are called **checkpoints**. Then it assesses each checkpoint's performance on the validation set. You'll find during gradient descent that the cost decreases as the number of epochs increases. After some epoch, the model can start overfitting, and the model's performance on the validation data can deteriorate. Remember the bias-variance illustration in Figure 5.10 in Chapter 5. By keeping a version of the model after each epoch, you can stop the training once you start observing a decreased performance on the validation set. Alternatively, you can keep running the training process for a fixed number of epochs, and then pick the best checkpoint. Some machine learning practitioners rely on this technique. Others try to properly regularize the model using appropriate techniques.

Batch normalization (which rather should be called batch standardization) consists of **standardizing** the outputs of each layer before the next layer receives them as input. In practice, batch normalization results in faster and more stable training, as well as some regularization effect. So, it's always a good idea to use batch normalization. In popular neural network libraries, you can often insert a batch normalization layer between two subsequent layers.

Another regularization technique that can be applied to any learning algorithm is **data augmentation**. This technique is often used to regularize models that work with images. In practice, applying data augmentation often results in an increased model performance.

6.1.7 Network Size Search and Hyperparameter Tuning

Step 5 of the deep model training strategy is similar to that in the shallow model training strategy — choose a hyperparameter tuning strategy T.

It step 6, we pick a combination of hyperparameter values using strategy T. Typical parameters include the size of the minibatch, the value of the learning rate (if you use the vanilla minibatch SGD), or an algorithm that automatically updates the learning rate, such as Adam. You also decide the initial number of layers and units per layer. It's recommended to start

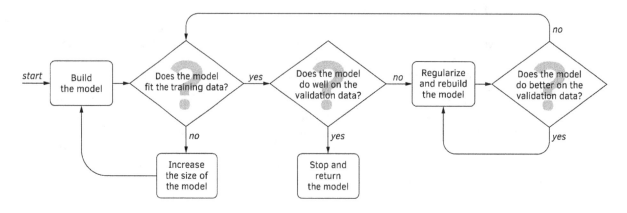

Figure 6.3: The neural network model training flowchart.

with something reasonable that would allow us to build the first model fast enough. For example, two hidden layers and 128 units per layer might be a good starting point.

Step 7 reads, "Build the training model M, using algorithm A, parametrized with hyper-parameters H, to optimize the cost function C." This is the main difference with shallow learning. When you work with a shallow learning algorithm or a model, you can only tweak some built-in hyperparameters. You don't have much control over the model architecture and complexity. With neural networks, you have all the control, and training a model is more a process than a single action. To build a deep model, you start with a reasonably-sized model, and then you follow the flowchart shown in Figure 6.3.

Observe that you start with some model, and then increase its size until it fits the training data well. Then you evaluate the model on the validation data. If it performs well, according to the performance metric, you stop and return the model. Otherwise, you regularize and retrain the model.

As we have seen, regularization in neural networks is usually achieved in several ways. The most effective is **dropout**, where you randomly remove some units from the network and make it simpler and "dumber." A simpler model would work better on the holdout data, and this is your goal.

Suppose, after several loops of regularization and model retrains, you don't see any improvement in the model performance on the validation data. Check if it still fits the training data. If it doesn't, increase the size of the model, by increasing the size of individual layers, or by adding another layer. Continue until the model fits the training data again. Then evaluate it again on the validation data. The process continues until a larger model doesn't result in better validation data performance, no matter your actions. Then you stop and return the model, if validation data performance is satisfactory.

If you are not satisfied with this performance, you can pick a different combination of hyperparameters for step 8, and build a different model. You will continue to test different values of hyperparameters until there are no more values to test. Then you keep the best model among those you trained in the process. If the performance of the best model is still not satisfactory, try a different network architecture, add more labeled data, or try **transfer learning**. We talk more on transfer learning in Section 6.1.10.

The properties of a trained neural network depend a lot on the choice of the values of hyperparameters. But before you choose specific values of hyperparameters, train a model, and validate its properties on the validation data, you must decide which hyperparameters are important enough for you to spend the time on.

Obviously, if you had infinite time and computing resources, you would tune all hyperparameters. However, in practice, you have finite time and, often, relatively modest resources. Which hyperparameters to tune?

While there is no definitive answer to that question, there are several observations that might help you in choosing the hyperparameters to tune when you work on a specific model:

- your model is more sensitive to some hyperparameters than to others; and
- the choice is often between using the default value of a hyperparameter or changing it.

The libraries for training neural networks often come with default values for hyperparameters: stochastic gradient descent version (often, **Adam**), the parameter initialization strategy (often, **random normal** or **random uniform**), minibatch size (often, 32), and so on. Those defaults were chosen based on observations from practical experience. Open-source libraries and modules are often the fruit of the collaboration of many scientists and engineers. These talented and experienced people established "good" defaults for many hyperparameters when working with various datasets and practical problems.

If you decide to tune a hyperparameter, as opposed to using the default value, it makes more sense to tune the hyperparameters to which the model is sensitive. Table 6.1 shows[2] several hyperparameters and approximate sensitivity of a neural network to those hyperparameters.

6.1.8 Handling Multiple Inputs

In practice, machine learning engineers often work with multimodal data. For example, the input could be an image and a text, and the binary output could indicate whether the text describes the given image.

It's hard to adapt **shallow learning** algorithms to work with multimodal data. For example, you can try to vectorize each input, by applying the corresponding feature engineering method. Then, concatenate two feature vectors to form one wider feature vector. If your image has features $[i^{(1)}, i^{(2)}, i^{(3)}]$, and your text has features $[t^{(1)}, t^{(2)}, t^{(3)}, t^{(4)}]$, your concatenated feature vector will be $[i^{(1)}, i^{(2)}, i^{(3)}, t^{(1)}, t^{(2)}, t^{(3)}, t^{(4)}]$.

---

[2]Taken from the talk "Troubleshooting Deep Neural Networks" by Josh Tobin et al., January 2019.

Hyperparameter	Sensitivity
Learning rate	High
Learning rate schedule	High
Loss function	High
Units per layer	High
Parameter initialization strategy	Medium
Number of layers	Medium
Layer properties	Medium
Degree of regularization	Medium
Choice of optimizer	Low
Optimizer properties	Low
Size of minibatch	Low
Choice of non-linearity	Low

Table 6.1: Approximate sensitivity of a model to some hyperparameters.

With neural networks, you have substantially more flexibility. You can build two **subnetworks**, one for each input type. For example, a **CNN** subnetwork reads the image, while an **RNN** subnetwork reads the text. Both subnetworks have, as their last layer, an **embedding**. CNN has an image embedding, and RNN has a text embedding. You then concatenate the two embeddings, and finally add a classification layer, such as **softmax** or **logistic sigmoid**, on top of the concatenated embeddings.

Neural network libraries provide simple-to-use tools that allow concatenating or averaging layers from several subnetworks.

6.1.9 Handling Multiple Outputs

Sometimes, you would like to predict multiple outputs for one input. Some problems with multiple outputs can be effectively converted into a multi-label classification problem. Those with labels of the same nature (like tags in social networks), or fake labels can be created as a full enumeration of combinations of original labels.

However, in many cases, the outputs are multimodal, and their combinations cannot be effectively enumerated. Consider the following example: you want to build a model that detects an object on an image, and returns its coordinates. In addition, the model has to return a tag describing the object, such as "person," "cat," or "hamster." Your training example will be a feature vector representing an image and a label. The label could be represented as a vector of coordinates of the object, and another vector with a **one-hot encoded** tag.

For this, you can create one subnetwork that works as an encoder. It will read the input image using, for example, one or several convolution layers. The encoder's last layer is the image embedding. Then you add two other subnetworks on top of the embedding layer: 1) one takes the embedding vector as input, and predicts the coordinates of the object, and 2) the other takes the embedding vector as input, and predicts the tag.

The first subnetwork can have a **ReLU** as the last layer, which is good for predicting positive real numbers, such as coordinates. This subnetwork can use the mean squared error cost C_1. The second subnetwork will take the same embedding vector as input, and will predict the probabilities for each tag. It can have a **softmax** as the last layer, which is appropriate for the **multiclass classification**, and use the averaged **negative log-likelihood cost** C_2 (also called **cross-entropy** cost). Alternatively, the coordinates could be in the range $[0, 1]$ (in which case the layer that predicts coordinates will have four **logistic sigmoid** outputs and average four **binary cross-entropy** cost functions), while the layer that predicts tags might solve a **multi-label classification** problem (in which case it would also have several sigmoid outputs and average several binary cross entropy costs, one per tag).

Obviously, you are interested in accurate predictions of both the coordinates and the tags. However, it is impossible to optimize two cost functions at once. By trying to improve one, you risk hurting the other one, and vice-versa. What you can do is add another hyperparameter γ, in the range $(0, 1)$, and define the combined cost function as $\gamma \times C_1 + (1 - \gamma) \times C_2$. Then you tune the value for γ on the validation data, just like any other hyperparameter.

6.1.10 Transfer Learning

Recall, **transfer learning** consists of using a pre-trained model to build a new model. Pre-trained models are usually created using big data available to its creators, usually large organizations, but not necessarily available to you. The parameters learned by the pre-trained models can be useful for your task.

A pre-trained model can be used in two ways:

1) its learned parameters can be used to initialize your own model, or
2) it can be used as a feature extractor for your model.

Using Pre-Trained Model as Initializer

As discussed, the choice of parameter initialization strategy affects the properties of the learned model. Pre-trained models, whether available on the Internet, or trained by you, usually perform well for solving the original learning problem.

If your current problem is similar to the one solved by the pre-trained model, chances are high that the optimal parameters for your current problem will not be too different from the pre-trained parameters, especially in the initial neural network layers (those closest to the input).

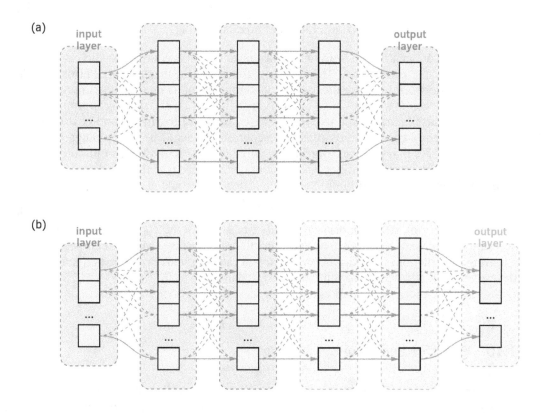

Figure 6.4: An illustration of transfer learning: (a) a pre-trained model and (b) your model, where you used the left part of the pre-trained model, and added new layers, including a different output layer tailored for your problem.

The learning might go faster for your problem because gradient descent will search for the optimal parameter values in a smaller region of potentially good values.

If the pre-trained model was built using a training set much bigger than yours, searching in a region of potentially good values might also lead to a better generalization. Indeed, if some behavior of the model you want to build is not reflected in your training examples, this behavior could still be "inherited" from the pre-trained model.

Using Pre-Trained Model as Feature Extractor

If you use a pre-trained model as an initializer for your model, it gives you more flexibility. The gradient descent will modify the parameters in all layers, and, potentially, reach a better performance for your problem. The downside of that is you will often end up training a very deep neural network.

Some pre-trained models contain hundreds of layers and millions of parameters. Training a large network like that can be challenging. It will definitely require a significant amount of computational resources. In addition, the problem of the vanishing gradient is more severe in a deep neural network than one with a couple hidden layers.

If you have a limited amount of computational resources, you might prefer using some layers of the pre-trained model as **feature extractors** for your model. In practice, it means that you only keep several initial layers of the pre-trained model, those closest to and including the input layer. You keep their parameters "frozen," that is, unchanged and unchangeable. Then you add new layers on top of the frozen layers, including the output layer appropriate for your task. Only the parameters of the new layers will be updated by gradient descent during training on your data.

An illustration of the process is shown in Figure 6.4. The blue neural network is a pre-trained model. Some of the blue layers are reused in the new model with their parameters frozen; the green layers are added by the analyst and tailored to the problem at hand.

The analyst might decide to freeze the parameters of the entire blue part of the new network, and only train the parameters of the green part. Alternatively, several right-most blue layers could be set as trainable.

How many layers of the pre-trained model to use in the new model? Freeze how many layers? This is up to the analyst: it's part of the decisions you'll make about the architecture that will work best for your problem.

6.2 Stacking Models

Ensemble learning is training an ensemble model, which is a combination of several **base models**, each individually performing worse than the ensemble model.

6.2.1 Types of Ensemble Learning

There are ensemble learning algorithms, such as **random forest learning** and gradient boosting. They train an ensemble of several hundred to thousands of **weak models**, and obtain a **strong model** that has a significantly better performance than the performance of each weak model. We will not discuss these algorithms here. If you are missing this knowledge, it can easily be found in a specialized machine learning book.[3]

The reason why combining multiple models can bring better performance is that, when several uncorrelated models agree, they are more likely to agree on the correct outcome. The key word here is "uncorrelated." Ideally, base models should be obtained by using different features, or be of a different nature — for example, SVM and random forest. Combining

---

[3]You can read about ensemble learning algorithms in Chapter 7 of The Hundred-Page Machine Learning Book.

different versions of the decision tree learning algorithm, or several SVMs with different hyperparameters, may not result in a significant performance boost.

The goal of ensemble learning is to learn to combine the strengths of each base model. There are three ways to combine weakly correlated models into an ensemble model: 1) averaging, 2) majority vote, and 3) model stacking.

Averaging works for regression, as well as those classification models that return classification scores. It consists of applying all your base models to the input $\mathbf{x}$, and then averaging the predictions. To see if the averaged model works better than each individual algorithm, you can test it on the validation set using a metric of your choice.

Majority vote works for classification models. It consists of applying all your base models to the input $\mathbf{x}$, and then returning the majority class among all predictions. In the case of a tie, you can either randomly pick one of the classes, or return an error message if misclassifying would incur a significant loss for the business.

Model stacking is an ensemble learning method that trains a strong model by inputting the outputs of other strong models. Let's go into more detail about model stacking.

6.2.2   An Algorithm of Model Stacking

Say you want to combine classifiers f_1, f_2, and f_3, all predicting the same set of classes. To create a synthetic training example $(\hat{\mathbf{x}}_i, \hat{y}_i)$ for the stacked model from the original training example $(\mathbf{x}_i, y_i)$, set $\hat{\mathbf{x}}_i \leftarrow [f_1(\mathbf{x}), f_2(\mathbf{x}), f_3(\mathbf{x})]$, and $\hat{y}_i \leftarrow y_i$. This is illustrated in Figure 6.5.

If some of your base models return a class plus a class score, you can use those scores as additional input features for the stacked model.

To train the stacked model, use synthetic examples, and tune the hyperparameters of the stacked model using cross-validation. Make sure your stacked model performs better on the validation set than each of the stacked base models.

In addition to using different machine learning algorithms and models, some base models, to be weakly correlated, can be trained by randomly sampling the examples and features of the original training set. Furthermore, the same learning algorithm, trained with very different hyperparameter values, could produce sufficiently uncorrelated models.

6.2.3   Data Leakage in Model Stacking

To avoid **data leakage**, be careful when training a stacked model. To create the synthetic training set for the stacked model, follow a process similar to cross-validation. First, split all training data into ten or more blocks. The more blocks the better, but the process of training the model will be slower.

Temporarily exclude one block from the training data, and train the base models on the remaining blocks. Then apply the base models to the examples in the excluded block. Obtain

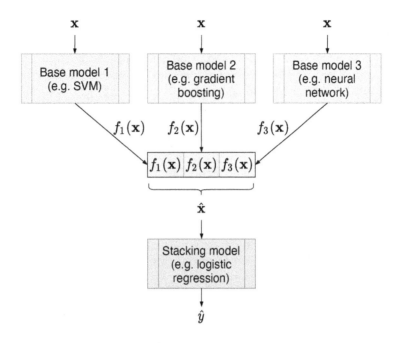

Figure 6.5: A stacking of three weakly correlated strong models.

the predictions, and build the synthetic training examples for the excluded block by using the predictions from the base models.

Repeat the same process for each of the remaining blocks, and you will end up with the training set for the stacking model. The new synthetic training set will be of the same size as that of the original training set.

6.3   Dealing With Distribution Shift

Recall that the holdout data must resemble the data you will observe in production. Sometimes, however, it is not available in sufficiently large quantities. At the same time, you might have access to labeled data that is similar to the production data, but not exactly the same. For example, you might have lots of labeled images from the Web crawl collection, but your goal is to train a classifier for Instagram photos. You might not have enough labeled Instagram photos for training, so you hope to train the model by using the Web crawl data, and then be able to use that model to classify the Instagram photos.

6.3.1 Types of Distribution Shift

When the distributions of the training data and test data are not the same, we call it **distribution shift**. Dealing with a distribution shift is currently an open research area. Researchers distinguish three types of distribution shift:

- **covariate shift** — shift in the values of features;
- **prior probability shift** — shift in the values of the target; and
- **concept drift** — shift in the relationship between the features and the label.

You may know your data is affected by a distribution shift, but you don't usually know what type of shift it is.

If the number of examples in the test set is relatively high compared to the size of the training set, you could randomly pick a certain fraction of test examples and transfer some to the training set and some to the validation set. Then you would train the model as usual. However, often you have a very high number of training examples and relatively few test examples. In that case, a more effective approach is to use **adversarial validation**.

6.3.2 Adversarial Validation

We prepare for adversarial validation as follows. We assume that the feature vectors in a training and a test examples contain the same number of features, and those features represent the same information. Split your original training set into two subsets: Training Set 1 and Training Set 2.

Create a Modified Training Set 1 by transforming the examples from Training Set 1 as follows. To each example in Training Set 1, add the original label as an additional feature, then assign the new label "Training" to that example.

Create a Modified Test Set by transforming the examples from the original test set as follows. To each example in the test set, add the original label as an additional feature, then assign the new label "Test" to that example.

Merge the Modified Training Set 1 and the Modified Test Set to obtain a new Synthetic Training Set. You will use it for solving a binary classification problem of distinguishing the "Training" examples from the "Test" examples. Use that Synthetic Training Set, and train a binary classifier that returns a prediction score.

Observe that the binary classifier we have trained will predict, for a given original example, whether it's a training or a test example. Apply that binary classifier to the examples from Training Set 2. Identify the examples predicted as "Test," which the binary model is most certain about. Use those examples as validation data for your original problem.

Remove the examples from Training Set 1 which the binary model predicted "Training" with the highest certainty. Use the remaining examples in Training Set 1 as the training data for your original problem.

You must experiment to find out what is the ideal way to split the original training set into Training Set 1 and Training Set 2. You also must find out how many examples from Training Set 1 to use for training, and how many of them to use for validation.

6.4 Handling Imbalanced Datasets

In Section 3.9 of Chapter 3, we considered some techniques to handle **imbalanced datasets**, such as over- and undersampling, and generating synthetic data.

In this section, we will consider additional techniques that are applied during learning, as opposed to in the data collection and preparation stage.

6.4.1 Class Weighting

Some algorithms and models, such as **support vector machine** (SVM), **decision trees**, and **random forests**, allow the data analyst to provide weights for each class. The loss in the cost function is typically multiplied by the weight. The data analyst may, for example, provide greater weight to the minority class. This makes it harder for the learning algorithm to disregard examples of the minority class, because it would result in much higher cost than without class weighting.

Let's see how it works in support vector machines. Our problem is distinguishing between genuine and fraudulent e-commerce transactions. The examples of genuine transactions are much more frequent. If you use SVM with **soft margin**, you can define a cost for misclassified examples. The SVM algorithm tries to move the hyperplane to reduce the number of misclassified examples. If the misclassification cost is the same for both classes, the "fraudulent" examples, in the minority, risk being misclassified to allow classifying more of the majority class correctly. This situation is illustrated in Figure 6.6a. This problem is observed for most learning algorithms applied to imbalanced datasets.

If you set higher the loss of minority misclassification, then the model will try harder to avoid misclassifying those examples. But this will incur the cost of misclassification of some majority class examples, as illustrated in Figure 6.6b.

6.4.2 Ensemble of Resampled Datasets

Ensemble learning is another way of mitigating the class imbalance problem. The analyst randomly chunks majority examples into H subsets, then creates H training sets. After training H models, the analyst then makes predictions by averaging (or taking the majority) of the outputs of H models.

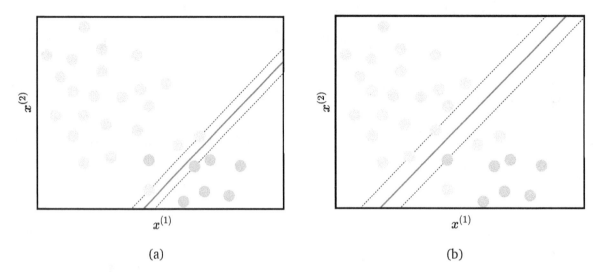

Figure 6.6: An illustration of an imbalanced problem. (a) Both classes have the same weight; (b) examples of the minority class have a higher weight.

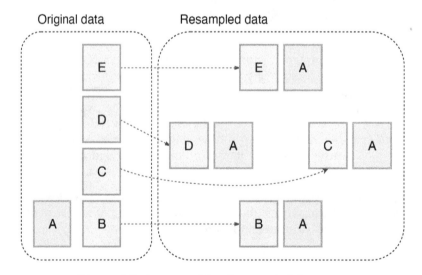

Figure 6.7: An ensemble of resampled datasets.

The process for $H = 4$ is illustrated in Figure 6.7. Here, we transformed our imbalanced binary learning problem into four balanced problems by chunking the examples of the majority class into four subsets. The examples of the minority class are copied four times in their entirety.

This approach is simple and scalable: you can train and run your models on different CPU cores or cluster nodes. Ensemble models also tend to produce a better prediction than each individual model in the ensemble.

6.4.3 Other Techniques

If you use stochastic gradient descent, the class imbalance can be tackled in several ways. First, you can have different learning rates for different classes: a lower value for the examples of the majority class, and a higher value otherwise. Second, you can make several consecutive updates of the model parameters each time you encounter an example of a minority class.

For imbalanced learning problems, the performance of the model is measured using adapted performance metrics such as **per-class accuracy** and **Cohen's kappa statistic** that we considered in Section 5.5.2 in the previous chapter.

6.5 Model Calibration

Sometimes it is important that the classification model returns not just the predicted class, but also the probability that the predicted class is correct. Some models return a score along with the predicted class. Even if its value ranges between 0 and 1, it's not always a probability.

6.5.1 Well-Calibrated Models

We say that the model is **well-calibrated** when, for input example $\mathbf{x}$ and predicted label $\hat{y}$, it returns the score that can be interpreted as the true probability for $\mathbf{x}$ to belong to class $\hat{y}$.

For instance, a well-calibrated binary classifier would generate a score of 0.8 for approximately 80% of the examples actually belonging to the positive class.

Most machine learning algorithms train models that are not well-calibrated, as shown[4] by the **calibration plots** in Figure 6.8.

A calibration plot for a binary model allows seeing how well the model is calibrated. On the X-axis, there are bins that group examples by the predicted score. For example, if we have 10 bins, the left-most bin groups all examples for which the predicted score is in the range $[0, 0.1)$ while the right-most bin groups all examples for which the predicted score is in the range $[0.9, 1.0]$. On the Y-axis, there are the fractions of positive examples in each bin.

---

[4]The graph is adapted from https://scikit-learn.org/stable/modules/calibration.html.

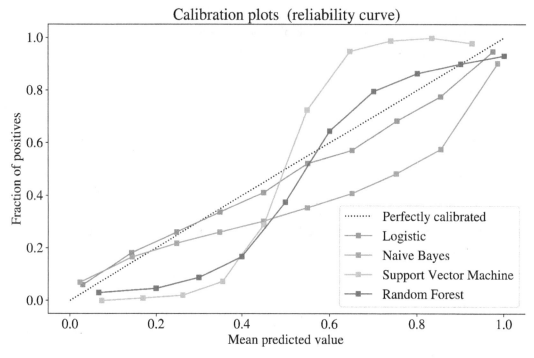

Figure 6.8: Calibration plots for models trained by several machine learning algorithms applied to a random binary dataset.

For multiclass classification, we would have one calibration plot per class in a **one-versus-rest** way. One-versus-rest is common strategy for converting a binary classification learning algorithm for solving multiclass classification problems. The idea is to transform a multiclass problem into C binary classification problems and build C binary classifiers. For example, if we have three classes, $y \in \{1, 2, 3\}$, we create three original dataset copies, and modify them. In the first copy, we replace all labels not equal to 1 with a 0. In the second copy, we replace all labels not equal to 2 with a 0. In the third copy, we replace all labels not equal to 3 with a 0. Now we have three binary classification problems where we want to learn to distinguish between labels 1 and 0, 2 and 0, and 3 and 0. As you can see, in each of the three binary classification problems, the label 0 denotes the "rest" in "one-versus-rest."

When the model is well-calibrated, the calibration plot oscillates around the diagonal (shown as a dotted line in Figure 6.8). The closer the calibration plot is to the diagonal, the better the model is calibrated. Because a logistic regression model returns the true probabilities of the positive class, its calibration plot is closest to the diagonal. When the model is not well-calibrated, the calibration plot usually has a sigmoid-shape, as shown by the **support vector machine** and **random forest** models.

186

6.5.2 Calibration Techniques

There are two techniques often used to calibrate a binary model: **Platt scaling** and **isotonic regression**. The two are based on similar principles.

Let us have a model f that we want to calibrate. First of all, we need a holdout dataset specifically set aside for calibration. To avoid overfitting, we cannot use training or validation data for calibration. Let this calibration dataset be of size M. Then, we apply the model f to each example $i = 1, \ldots, M$ and obtain, for each example i, the prediction f_i. We build a new dataset $\mathcal{Z}$, where each example is a pair (f_i, y_i), y_i is the true label of example i, and labels have the values in the set $\{0, 1\}$.

The only difference between Platt scaling and isotonic regression is that the former builds a logistic regression model by using the dataset $\mathcal{Z}$, while the latter builds the isotonic regression of $\mathcal{Z}$, that is, a non-decreasing function as close to the examples as possible. Once we have the calibration model z, obtained either using Platt scaling or isotonic regression, we can predict the calibrated probability for an input $\mathbf{x}$ as $z(f(\mathbf{x}))$.

Notice that a calibrated model may or may not result in better quality prediction for your problem. That depends on the chosen model performance metric.

According to experiments:[5] Platt scaling is most effective when the distortion in the predicted probabilities is sigmoid-shaped. Isotonic regression can correct a wider range of distortions. Unfortunately, this extra power comes at a price. Analysis has shown that isotonic regression is more prone to overfitting, and thus performs worse than Platt scaling when data is scarce.

Experiments with eight classification problems also suggested that random forests, neural networks, and bagged decision trees are the best learning methods for predicting well-calibrated probabilities prior to calibration, but after calibration, the best methods are boosted trees, random forest, and SVM.

6.6 Troubleshooting and Error Analysis

Troubleshooting a machine learning pipeline is hard. It's difficult to differentiate whether the model performs poorly because your code contains a bug, or if there are problems with your training data, learning algorithm, or the way you designed your pipeline. Moreover, the same degradation in performance can be explained by various reasons. The results of the learning can be sensitive to small changes in hyperparameters or dataset makeup.

Because of these challenges, model training is usually an iterative process, where an analyst trains a model, observes its behavior, and makes adjustments based on observations.

---

[5]Alexandru Niculescu-Mizil and Rich Caruana, "Predicting Good Probabilities With Supervised Learning", appearing in Proceedings of the 22nd International Conference on Machine Learning, Bonn, Germany, 2005.

6.6.1 Reasons for Poor Model Behavior

If your model does poorly on the training data (underfits it), common reasons are:

- the model architecture or learning algorithm are not expressive enough (try more advanced learning algorithm, an **ensemble method**, or a deeper **neural network**);
- you regularize too much (reduce **regularization**);
- you have chosen suboptimal values for hyperparameters (**tune hyperparameters**);
- the features you engineered don't have enough **predictive power** (add more informative features);
- you don't have enough data for the model to generalize (try to get more data, use **data augmentation**, or **transfer learning**); or
- you have a bug in your code (debug the code that defines and trains the model).

If your model does well on the training data, but poorly on the holdout data (overfits the training data), common reasons are:

- you don't have enough data for generalization (add more data or use data augmentation);
- your model is under-regularized (add regularization or, for neural networks, both regularization and **batch normalization**);
- your training data distribution is different from the holdout data distribution (reduce the **distribution shift**);
- you have chosen suboptimal values for hyperparameters (tune hyperparameters); or
- your features have low predictive power (add features with high predictive power).

6.6.2 Iterative Model Refinement

If you have access to new labeled data (for example, you can label examples yourself, or easily request the help of a labeler) then, you can refine the model using a simple iterative process:

1. Train the model using the best values of hyperparameters identified so far.
2. Test the model by applying it to a small subset of the validation set (100 − 300 examples).
3. Find the most frequent error patterns on that small validation set. Remove those examples from the validation set, because your model will now overfit to them.
4. Generate new features, or add more training data to fix the observed error patterns.
5. Repeat until no frequent error patterns are observed (most errors look dissimilar).

Iterative model refinement is a simplified version of **error analysis**. A more principled approach is described below.

6.6.3   Error Analysis

Errors can be:

- uniform, and appear with the same rate in all use cases, or
- focused, and appear more frequently in certain types of use cases.

Focused errors following a specific pattern are those that merit special attention. By fixing an error pattern, you fix it once for many examples. Focused errors, or error trends, usually happen when some use cases aren't well-represented in the training data. For example, a face detection system developed by a major web camera provider worked better for white users than for black users. In another case, a human presence detection system equipped with a night vision system worked better during the day than at night, simply because the night training examples were less frequent in the training data.

Uniform errors cannot be entirely avoided, but important focused errors should be discovered before the model is deployed in production. This can be done by clustering test examples, and by testing the model on examples coming from different clusters. The distribution of the production (online) data can be significantly different from the offline data distribution used for model training/pre-deployment tests. So, the clusters that contain few examples in the offline data might represent much more frequent use cases in the online scenario.

In Section 4.8 of Chapter 4, we discussed several techniques for dimensionality reduction. In addition to using clustering for spotting error trends, uniform manifold approximation and projection (**UMAP**) or **autoencoder** can be used. Use those techniques to reduce the dimensionality of the data to 2D, and then visually inspect the distribution of errors across a dataset.

More specifically, you can visualize the data on a 2D scatter plot, using different colors for examples of different classes. To identify error trends on a scatter plot, use different markers depending on whether a model's prediction was correct or not. For example, use circles to denote examples whose label was predicted correctly, and squares otherwise. This will allow you to see the regions of poor model performance. If you work with perceptive data, such as images or text, it is also helpful to visually examine some examples from those poor performance regions.

Whether you are satisfied or dissatisfied by the model's performance on the holdout data, you can always improve the model by analyzing individual errors. As discussed, the best way is to work iteratively, by considering $100 - 300$ examples at a time. By considering a small number of examples at a time, you can iterate quickly, by retraining the model after each iteration, but still consider enough examples to spot obvious patterns.

How do you decide whether an error pattern is worth spending time to fix it? You can base that decision on the **error pattern frequencies**. Let's see how it works.

Let your model have an accuracy of 80%, which corresponds to an error rate of 20%. If you fix all error patterns, you can improve the model's performance by at most 20 percentage points. If your small error-analysis batch was of 300 examples, your model made $0.2 \times 300 = 60$ errors.

Observe the errors one by one, and try to get an idea of what particularities in the input led to a misclassification of those 60 examples. To be even more concrete, let our classification problem be to detect pedestrians-on-the-street images. Assume that in 60 out of the 300 images, the model failed to detect a pedestrian. After closer analysis, you discover two patterns: 1) the image is blurry in 40 examples, and 2) the picture was taken during the nighttime in 5 examples. Now, should you spend time addressing both problems?

If you address the blurry-image problem (for example, by adding more labeled blurry images to your training data), you can hope to decrease your error by $(40/60) \times 20 = 13$ percentage points. In the best-case scenario, after you solve the blurry-image misclassification problem, your error becomes $20 - 13 = 7$ percent, a significant decrease from the initial 20% error.

On the other hand, if you solve the nighttime image problem, you can hope to decrease your error by $5/60 \times 20 = 1.7$ percentage points. So, in the best-case scenario, your model will make $20 - 1.7 = 18.3$ percent errors, which might be significant for some problems, or insignificant for others. The cost of gathering additional labeled night-time images can be significant and might not be worth the effort.

To fix an error pattern, you can use one or a combination of techniques:

- preprocessing the input (e.g. image background removal, text spelling correction);
- data augmentation (e.g., blurring or cropping of images);
- labeling more training examples; and
- engineering new features that would allow the learning algorithm to distinguish between "hard" cases.

6.6.4   Error Analysis in Complex Systems

Let's say you work on a complex document classification system that consists of three chained models as shown below:

Figure 6.9: A complex document classification system.

Let the accuracy of the entire system be 73%. If the classification is binary, the accuracy of 73% doesn't seem high. On the other hand, if the classification model (the rightmost block in Figure 6.9) supports thousands of classes, then the accuracy of 73% doesn't seem too low. For some business cases, however, the user might expect human-like, or even superhuman performance.

Imagine that you are in a position, where the business expects a higher than 73% performance from the document classification system you have built. To get the most out of your additional effort, you must decide which part of the system needs improvement in the first place.

When the decision about something is made on several chained levels, like in the problem shown in Figure 6.9, and when those decisions are independent of one another, the accuracy multiplies. For example, if the language predictor accuracy was 95%, the machine translation model accuracy[6] was 90%, and the classifier accuracy was 85%, then, in the case of independence of the three models, the overall accuracy of the entire three-stage system would be $0.95 \times 0.90 \times 0.85 = 0.73$, or 73 percent. At first glance, it seems obvious that the most gain in the entire system's accuracy would come from maximizing the accuracy of the third model — the classifier. However, in practice, some errors made by a given model might not significantly affect the overall performance of the system. For example, if the language predictor often confuses Spanish and Portuguese, the machine translation model could still be capable of generating an adequate translation for the third-stage classification model.

While working on the third-stage classifier, you might have concluded that you reached its maximum performance, so it doesn't make sense to continue. Now, which of the previous two models, the language detector and/or the machine translator, should you improve to increase the quality of the entire three-stage system?

One way to determine the upper bound of an entire system's potential is to perform the **error analysis by parts**. You replace one model's predictions with perfect labels, such as human-provided labels. Then you calculate how the entire system performs. For example, instead of using the machine translation system at stage two in Figure 6.9, you can ask a professional human translator to translate the text from the predicted language (if the prediction of the language was correct), or keep the original text (if the prediction of the language was wrong).

Let's say you asked a professional for a hundred translations. Now you can measure how perfect translations affect the overall system performance. Let the accuracy of the entire system's output become 74%. So, the potential gain from improved translation in overall system performance is only one percentage point. Reaching the human-level performance for a machine translation model can turn out to be a daunting task, not worth the effort, especially when what we can achieve in the end is one percentage point gain for the entire system. So, you might prefer spending more time on building a better language predictor in stage 1, if the potential gain in overall system performance prediction quality is higher.

6.6.5 Using Sliced Metrics

If the model will be applied to different segments of the use cases, it should be separately tested for each segment. For example, if you want to predict the solvency of borrowers, you would want your model to be equally accurate for both male and female borrowers. To

---

[6]Measuring the error of the machine translation system in practice is tricky as a translation is rarely entirely accurate or inaccurate. Instead, measures, such as BLEU (for Bilingual Evaluation Understudy Score) score, are used.

achieve that, you can split your validation data into several subsets, one subset per segment. Then compute the performance metric by separately applying your model to each subset.

Alternatively, you can separately evaluate the model on each class by applying precision and recall metrics. Remember these metrics are defined only for binary classification. By isolating one class in your multiclass classification problem, and labeling the other classes "Other," you can individually compute the precision and recall for each class.

If you see that the value of the performance metric changes between segments or classes, you can try to fix the problem by adding more labeled data to the segments or classes, where the performance of the model is unsatisfactory, or engineer additional features.

6.6.6   Fixing Wrong Labels

When humans label the training examples, the assigned labels can be wrong. This can cause poor model performance on the model on both training and holdout data. Indeed, if similar examples have conflicting labels — some correct and some incorrect — the learning algorithm can learn to predict the wrong label.

Here is a simple way to identify the examples that have wrong labels. Apply the model to the training data from which it was built, and analyze the examples for which it made a different prediction as compared to the labels provided by humans. If you see that some predictions are indeed correct, change those labels.

If you have time and resources, you could also examine the predictions with the score close to the decision threshold. Those are often mislabeled cases too.

If wrong labels in the training data is a serious issue, you can avoid it by asking several individuals to provide labels for the same training example. Only accept it if all individuals assigned the same label to that example. In less demanding situations, you can accept a label if the majority of individuals assigned it.

6.6.7   Finding Additional Examples to Label

As discussed above, error analysis can reveal that more labeled data is needed from specific regions of feature space. You might have an abundance of unlabeled examples. How should you decide which examples to label so as to maximize the positive impact on the model?

If your model returns a prediction score, an effective way is to use your best model to score the unlabeled examples. Then label those examples, whose prediction score is close to the prediction threshold.

When the error analysis has revealed error patterns by means of visualization, then choose those examples which are surrounded by many examples with prediction errors.

6.6.8 Troubleshooting Deep Learning

To avoid problems when training a deep model, follow a workflow shown below:

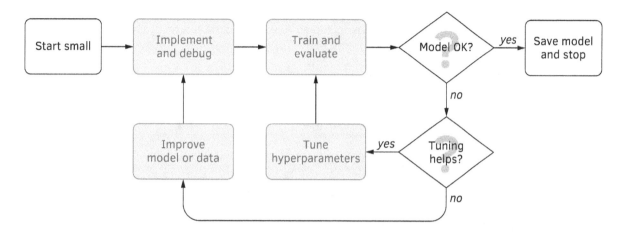

Figure 6.10: A deep learning troubleshooting workflow.

When possible, start small, for example, with a simple model using a high-level library, such as **Keras**. It should be very easy to validate visually, ideally fitting on at most two screens.

Alternatively, reuse an existing open-source architecture that was proven to work (pay attention to the code license!). Start with:

- a small, normalized dataset fitting in memory,
- the most simple to use cost-function optimizer (e.g., **Adam**),
- an initialization strategy (e.g., **random normal**),
- the default values of the sensitive hyperparameters of both the cost-function optimizer and the layers, and
- no regularization.

Once you have your first simplistic model architecture and dataset, temporarily reduce your training dataset even further, to the size of one **minibatch**. Then start the training. Make sure your simplistic model is capable of **overfitting** this training minibatch. If the overfitting of the minibatch doesn't happen, it is a solid indicator that something is wrong with your code or data. Look for the following signs[7] and their probable causes:

---

[7]Adapted from the talk "Troubleshooting Deep Neural Networks" by Josh Tobin et al., January 2019.

Sign	Probable causes
Error goes up	Flipped the sign of the loss function or gradient
	Learning rate too high
	Softmax taken over wrong dimension
Error explodes	Numerical issue
	Learning rate too high
Error oscillates	Data or labels corrupted (e.g. zeroed or incorrectly shuffled)
	Learning rate too high
Error plateaus	Learning rate too low
	Gradient not flowing through the whole model
	Too much regularization
	Incorrect input to loss function
	Data or labels corrupted

Table 6.2: Common issues and most common causes of problems with getting to overfit one minibatch by a neural network model.

Once your model overfits one minibatch, get back to the entire dataset, and train, evaluate, then tune hyperparameters until no improvements on the validation data are possible.

If the performance of the model is still unsatisfactory, update the model (e.g., by increasing its depth or width), or the training data (e.g., by changing the pre-processing, or adding features). Debug the change by overfitting one minibatch once again, then train, evaluate, and tune the new model. Keep iterating until you're satisfied with the quality of the model.

While you are searching for the best architecture for your model, it's convenient not just to use a smaller training set, but also to simplify the problem by either,

- creating a simple synthetic training set, or
- reducing the number of classes or the resolution of input images (or video fragments), size of the texts, bitrate of the sound frequencies, and so on.

At the evaluation step of the deep learning troubleshooting workflow shown in Figure 6.10, verify if the poor model performance could be caused by one of the reasons listed in Section 6.6.1. Choose the next step depending on whether the performance can be improved by tuning hyperparameters, updating the model, features, or the training data.

6.7 Best Practices

In this section, I gathered practical advice on training machine learning models. The best practices below aren't strict prescriptions. They are rather recommendations that often save time, effort, and might lead to higher quality results.

6.7.1 Deliver a Good Model

What is a good model? A good model has two properties:

- it has the desired quality according to the performance metric; and
- it is safe to serve in a production environment.

For a model to be safe-to-serve means satisfying the following requirements:

- it will not crash or cause errors in the serving system when being loaded, or when loaded with bad or unexpected inputs;
- it will not use an unreasonable amount of resources (such as CPU, GPU, or RAM).

6.7.2 Trust Popular Open Source Implementations

Modern open-source libraries and modules for machine learning in popular modern programming languages and platforms, such as Python, Java, and .NET, contain efficient, industry-standard implementations of popular machine learning algorithms. They usually have permissive licenses. Additionally, open-source libraries and modules exist specifically for training neural networks.

It is only considered reasonable to create your own machine learning algorithms if you use an exotic or very new programming language. In addition, you might program from scratch if the model is intended to be executed in a very resource-constrained environment, or you need to run your model with a speed no existing implementation can provide.

Avoid using multiple programming languages in the same project. Using different programming languages increases the cost of testing, deployment, and maintenance. It also makes it difficult to transfer project ownership between employees.

6.7.3 Optimize a Business-Specific Performance Measure

Learning algorithms try to reduce training data error. The data analyst, in turn, wants to minimize test data error. However, your client or employer typically wants you to optimize a **business-specific performance metric**.

When you have minimized the validation error rate, focus on tuning hyperparameters that optimize a business-specific metric, even if it causes the validation error rate to increase.

6.7.4 Upgrade From Scratch

Once deployed to production, some models have to be periodically updated with new data to adapt to the user's needs. This new training data must be automatically collected by using scripts (as we discussed in Chapter 3 in Section 3.12 about **reproducibility**).

Each time the data is updated, the hyperparameters must be tuned from scratch. Otherwise, the new data may yield suboptimal performance with old hyperparameters.

Some models, such as neural networks, may be iteratively upgraded. However, avoid the practice of **warm-starting**. It consists of iteratively upgrading the existing model by using only new training examples and running additional training iterations.

Furthermore, frequent model upgrades without retraining from scratch can lead to **catastrophic forgetting**. It's a situation in which the model that was once capable of something, "forgets" that capability because of learning something new.

Note that upgrading the model is not the same as **transfer learning**. Analysts use transfer learning when the data used to build the pre-trained model, or adequate computing resources, are not available.

6.7.5 Avoid Correction Cascades

You might have model m_A that solves problem A, but you need a solution m_B for a slightly different problem B. It can be tempting to use the output of m_A as input for m_B, and only train m_B on a small sample of examples that "correct" the output of m_A for solving problem B. Such technique is called **correction cascading**, and it is not recommended.

Model cascading makes it impossible to update model m_A, without also updating model m_B (and the rest of the cascade). The effect a change in m_A might have on m_B is impossible to predict, but most likely it will be negative. Furthermore, the developer of model m_B might not know about the change in model m_A, and the developer of model m_A might not know that model m_B depends on it. The negative effect on m_B of the change in model m_A may go unnoticed for a long time.

Instead of building a correction cascade, it is recommended to update model m_A to include the use cases for solving problem B. It would be wise to add features allowing the model to distinguish between the examples of problem B. One might also use transfer learning, or build an entirely independent model for solving problem B.

6.7.6 Use Model Cascading With Caution

It's important to note that **model cascading** is not always a bad practice. Using the output of one model, as one of many inputs for another model, is common. It might significantly reduce time to market. However, cascading must be used with caution, because the update of one model in a cascade must involve an update of all models in the cascade, which can end up being costly in the long-term.

To mitigate the negative effect of model cascading, two strategies are beneficial:

1. Analyze the information flow in your software system and update, or retrain, the entire chain. Model m_A's updated output must be reflected in the training data for model m_B.

2. Control who can and who cannot make calls to model m_A to prevent undeclared consumers from creating this issue. As Google's engineers mentioned:[8] "In the absence of barriers, engineers will naturally use the most convenient signal at hand, especially when working against deadline pressures."

Furthermore, a prediction output by a model should not be a plain number or a string. It should come with information about the production model, and how it should be consumed.

6.7.7 Write Efficient Code, Compile, and Parallelize

By writing fast and efficient code, you can speed up the training by an order of magnitude, as compared to an inefficient quick-and-dirty script you implemented during experimentation, just "to make it work." Modern datasets are large, so you might wait for hours, even days, for data preprocessing. Training also can take days, or sometimes weeks.

Always write the code with efficiency in mind, even if it seems to be a function, a method, or a script that you will not run frequently. Some code that was supposed to run once might be called in a loop millions of times.

Avoid using loops. For example, if you need to compute a **dot product** of two vectors, or multiply a matrix by a vector, use fast and efficient dot-product or matrix-multiplication methods in scientific libraries and modules. Examples of such efficient implementations are Python's **NumPy** and **SciPy** libraries. Talented and skilled software engineers and scientists created these libraries and modules. They rely on low-level programming languages such as C, as well as hardware acceleration, and work blazingly fast.

Where possible, compile the code before executing it. Such libraries as **PyPy** and **Numba** for Python, or **pqR** for R, would compile the code into the OS (operating system) native binary code, which can significantly increase the speed of data processing and model training.

Another important aspect is parallelization. If you work with modern libraries and modules, you can find learning algorithms that exploit multicore CPUs. Some allow GPUs to speed up the training of neural networks and many other models. Training of some models, such as SVM, cannot be effectively parallelized. In such cases, you can still exploit a multicore CPU by running multiple experiments in parallel. Run one experiment for each combination of hyperparameter values, geographical region, or user segment. Furthermore, compute each cross-validation fold in parallel with other folds.

Where possible, use a solid-state drive (SSD) to store the data. Use distributed computing; some implementations of learning algorithms are designed to run in distributed computing environments, such as Spark. Try to put all the needed data into the RAM of your laptop or server. It's not uncommon today for data analysts to work on a server with 512 gigabytes or even one or more terabytes of RAM.

---

[8]"Hidden Technical Debt in Machine Learning Systems" by Sculley et al. (2015).

By reducing to a minimum the time needed to train a model, you can spend more time tweaking your model, testing data pre-processing ideas, feature engineering, neural network architectures, and other creative activities. The greatest benefit for the machine learning project lies in the human touch and intuition. The more you, as a human, can work instead of waiting, the higher the chances that your machine learning project will be a success.

Reduce **glue code** to a minimum. This how Google engineers put it. Machine learning researchers tend to develop general purpose solutions as self-contained packages. A wide variety of these are available as open-source packages or from in-house code, proprietary packages, and cloud-based platforms. Using generic packages often results in a glue-code system design pattern, in which a massive amount of supporting code is written to get data into and out of general-purpose packages.

Glue code is costly in the long term. It tends to freeze a system to the peculiarities of a specific package. Testing alternatives may become prohibitively expensive. Using a generic package this way inhibits improvements. It becomes harder to take advantage of domain-specific properties, or to tweak the objective function, and to achieve a domain-specific goal. A mature system might become (at most) 5% machine learning code and (at least) 95% glue code. It may be less costly to create a clean native solution, rather than re-use a generic package.

An important strategy for combating glue code is to wrap black-box machine learning packages into common APIs used by the entire organization. Infrastructure becomes more reusable and it reduces the cost of changing packages.

It is recommended to learn to switch between at least two programming languages: one for fast prototyping (like Python) and one for fast implementation (like C++). Modern languages like Go, Kotlin, and Julia may work well for both cases, but at the time of the writing of this book, these two languages have not developed an ecosystem of machine learning projects, as compared to more established counterparts.

6.7.8 Test on Both Newer and Older Data

If you used a data dump from some time ago to create training, validation, and test sets, observe how your model behaves with data collected before and after this period. If it's radically worse, there's a problem.

Data leakage and **distribution shift** could be among the most likely reasons. Recall that data leakage is when information unavailable in the future or in the past was used to engineer a feature. Distribution shift is when properties of the data change over time.

6.7.9 More Data Beats Cleverer Algorithm

When confronted to insufficient model performance, to improve the performance of the model, analysts are often tempted into crafting a more sophisticated learning algorithm or a pipeline.

In practice, however, better results often come from getting more data, specifically, more labeled examples. If designed well, the data labeling process can allow a labeler to produce several thousand training examples daily. It can also be less expensive, compared to the expertise needed to invent a more advanced machine learning algorithm.

6.7.10   New Data Beats Cleverer Features

If, despite adding more training examples and designing clever features, the performance of your model plateaus, think about different information sources.

For example, if you want to predict whether user U will like a news article, try to add historical data about the user U as features. Or cluster all the users, and use the information on the k-nearest users to user U as new features. This is a simpler approach compared to programming very complex features, or combining existing features in a complex way.

6.7.11   Embrace Tiny Progress

Many tiny improvements to your model may give the expected result faster than looking for one revolutionary idea.

Furthermore, by trying different ideas, the analyst gets to know the data better, which might indeed help in finding that revolutionary idea.

6.7.12   Facilitate Reproducibility

Most machine learning algorithms are stochastic. For example, when we train a neural network, we initialize model parameters randomly; the minibatch stochastic gradient descent generates minibatches randomly; the decision trees in a random forest are built randomly; when we shuffle examples before splitting the data into three sets, we do it randomly; and so on. This means that when you train a model on the same data twice, you might end up having two different models. In order to facilitate reproducibility, it's recommended to set the value of the **random seed** used to initialize the pseudorandom number generator. If your random seed remains the same, then, if your data doesn't change, you will obtain exactly the same model each time you train.

The random seed can be set as `np.random.seed(15)` (in NumPy and scikit-learn), `tf.random.set_seed(15)` in TensorFlow, `torch.manual_seed(15)` (in PyTorch), and `set.seed(15)` (in R). The seed value doesn't matter as long as it remains constant.

Even if a machine learning framework allows us to set the value of the random seed, there's no guarantee that the code of the framework that uses randomization doesn't change between versions of the framework. For reproducibility, each project's dependencies should be isolated. It can be done in many ways: either by using tools such as **virtualenv** in Python and **Packrat** in R, or by running machine learning experiments in standardized **virtual machines** or **containers**. We will talk more about virtualization in Section 8.3 in Chapter 8.

When delivering the model, make sure it's accompanied by all relevant information for **reproducibility**. Besides the description of the dataset and features, such as documentation and metadata considered in Sections 3.11 and 4.11, each model should contain the documentation with the following details:

- a specification of all hyperparameters, including the ranges considered, and the default values used,
- the method used to select the best hyperparameter configuration,
- the definition of the specific measure or statistics used to evaluate the candidate models, and the value of it for the best model,
- a description of the computing infrastructure used, and
- the average runtime for each trained model, and an estimated cost of the training.

6.8 Summary

The deep model training strategy has more moving parts, as compared to training shallow models. At the same time, it's more principled and amenable to automation.

Instead of training your model from scratch, it can be useful to start with a pre-trained model. Organizations with access to big data have trained and open-sourced very deep neural networks with architectures optimized for image or natural language processing tasks.

A pre-trained model can be used in two ways: 1) its learned parameters can be used to initialize your own model, or 2) it can be used as a feature extractor for your model.

Using a pre-trained model to build your own is called transfer learning. The fact that deep models allow for transfer learning is one of the most important properties of deep learning.

Minibatch stochastic gradient descent and its variants are the most frequently used **cost function** optimization algorithms for deep models.

The backpropagation algorithm computes the partial derivatives of each deep model parameter, using the chain rule for derivatives of complex functions. At each epoch, gradient descent updates all parameters using partial derivatives. The learning rate controls the significance of an update. The process continues until convergence, the state where parameters' values don't change much after each epoch. Then the algorithm stops.

There are several popular upgrades to minibatch stochastic gradient descent, such as Momentum, RMSProp, and Adam. These algorithms update the learning rate automatically, based on the performance of the learning process. You do not need to choose the initial value of the learning rate, the decay schedule and rate, or the values of other related hyperparameters. These algorithms have demonstrated good performance in practice, and practitioners often use them instead of trying to manually tune the learning rate.

In addition to L1 and L2 regularization, neural networks benefit from neural network-specific regularizers: dropout, early stopping, and batch-normalization. Dropout is a simple but very effective regularization method. Using batch-normalization is a best practice.

Ensemble learning is training an ensemble model, which is a combination of several base models, each individually performing worse than the ensemble model. There are ensemble learning algorithms, such as random forest and gradient boosting, that build an ensemble of several hundred to thousands of weak models, and obtain a strong model that has a significantly better performance than the performance of each weak model.

Strong models can be combined into an ensemble model by averaging their outputs (for regression) or by taking a majority vote (for classification). Model stacking, being the most effective of the ensembling methods, consists of training a meta-model that takes the output of base models as input.

In addition to using over- and undersampling, imbalanced learning problems can be solved by applying class weighting and ensemble of resampled datasets. If you train your model using stochastic gradient descent, the class imbalance can be tackled in two additional ways: 1) by setting different learning rates for different classes, and 2) by making several consecutive updates of the model parameters each time you encounter an example of a minority class.

For imbalanced learning problems, the performance of the model is measured using adapted performance metrics such as per-class accuracy and Cohen's kappa statistic.

Troubleshooting a machine learning pipeline can be hard. Poor performance can be caused by a bug in your code, training data errors, learning algorithm issues, or pipeline design. In addition, learning can be sensitive to small changes in hyperparameters and dataset makeup.

Errors made by a machine learning model can be uniform and appear in all use cases with the same rate, or focused and appear in just certain types of use cases.

Focused errors are those that merit special attention, because by fixing an error pattern, you fix it once for many examples.

The performance of the model can be iteratively improved using the following simple process:

1. Train the model using the best values of hyperparameters identified so far.
2. Test the model by applying it to a small subset of the validation set ($100 - 300$ examples).
3. Find the most frequent error patterns on that small validation set. Remove those examples from the validation set, because your model will now overfit to them.
4. Generate new features, or add more training data to fix the observed error patterns.
5. Repeat until no frequent error patterns are observed (most errors look dissimilar).

In complex machine learning systems, the error analysis is done by parts. We first substitute the predictions of one model for the perfect labels (such as human-provided labels), and see how the performance of the entire system improves. If it improves significantly, then more effort must be put in improving that specific model.

For reproducibility, set the random seed and make sure the model is accompanied by all relevant information.

Chapter 7

Model Evaluation

Statistical models play an increasingly important role in the modern organization. When applied in a business context, a model can affect the organization's financial indicators. However, it may also present a liability risk. Therefore, any model running in production must be carefully and continuously evaluated.

Model evaluation is the fifth stage in the machine learning project life cycle:

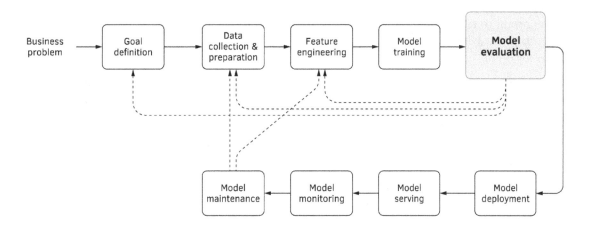

Figure 7.1: Machine learning project life cycle.

Depending on the model's applicative domain and the organization's business goals and constraints, model evaluation may include the following tasks:

- Estimate legal risks of putting the model in production. For example, some model predictions may indirectly communicate confidential information. Cyber attackers or competitors may attempt to reverse engineer the model's training data. Additionally, when used for prediction, some features, such as age, gender, or race, might result in the organization being considered as biased or even discriminatory.
- Study the main properties of distributions of the training data versus the production data. By comparing the statistical distribution of examples, features, and labels, in both training and production data, is how distribution shift is detected. A significant difference between the two indicates a need to update the training data, and retrain the model.
- Evaluate the performance of the model. Before the model is deployed in production, its predictive performance must be evaluated on the external data, that is, data not used for training. The external data must include both historical and online examples from the production environment. The context of evaluation on the real-time, online data should closely resemble the production environment.
- Monitor the performance of the deployed model. The model's performance may degrade over time. It is important to be able to detect this and, either upgrade the model by adding new data, or train an entirely different model. Model monitoring must be a carefully designed automated process, and might include a human in the loop. We consider this in more detail in Chapter 9.

In this chapter, we look at *some* examples of the kinds of tricks that statisticians use during the model evaluation phase. Machine learning engineering is a developing discipline, and some questions still don't have well established and easy to apply answers. In particular, the evaluation is presented from the point of view of an engineer, while each business has its own success criteria, which are unique. Before evaluating a machine learning solution, it is very important to ensure that the right people have done the most difficult work in the project: figuring out what success looks like and what are the right questions to ask in the form of business-appropriate metrics and objectives.

A common reason for failure is engineers answering convenient questions with basic tools instead of answering the right questions with custom tools — something that may require consultation with a professional statistician after your project's leaders and stakeholders have completed their part in your project. Note that some methods highlighted in this chapter, specifically those used in A/B testing (Section 7.2), are provided as examples only and might not be appropriate for your specific business problem. On important large-scale projects, it would be a mistake to try to do everything yourself. Timely collaboration with your leadership team and consulting a statistician is essential.

7.1 Offline and Online Evaluation

In Section 5.5, we overviewed the evaluation techniques applied in what's called **offline model evaluation**. An offline model evaluation happens when the model is being trained by the analyst. The analyst tries out different features, models, algorithms, and hyperparameters.

Tools like confusion matrix and various performance metrics, such as precision, recall, and AUC, allow comparing candidate models, and guide the model training in the right direction.

First, validation data is used to assess the chosen performance metric and compare models. Once the best model is identified, the test set is used, also in offline mode, to again assess the best model's performance. This final offline assessment guarantees post-deployment model performance. In this chapter, we talk, among other topics, about establishing statistical bounds on the offline test performance of the model.

A significant part of the chapter is devoted to the **online model evaluation**, that is, testing and comparing models in production by using online data. The difference between offline and online model evaluation, as well as the placement of each type of evaluation in a machine learning system, is illustrated in Figure 7.2.

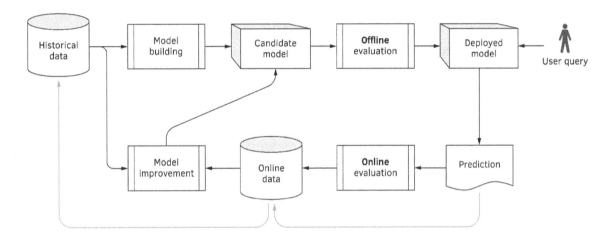

Figure 7.2: The placement of offline and online model evaluations in a machine learning system.

In Figure 7.2, the historical data is first used to train a deployment candidate. Then it is evaluated offline, and, if the result is satisfactory, deployment candidate becomes the deployed model, and starts accepting user queries. Then, user queries and the model predictions are used for an online evaluation of the model. The online data is then used to improve the model. To close the loop, the online data is permanently copied to the offline data repository.

Why do we evaluate both offline and online? The offline model evaluation reflects how well the analyst succeeded in finding the right features, learning algorithm, model, and values of hyperparameters. In other words, the offline model evaluation reflects how good the model is from an engineering standpoint.

Online evaluation, on the other hand, focuses on measuring business outcomes, such as customer satisfaction, average online time, open rate, and click-through rate. This information may not be reflected in historical data, but it's what the business really cares about. Furthermore, offline evaluation doesn't allow us to test the model in some conditions that can be observed online, such as connection and data loss, and call delays.

The performance results obtained on the historical data will hold after deployment only if the distribution of the data remains the same over time. In practice, however, it's not always the case. Typical examples of a **distribution shift** include the ever-changing interests of the user of a mobile or online application, instability of financial markets, climate change, or wear of a mechanical system whose properties the model is intended to predict.

As a consequence, the model must be continuously monitored once deployed in production. When a distribution shift happens, the model must be updated with new data and re-deployed. One way of doing such monitoring is to compare the performance of the model on online and historical data. If the performance on online data becomes significantly worse, as compared to historical, it's time to retrain the model.

There are different forms of online evaluation, each serving a different purpose. For example, runtime monitoring is checking whether the running system meets the runtime requirements.

Another common scenario is to monitor user behavior in response to different versions of the model. One popular technique used in this scenario is A/B testing. We split the users of a system into two groups, A and B. The two groups are served the old and the new models, respectively. Then we apply a statistical significance test to decide whether the performance of the new model is better than the old one.

Multi-armed bandit (MAB) is another popular technique of online model evaluation. Similar to A/B testing, it identifies the best performing models by exposing model candidates to a fraction of users. Then it gradually exposes the best model to more users, by keeping gathering performance statistics until it's reliable.

7.2 A/B Testing

A/B testing is one of the most frequently used statistical techniques. When applied to online model evaluation, it allows us to answer such questions as, "Does the new model m_B work better in production than the existing model m_A?" or, "Which of the two model candidates works better in production?"

A/B testing is often used on websites and mobile applications to test whether a specific change in the design or wording positively affects business metrics such as user engagement, click-through rate, or sales rate.

Imagine we want to decide whether to replace an existing (old) model in production with a new model. The live traffic that contains input data for the model is split into two disjoint groups: A (control) and B (experiment). Group A traffic is routed to the old model, while group B traffic is routed to the new model.

By comparing the performance of the two models, a decision is made about whether the new model performs better than the old model. The performance is compared using **statistical hypothesis testing**.

In general, statistical hypothesis testing maintains a **null hypothesis** and an **alternative hypothesis**. An A/B test is usually formulated to answer the following question: "Does the new model lead to a statistically significant change in this specific business metric?" The null hypothesis states that the new model doesn't change the average value of the business metric. The alternative hypothesis states that the new model changes the average value of the metric.

A/B test is not one test, but a family of tests. Depending on the business performance metric, a different statistical toolkit is used. However, the principle of splitting the users into two groups, and measuring the statistical significance of the difference in the metric values between different groups, remains the same.

The description of all formulations of A/B tests is beyond the scope of this book. Here we will consider only two formulations, but they apply to a wide range of practical situations.

7.2.1 G-Test

The first formulation of A/B test is based on the **G-test**. It is appropriate for a metric that counts the answer to a "yes" or "no" question. An advantage of the G-test is that you can ask any question, as long as only two answers are possible. Examples of questions:

- Whether the user bought the recommended article?
- Whether the user has spent more than $50 during a month?
- Whether the user renewed the subscription?

Let's see how to apply it. We want to decide whether the new model works better than the old one. To do that, we formulate a yes-or-no question that defines our metric. Then we randomly divide the users into groups A and B. The users of group A are routed to the environment running the old model, while the group's B traffic is routed to the new model. Observe the actions of each user and record the answer as "yes" or "no." Fill the following table:

	Yes	No	
A	$\hat{a}_{yes}$	$\hat{a}_{no}$	n_a
B	$\hat{b}_{yes}$	$\hat{b}_{no}$	n_b
	n_{yes}	n_{no}	n_{total}

Figure 7.3: The counts of answers to the yes-or-no question by users from groups A and B.

In the above table, $\hat{a}_{yes}$ is the number of users in group A, for which the answer to the question is "yes," $\hat{b}_{yes}$ is the number of users in group B, for which the answer to the question is "yes," $\hat{a}_{no}$ is the number of users in group A, for which the answer to the question is "no," and so on. Similarly, $n_{yes} = \hat{a}_{yes} + \hat{b}_{yes}$, $n_{no} = \hat{a}_{no} + \hat{b}_{no}$, $n_a = \hat{a}_{yes} + \hat{a}_{no}$, $n_b = \hat{b}_{yes} + \hat{b}_{no}$, and, finally $n_{total} = n_{yes} + n_{no} = n_a + n_b$.

Now, find the expected numbers of "yes" and "no" answers for A and B, i.e. the number of "yes" and "no" we would get if versions A and B were equivalent.

$$
\begin{aligned}
a_{yes} &\stackrel{\text{def}}{=} n_a \, \frac{n_{yes}}{n_{total}}, \\
a_{no} &\stackrel{\text{def}}{=} n_a \, \frac{n_{no}}{n_{total}}, \\
b_{yes} &\stackrel{\text{def}}{=} n_b \, \frac{n_{yes}}{n_{total}}, \\
b_{no} &\stackrel{\text{def}}{=} n_b \, \frac{n_{no}}{n_{total}}.
\end{aligned}
\tag{7.1}
$$

Now, find the value of the G-test as,[1]

$$
G \stackrel{\text{def}}{=} 2 \left(\hat{a}_{yes} \ln \left(\frac{\hat{a}_{yes}}{a_{yes}} \right) + \hat{a}_{no} \ln \left(\frac{\hat{a}_{no}}{a_{no}} \right) + \hat{b}_{yes} \ln \left(\frac{\hat{b}_{yes}}{b_{yes}} \right) + \hat{b}_{no} \ln \left(\frac{\hat{b}_{no}}{b_{no}} \right) \right).
$$

G is a measure of how different the samples from A and B are. Statistically speaking, under the null hypothesis (A and B are equal), G follows a **chi-square distribution** with one degree of freedom:

$$
G \sim \chi_1^2
$$

In other words, if A and B were equal, we expect G to be small. A large value of G would make us suspicious that one of the models performs better than the other. For example, imagine you calculated $G = 3.84$. If A and B were equal (i.e. under the null hypothesis) the probability of observing $G \geq 3.84$ is about 5%. We often refer to this probability as the p-value.

If the p-value is small enough (e.g., below 0.05) then the performances of the new and the old model are very likely different (the null hypothesis is rejected). In this case, if b_{yes} is higher than a_{yes}, then the new model is very likely to work better than the old model; otherwise, the old model is better.

If the p-value corresponding to the value of G is not small enough then the observed difference of performance between the new and the old model is not statistically significant, and you can keep the old model in production.

---

[1] More details on the derivation of the above formula can be found in a statistics textbook or on Wikipedia.

It is convenient to find the p-value of the G-test using a programming language of your choice. In Python, it can be done in the following way:

```python
from scipy.stats import chi2
def get_p_value(G):
    p_value = 1 - chi2.cdf(G, 1)
    return p_value
```

The following code will work for R:

```r
get_p_value <- function(G) {
  p_value <- pchisq(G, df=1, lower.tail=FALSE)
  return(p_value)
}
```

Statistically, the result of the G-test is valid if we have at least 10 "yes" and "no" results in each of the two groups, though this estimate should be taken with a grain of salt. If testing is not too expensive, then having about 1000 "yes" and "no" results in each of the two groups, with at least 100 answers of each type in each group, should be enough. Note that the total number of answers in the two groups can be different.

If you can't reach at least 100 answers of each type in each group at a reasonable cost, you can use an approximation of the p-value of a very similar test using **Monte-Carlo simulation**.

The following code will work for R:

```r
p_value <- chisq.test(x,
             simulate.p.value = TRUE)$p.value
}
```

Where x is the 2×2 contingency table shown in Figure 7.3.

Note that it is possible to test more than two models (e.g. models A, B, and C) and more than two possible answers to the question that define our metric (e.g., "yes," "no," "maybe"). If we want to test k different models and l different possible answers, the G statistic would follow a chi-square distribution with $(k - 1) \times (l - 1)$ degrees of freedom. The problem here is that a test with multiple models and answers will tell you whether there is something different somewhere between your models, but it will not tell you where is the difference. In practice, it is easier to compare your current model with only one new model and to formulate a question metric with a binary answer. More complex experiment testing is outside the scope of this book.

Note that it could be tempting, when we have more than two models, to do binary comparisons of pairs of models using a test designed for comparing two models. This is not recommended, however, as it could be scientifically wrong. It's better to consult a statistician.

7.2.2 Z-Test

The second formulation of A/B test applies when the question for each user is, "How many?" or, "How much?" (as opposed to a yes-or-no question considered in the previous subsection). Examples of questions include:

1. How much time a user has spent on the website during a session?
2. How much money a user has spent during a month?
3. How many news articles a user has read during a week?

For simplicity of illustration, let's measure the time a user spends on a website where our model is deployed. As usual, users are routed to versions A and B of the website, where version A serves the old model and version B serves the new model. The null hypothesis is that users of both versions spend, on average, the same amount of time. The alternative hypothesis is that they spend more time on website B than on website A. Let n_A be the number of users routed to version A and n_B be the number of users routed to version B. Let i and j denote users from groups A and B respectively.

To compute the value of the Z-test, we first compute sample mean and sample variance for A and B. The sample mean is given by:

$$\hat{\mu}_A \stackrel{\text{def}}{=} \frac{1}{n_A} \sum_{i=1}^{n_A} a_i,$$

$$\hat{\mu}_B \stackrel{\text{def}}{=} \frac{1}{n_B} \sum_{j=1}^{n_A} b_j,$$

$$(7.2)$$

where a_i and b_j is the time spent on the website by, respectively, users i and j.

The sample variance for A and B is given, respectively, by,

$$\hat{\sigma}_A^2 \stackrel{\text{def}}{=} \frac{1}{n_A} \sum_{i=1}^{n_A} (\hat{\mu}_A - a_i)^2,$$

$$\hat{\sigma}_B^2 \stackrel{\text{def}}{=} \frac{1}{n_B} \sum_{j=1}^{n_B} (\hat{\mu}_B - b_j)^2.$$

$$(7.3)$$

The value of the Z-test is then given by,

$$Z \stackrel{\text{def}}{=} \frac{\hat{\mu}_B - \hat{\mu}_A}{\sqrt{\frac{\hat{\sigma}_B^2}{n_B} + \frac{\hat{\sigma}_A^2}{n_A}}}.$$

The larger Z, the more likely the difference between A and B is significant. Under the null hypothesis (i.e. A and B are equivalent), Z approximately follows a standardized normal distribution,

$$Z \approx \mathcal{N}(0, 1)$$

This is true only if the sample size is large and if $\sigma_A^2 \approx \sigma_B^2$. If not, it is recommended to ask advice from a statistician.

As for the G-test, we will use the p-value to decide whether or not Z is large enough to think that the time spent on B is really greater than time spent on A. To compute the p-value, you check the probability of getting a Z-value from this distribution that is at least as extreme (out of line with the null hypothesis) as the Z-value you calculated. For example, let's imagine your sample gave you $Z = 2.64$. If A and B were equal, the probability of observing $Z \geq 2.64$ is about 5%.

To see the result of the test, you compare the p-value with the significance level you chose. If your significance level is 5%, then if the p-value is below 0.05, we reject the null hypothesis that says that the difference in performance of the two models is not statistically significant. Thus, the new model works better than the old one.

If the p-value is above or equal to 0.05, then we do not reject the null hypothesis. Note that this is not the same as accepting the null hypothesis. The two models could still be different, we just didn't get evidence in support of that. In this case, we will stick with the old model unless evidence changes our mind. No evidence means we keep doing what we were doing. Note also that we cannot simply keep gathering evidence until the p-value goes below 0.05, as it would not be scientifically sound. It's recommended to consult a statistician and design a different test.

As for significance levels, there's no universal consensus on which threshold is optimal. The values of 0.05 or 0.01 are commonly used in practice. They were favorites of a trendsetting statistician Ronald Fisher in the 1920s. You should select a higher or a lower value if it's appropriate for your application. The lower the value, the more evidence it takes to change your mind.

Similar to the G-test, it is convenient to find the p-value of the Z-test using a programming language. In Python, it can be done in the following way:

```
from scipy.stats import norm
def get_p_value(Z):
    p_value = norm.sf(Z)
    return p_value
```

The following code will work for R:

```
1  get_p_value <- function(Z) {
2    p_value <- 1-pnorm(Z)
3    return(p_value)
4  }
```

For best results, it is recommended to set n_A and n_B to a value 1000 or higher.

7.2.3 Concluding Remarks and Warnings

As mentioned in the beginning of this chapter, some methods highlighted in this chapter are provided as examples only and might not be appropriate for your specific business problem. In particular, the two statistical tests presented above are taught in schools and are indeed often used in practice, but, unfortunately, not all of those uses are appropriate for your business problem. While pointing this out, Cassie Kozyrkov, the Chief Decision Scientist at Google and one of the reviewers of this chapter, emphasized that the above two tests are rarely a good idea to apply in practice because they only show that two models are different, but they don't show whether the difference is "of at least x." If replacing the old model with the new one has a significant cost or poses a risk, then just knowing that the new model is "somewhat" better is not enough to make a replacement decision. In this case, an adjusted test must be specifically crafted for the problem at hand, and the best way to do is to consult a statistician.[2]

Carefully test the programming code of your A/B test. You will only have a valid model evaluation if you implemented everything right. Otherwise, you will not know that something is wrong: your test will not reveal that it's broken.

Also, make sure to apply measurements in groups A and B at the same time. Remember that traffic on a website behaves differently at different times of the day, or at different days of the week. For the purity of the experiment, avoid comparing measurements from different times. The same reasoning applies to other possible measurable parameters that might significantly affect user behavior, such as country of residence, speed of internet connection, or version of web browser.

7.3 Multi-Armed Bandit

A more advanced, and often preferable way of online model evaluation and selection, is **multi-armed bandit** (MAB). A/B testing has one major drawback. The number of test results in groups A and B you need to calculate the value of the A/B test is high. A significant portion of users routed to a suboptimal model would experience suboptimal behavior for a long time.

---

[2]Unfortunately, in a compact book describing all special cases and tests would be impractical. Please consult the book's companion wiki from time to time. More statistical tests will be added over time.

Ideally, we would like to expose a user to a suboptimal model as few times as possible. At the same time, we need to expose users to each of the two models a number of times sufficient to get reliable estimates of both models' performance. This is known as the **exploration-exploitation dilemma**: on one hand, we want to explore the models' performance enough to be able to reliably choose the better one. On the other hand, we want to exploit the performance of the better model as much as possible.

In probability theory, the multi-armed bandit problem is a problem in which a fixed and limited set of resources must be allocated between competing choices in a way that maximizes the expected reward. Each choice's properties are only partially known at the time of allocation, and may become better understood as time passes and we allocate resources to the choice.

Let's see how the multi-armed bandit problem applies to an online evaluation of two models. (The approach for more than two models is the same.)

The limited set of resources we have are the users of our system. The competing choices, also called "arms," are our models. We can allocate a resource to a choice (in other words, we can "play an arm") by routing a user to a version of the system running a specific model. We want to maximize the expected reward, where the reward is given by the business performance metric. Examples might be the average amount of time spent on the website during a session, the average number of news articles read during a week, the percentage of users who purchased the recommended article, etc.

UCB1 (for Upper Confidence Bound) is a popular algorithm for solving the multi-armed bandit problem. The algorithm dynamically chooses an arm, based on the performance of that arm in the past, and how much the algorithm knows about it. In other words, UCB1 routes the user to the best performing model more often when its confidence about the model performance is high. Otherwise, UCB1 might route the user to a suboptimal model so as to get a more confident estimate of that model's performance. Once the algorithm is confident enough about the performance of each model, it almost always routes users to the best performing model.

The mathematics of UCB1 works as follows. Let c_a denote the number of times the arm a was played since the beginning, and let v_a denote the average reward obtained from playing that arm. The reward corresponds to the value of the business performance metric. For the purpose of illustration, let the metric be the average time spent by the user in the system during one session. The reward for playing an arm is, thus, a particular session duration.

In the beginning, c_a and v_a are zero for all arms, $a = 1, \ldots, M$. Once an arm a is played, a reward r is observed, and c_a is incremented by 1; v_a is then updated as follows:

$$v_a \leftarrow \frac{c_a - 1}{c_a} \times v_a + \frac{r}{c_a}.$$

At each time step (that is, when a new user logs in), the arm to play (that is, the version of the system the user will be routed to) is chosen as follows. If $c_a = 0$ for some arm a, then this arm is played; otherwise, the arm with the greatest UCB value is played. The UCB value of an arm a, denoted as u_a, is defined as follows:

$$u_a \overset{\text{def}}{=} v_a + \sqrt{\frac{2 \times \log(c)}{c_a}}, \text{ where } c \overset{\text{def}}{=} \sum_a^M c_a.$$

The algorithm is proven to converge to the optimal solution. That is, UCB1 will end up playing the best performing arm most of the time.

In Python, the code that implements UCB1, would look as follows:

```python
class UCB1():
    def __init__(self, n_arms):
        self.c = [0]*n_arms
        self.v = [0.0]*n_arms
        self.M = n_arms
        return

    def select_arm(self):
        for a in range(self.M):
            if self.c[a] == 0:
                return a
        u = [0.0]*self.M
        c = sum(self.c)
        for a in range(self.M):
            bonus = math.sqrt((2 * math.log(c)) / float(self.c[a]))
            u[a] = self.v[a] + bonus
        return u.index(max(u))

    def update(self, a, r):
        self.c[a] += 1
        v_a = ((self.c[a] - 1) / float(self.c[a])) * self.v[a] \
                + (r / float(self.c[a]))
        self.v[a] = v_a
        return
```

The corresponding code in R would look as shown below:

```r
setClass("UCB1", representation(count="numeric", value="numeric", M="numeric"))

setGeneric("select_arm", function(x) standardGeneric("select_arm"))
setMethod("select_arm", "UCB1", function(x) {
    for (a in seq(from = 1, to = x@M, by = 1)) {
        if(x@count[a] == 0) {
            return(a)
```

```
 8              }
 9          }
10      u <- rep(0.0, x@M)
11      count <- sum(x@count)
12      for (a in seq(from = 1, to = x@M, by = 1)){
13          print(a)
14          bonus <- sqrt((2 * log(count)) / x@count[a])
15          u[a] <- x@value[a] + bonus
16      }
17      match(c(max(u)),u)
18 })
19
20 setGeneric("update", function(x, a, r) standardGeneric("update"))
21 setMethod("update", "UCB1", function(x, a, r) {
22      x@count[a] <- x@count[a] + 1
23      v_a <- ((x@count[a] - 1) / x@count[a]) * x@value[a] + (r / x@count[a])
24      x@value[a] <- v_a
25 })
26
27 UCB1 <- function(M) {
28      new("UCB1", count = rep(0, M), value = rep(0.0, M), M = M)
29 }
```

7.4   Statistical Bounds on the Model Performance

When reporting the model performance, sometimes, besides the value of the metric, it is required to also provide the statistical bounds, also known as the **statistical interval**.

A reader familiar with other books on machine learning or some popular online blogs might wonder, why we use the term "statistical interval" and not "confidence interval." The reason is that in some machine learning literature, what the authors call a "confidence interval" is in fact a "credible interval." The difference between the two is clear and important for a statistician because the two terms have different meanings in frequentist and Bayesian statistics. In this book, I decided not to burden the reader with the subtlety of the difference between the two terms. For a non-expert in statistics, it would be beneficial to think of the statistical interval as follows: a 95% statistical interval indicates that there's a 95% chance the parameter you're estimating is between the intervals bounds. Strictly speaking, this is the definition of the credible interval. A confidence interval's interpretation is subtly different, most newcomers to statistics won't start to appreciate the difference until they're a few textbooks in. For our purposes, the above interpretation of a statistical interval will suffice.

There are several techniques that allow establishing statistical bounds for a model. Some techniques apply to classification models, and some can be applied to regression models. We will consider several techniques in this section.

7.4.1 Statistical Interval for the Classification Error

If you report the error ratio "err" for a classification model (where err $\overset{\text{def}}{=} 1 -$ accuracy), then the following technique can be used to obtain the statistical interval for "err."

Let N be the size of the test set. Then, with probability 99%, "err" lies in the interval,

$$[\text{err} - \delta, \text{err} + \delta],$$

where $\delta \overset{\text{def}}{=} z_N \sqrt{\frac{\text{err}(1-\text{err})}{N}}$, and $z_N = 2.58$.

The value of z_N depends on the required **confidence level**. For the confidence level of 99%, $z_N = 2.58$. For other confidence level values, the values of z_N can be found in the table below:

confidence level	80%	90%	95%	98%	99%
z_N	1.28	1.64	1.96	2.33	2.58

As with p-values, it is convenient to find the value of z_N using a programming language. In Python, it can be done in the following way:

```
from scipy.stats import norm
def get_z_N(confidence_level): # a value in (0,100)
    z_N = norm.ppf(1-0.5*(1 - confidence_level/100.0))
    return z_N
```

The following code will work for R:

```
get_z_N <- function(confidence_level) {# a value in (0,100)
  z_N <- qnorm(1-0.5*(1 - confidence_level/100.0))
  return(z_N)
}
```

In theory, the above technique works even for very tiny test sets with $N \geq 30$. However, a more accurate rule of thumb for obtaining the minimum size N of the test set is as follows: find the value of N such that $N \times \text{err}(1 - \text{err}) \geq 5$. Intuitively, the greater the size of the test set, the lower our uncertainty about the true performance of the model.

7.4.2 Bootstrapping Statistical Interval

A popular technique for reporting the statistical interval for any metric, and which applies to both classification and regression, is based on the idea of **bootstrapping**. Bootstrapping is a statistical procedure that consists of building B samples of a dataset, and then training a model or computing some statistic using those B samples. In particular, the **random forest** learning algorithm is based on this idea.

Here's how bootstrapping applies for building a statistical interval for a metric. Given the test set, we create B random samples S_b, one for each $b = 1, \ldots, B$. To obtain a sample S_b for some b, we use **sampling with replacement**. Sampling with replacement means that we start with an empty set, and then pick at random an example from the test set and put its exact copy in S_b by keeping the original example in the test set. We keep picking examples at random and putting them to S_b until $|S_b| = N$.

Once we have B bootstrap samples of the test set, we compute the value of the performance metric m_b using each sample S_b as the test set. Sort the B values in ascending order. Then find the value S of the sum of all B values of the metric: $S \stackrel{\text{def}}{=} \sum_{b=1}^{B} m_b$. To obtain a c percent statistical interval for the metric, pick the tightest interval between a minimum a and a maximum b such that the sum of the values m_b that lie in that interval accounts for at least c percent of S. Our statistical interval is then given by $[a, b]$.

The above paragraph might sound vague, so let's illustrate it with an example. Let's have $B = 10$. Let the values of the metric, computed by applying the model to B bootstrap samples, be $[9.8, 7.5, 7.9, 10.1, 9.7, 8.4, 7.1, 9.9, 7.7, 8.5]$. First, we sort those values in the increasing order: $[7.1, 7.5, 7.7, 7.9, 8.4, 8.5, 9.7, 9.8, 9.9, 10.1]$. Let our confidence level c be 80%. Then, the minimum a of the statistical interval will be 7.46 and the maximum b will be 9.92. The above two values were found using the `percentile` function in Python:

```python
from numpy import percentile
def get_interval(values, confidence_level):
    # confidence_level is a value in (0,100)
    lower = percentile(values, (100.0-confidence_level)/2.0)
    upper = percentile(values, confidence_level+((100.0-confidence_level)/2.0))
    return (lower, upper)
```

The same can be done in R by using the `quantile` function:

```r
get_interval <- function(values, confidence_level) {
    # confidence_level is a value in (0,100)
    cl <- confidence_level/100.0
    quant <- quantile(values, probs = c((1.0-cl)/2.0, cl+((1.0-cl)/2.0)),
    names = FALSE)
    return(quant)
}
```

Once you have the boundaries $a = 7.46$ and $b = 9.92$ of the statistical interval, you can report that the value of the metric for your model lies in the interval $[7.46, 9.92]$ with confidence 80%.

In practice, analysts use confidence levels of either 95% or 99%. The higher the confidence, the wider the interval. The number B of bootstrap samples is usually set to 100.

7.4.3   Bootstrapping Prediction Interval for Regression

Until now, we considered the statistical interval for an entire model and a given performance metric. In this section, we will use bootstrapping to compute the **prediction interval** for a regression model and a given feature vector $\mathbf{x}$, which this model receives as input.

We want to answer the following question. Given a regression model f and an input feature vector $\mathbf{x}$, what is an interval of values $[f_{min}(\mathbf{x}), f_{max}(\mathbf{x})]$ such that the prediction $f(\mathbf{x})$ lies inside that interval with confidence c percent?

The bootstrapping procedure here is similar. The only difference is that now we build B bootstrap samples of the training set (and not the test set). By using B bootstrap samples as B training sets, we build B regression models, one per bootstrap sample. Let the input feature vector be $\mathbf{x}$. Fix a confidence level c. Apply B models to $\mathbf{x}$ and obtain B predictions. Now, by using the same technique as above, find the tightest interval between a minimum a and a maximum b such that the sum of the values of predictions that lie in the interval accounts for at least c percent of the sum of B predictions. Then return the prediction $f(\mathbf{x})$, and state that, with confidence c percent, it lies in the interval $[a, b]$.

As previously, the confidence level usually is either 95% or 99%. The number B of bootstrap samples is set to 100 (or as many as the time allows).

7.5   Evaluation of Test Set Adequacy

In traditional software engineering, tests are used to identify defects in the software. The collection of tests is constructed in such a way that they allow discovery of bugs in the code before the software reaches production. The same approach applies to the testing of all the code developed "around" the statistical model: the code that gets the input from the user, transforms it into features, and the code that interprets the outputs of the model, and serves the result to the user.

However, an additional evaluation must be applied to the model itself. The test examples used to evaluate the model must also be designed in such a way that they allow the discovery of the model's defective behavior before the model reaches production.

7.5.1 Neuron Coverage

When we evaluate a neural network, especially one to be used in a mission-critical scenario, such as a self-driving car or a space rocket, our test set must have good coverage. **Neuron coverage** of a test set for a neural network model is defined as the ratio of the units (neurons) activated by the examples from the test set, to the total number of units. A good test set has close to 100% neuron coverage.

A technique for building such a test set is to start with a set of unlabeled examples, and all units of the model uncovered. Then, iteratively, we

1) randomly pick an unlabeled example i and label it,
2) send the feature vector $\mathbf{x}_i$ to the input of the model,
3) observe which units in the model were activated by $\mathbf{x}_i$,
4) if the prediction was correct, mark those units as covered,
5) go back to step 1; continue iterating until the neuron coverage becomes close to 100%.

A unit is considered activated when its output is above a certain threshold. For ReLU, it's usually zero; for a logistic sigmoid, it's 0.5.

7.5.2 Mutation Testing

In software engineering, good test coverage for a **software under test** (SUT) can be determined using the approach known as **mutation testing**. Let's have a set of tests designed to test an SUT. We generate several "mutants" of the SUT. A mutant is a version of the SUT in which we randomly make some modifications, such as replacing in the source code, a "+" with a "−", a "<" with a ">", delete the `else` command in an `if-else` statement, and so on. Then we apply the test set to each mutant, and see if at least one test breaks on that mutant. We say that we kill a mutant if one test breaks on it. We then compute the ratio of killed mutants in the entire collection of mutants. A good test set makes this ratio equal to 100%.

In machine learning, a similar approach can be followed. However, to create a mutant statistical model, instead of modifying the code, we modify the training data. If the model is deep, we can also randomly remove or add a layer, or remove or replace an activation function. The training data can be modified by,

- adding duplicated examples,
- falsifying the labels of some examples,
- removing some examples, or
- adding random noise to the values of some features.

We say that we kill a mutant if at least one test example gets a wrong prediction by that mutant statistical model.

7.6 Evaluation of Model Properties

When we measure the quality of the model according to some performance metric, such as accuracy or AUC, we evaluate its **correctness** property. Besides this commonly evaluated property of the model, it can be appropriate to evaluate other properties of the model, such as robustness and fairness.

7.6.1 Robustness

The **robustness** of a machine learning model refers to the stability of the model performance after adding some noise to the input data. A robust model would exhibit the following behavior. If the input example is perturbed by adding random noise, the performance of the model would degrade proportionally to the level of noise.

Consider an input feature vector $\mathbf{x}$. Let us, before applying a model f to that input example, modify the values of some features, chosen randomly, by replacing them with a zero, to obtain a modified input $\mathbf{x}'$. Continue randomly choosing and replacing values of features in $\mathbf{x}$, as long as the **Euclidean distance** between $\mathbf{x}$ and $\mathbf{x}'$ remains below some δ. Then apply the model f to $\mathbf{x}$ and $\mathbf{x}'$ to obtain predictions $f(\mathbf{x})$ and $f(\mathbf{x}')$. Fix values of δ and ϵ. The model f is said to be ϵ-robust to a δ-perturbation of the input, if, for any $\mathbf{x}$ and $\mathbf{x}'$, such that $\|\mathbf{x} - \mathbf{x}'\| \leq \delta$, we have $|f(\mathbf{x}) - f(\mathbf{x}')| \leq \epsilon$.

If you have several models that perform similarly according to the performance metric, you would prefer to deploy in production a model that is ϵ-robust, when applied to the test data, with the smallest ϵ. However, in practice, it's not always clear how to set the appropriate value of δ. A more practical way to identify a robust model among several candidates is as follows.

Let us say that a certain test set is δ-perturbed if we obtained it by applying a δ-perturbation to all examples in a certain original test set. Pick the model f you want tested for robustness. Set a reasonable value of $\hat{\epsilon}$ such that, if the model prediction in production is not farther from the correct prediction than $\hat{\epsilon}$, you would consider that acceptable. Start with a small value of δ and build a δ-perturbed dataset. Find the minimum ϵ such that for each example $\mathbf{x}$ from the original test set and its counterpart $\mathbf{x}'$ from the δ-perturbed test set, $|f(\mathbf{x}) - f(\mathbf{x}')| \leq \epsilon$.

If $\epsilon \geq \hat{\epsilon}$, you have chosen too high a value for δ; set a lower value and start over.

If $\epsilon < \hat{\epsilon}$, then slightly increase δ, build a new δ-perturbed test set, find ϵ for this new δ-perturbed test set, and continue increasing δ as long as ϵ remains less than $\hat{\epsilon}$. Once you find the value of $\delta = \hat{\delta}$ where $\epsilon \geq \hat{\epsilon}$, note that the model f you are testing for robustness is $\hat{\epsilon}$-robust to $\hat{\delta}$-perturbation of the input. Now pick another model you want to test for robustness, and find its $\hat{\delta}$; continue like that until all models are tested.

Once you have the value of $\hat{\delta}$-perturbation for each model, deploy in production the model whose $\hat{\delta}$ is the greatest.

7.6.2 Fairness

Machine learning algorithms tend to learn what humans are teaching them. The teaching comes in the form of training examples. Humans have biases which may affect how they collect and label data. Sometimes, bias is present in historical, cultural, or geographical data. This, in turn, as we have seen in Section 3.2 in Chapter 3, may lead to biased models.

The attributes that are sensitive and need protection from unfairness are called **protected** or **sensitive attributes**. Examples of legally-recognized and protected attributes include race, skin color, gender, religion, national origin, citizenship, age, pregnancy, familial status, disability status, veteran status, and genetic information.

Fairness is often domain-specific, and each domain may have its own regulations. Regulated domains include credit, education, employment, housing, and public accommodation.

The definition of fairness varies greatly, depending on the domain. At the time of writing this book, there is no firm consensus, in the scientific and technical literature, on what is fairness. Most commonly cited concepts are demographic parity and equal opportunity.

Demographic parity (also known as **statistical parity**, or **independence parity**) means the proportion of each segment of a protected attribute receives a positive prediction from the model at equal rates.

Let a positive prediction mean "acceptance to university," or "granting a loan." Mathematically, demographic parity is defined as follows. Let G_1 and G_2 be the two disjoint groups belonging to the test data, divided by a sensitive attribute j, such as gender. Let $\mathbf{x}^{(j)} = 1$ if $\mathbf{x}$ represents a woman, and $\mathbf{x}^{(j)} = 0$ otherwise. A binary model f under test satisfies demographic parity if $\Pr(f(\mathbf{x}_i) = 1 | \mathbf{x}_i \in G_1) = \Pr(f(\mathbf{x}_k) = 1 | \mathbf{x}_k \in G_2)$. That is, as measured on the test data, the chance to predict 1 with the model f for women is the same as the chance to predict 1 for men.

The exclusion of the protected attributes from the feature vector in the training data doesn't guarantee that the model will have demographic parity, as some of the remaining features may be **correlated** with the excluded ones.

Equal opportunity means each group gets a positive prediction from the model at equal rates, assuming that people in this group qualify for it.

Mathematically, a binary model f under test satisfies equal opportunity if $\Pr(f(\mathbf{x}_i) = 1 | \mathbf{x}_i \in G_1$ and $y_i = 1) = \Pr(f(\mathbf{x}_k) = 1 | \mathbf{x}_k \in G_2$ and $y_k = 1)$, where y_i and y_k are the actual labels of the feature vectors $\mathbf{x}_i$ and $\mathbf{x}_k$, respectively. The above equality means that, as measured on the test data, the chance to predict 1 by the model f for women who qualify for that prediction is the same as the chance to predict 1 for men who also qualify. In the terms of the **confusion matrix**, equal opportunity requires the **true positive rate** (TPR) to be equal for each value of the protected attribute.

7.7 Summary

All statistical models running in production must be carefully and continuously evaluated.

Depending on the model's applicative domain and the organization's goals and constraints, model evaluation will include the following tasks:

- estimate legal risks of putting the model in production,
- understand the main properties of the distribution of the data used to train the model,
- evaluate the performance of the model prior to deployment, and
- monitor the performance of the deployed model.

An offline model evaluation happens after the model was trained. It is based on the historical data. The online model evaluation consists of testing and comparing models in the production environment using online data.

A popular technique of online model evaluation is A/B testing. When performing A/B testing, we split users into two groups, A and B. The two groups are served the old and the new models, respectively. Then we apply a statistical significance test to decide whether the new model is statistically different from the old model.

Multi-armed bandit is another popular technique of online model evaluation. We start by randomly exposing all models to the users. Then we gradually reduce the exposure of the least-performing models until only one, the best performing model, gets served most of the time.

In addition to reporting training model performance metrics, one may also need to provide the statistical bounds known as the statistical interval.

For both classification and regression models, a statistical interval for any metric can be computed using a popular technique called bootstrapping. It is a statistical procedure that consists of building B samples of a dataset, and then training a model and computing some statistic using each of those B samples.

The test examples used to evaluate the model must allow the discovery of defective behavior before the model reaches production. Such techniques as neuron coverage and mutation testing can be used to evaluate the test set.

When the model is used in a mission-critical system, or in regulated domains (such as credit, education, employment, housing, and public accommodation) accuracy, robustness, and fairness may have to be evaluated.

Chapter 8

Model Deployment

Once the model has been built and thoroughly tested, it can be deployed. Deploying a model means to make it available for accepting queries generated by the users of the production system. Once the production system accepts the query, the latter is transformed into a feature vector. The feature vector is then sent to the model as input for scoring. The result of the scoring then is returned to the user.

Model deployment is the sixth stage in the machine learning project life cycle:

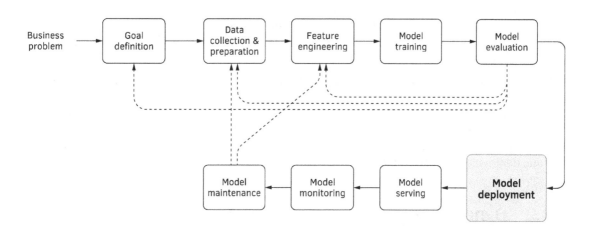

Figure 8.1: Machine learning project life cycle.

A trained model can be deployed in various ways. It can be deployed on a server, or on a user's device. It can be deployed for all users at once, or to a small fraction of users. Below, we consider all the options.

A model can be deployed following several **patterns**:

- statically, as a part of an installable software package,
- dynamically on the user's device,
- dynamically on a server, or
- via model streaming.

8.1 Static Deployment

The static deployment of a machine learning model is very similar to traditional software deployment: you prepare an installable binary of the entire software. The model is packaged as a resource available at the runtime. Depending on the operating system and the runtime environment, the objects of both the model and the feature extractor can be packaged as a part of a dynamic-link library (DLL on Windows), Shared Objects (*.so files on Linux), or be serialized and saved in the standard resource location for virtual machine-based systems, such as Java and .Net.

Static deployment has many advantages:

- the software has direct access to the model, so the execution time is fast for the user,
- the user data doesn't have to be uploaded to the server at the time of prediction; this saves time and preserves privacy,
- the model can be called when the user is offline, and
- the software vendor doesn't have to care about keeping the model operational; it becomes the user's responsibility.

However, a static deployment also has several drawbacks. First and foremost, the separation of concerns between the machine learning code and the application code isn't always obvious. This makes it harder to upgrade the model without also having to upgrade the entire application. Second, if the model has certain computational requirements for scoring (such as access to an accelerator or a GPU), it may add complexity and confusion as to where the static deployment can or cannot be used.

8.2 Dynamic Deployment on User's Device

A dynamic deployment on devices is similar to a static deployment, in the sense the user runs a part of the system as a software application on their device. The difference is that in dynamic deployment, the model is not part of the binary code of the application. Thus it achieves better separation of concerns. Pushing model updates is done without updating the whole application running on the user's device. Moreover, a dynamic deployment may allow the same piece of code to select the right model, based on the available compute resources.

Dynamic deployment can be achieved in several ways:

- by deploying model parameters,
- by deploying a serialized object, and
- by deploying to the browser.

8.2.1 Deployment of Model Parameters

In this deployment scenario, the model file only contains the learned parameters, while the user's device has installed a runtime environment for the model. Some machine learning packages, like **TensorFlow**, have a lightweight version that can run on mobile devices.

Alternatively, frameworks such as Apple's **Core ML** allow running models created using popular packages, including **scikit-learn**, **Keras**, and **XGBoost**, on Apple devices.

8.2.2 Deployment of a Serialized Object

Here, the model file is a serialized object that the application would deserialize. The advantage of this approach is that you don't need to have a runtime environment for your model on the user's device. All needed dependencies will be deserialized with the object of the model.

An evident drawback is that an update might be quite "heavy," which is a problem if your software system has millions of users.

8.2.3 Deploying to Browser

Most modern devices have access to a browser, either desktop or mobile. Some machine learning frameworks, such as **TensorFlow.js**, have versions that allow to train and run a model in a browser, by using JavaScript as a runtime.

It's even possible to train a TensorFlow model in Python, and then deploy it to, and run it in the browser's JavaScript runtime environment. Additionally, if a GPU (graphics processing unit) is available on the client's device, Tensorflow.js can leverage it.

8.2.4 Advantages and Drawbacks

The main advantage of dynamic deployment to users' devices is that the calls to the model will be fast for the user. It also reduces the impact on the organization's servers, as most computations are performed on the user's device. Additionally, if the model is deployed to the browser, the organization's infrastructure only needs to serve a web page that includes the model's parameters. A downside of the browser-based deployment is that the bandwidth cost and application startup time might increase. The users must download the model's parameters each time they start the web application, as opposed to doing it only once when they install an application.

Another drawback occurs during model updates. Recall, a serialized object can be quite voluminous. Some users may be offline during the update, or even turn off all future updates. In that case, you may end up with different users using very different model versions. Now it becomes difficult to upgrade the server-side part of the application.

Deploying models on the user's device means that the model easily becomes available for third-party analyses. They may try to reverse-engineer the model to reproduce its behavior. They may search for weaknesses by providing various inputs and observing the output. Or, they may adapt their data so the model predicts what they want.

Suppose the mobile application allows the user to read news related to their interests. A content provider might try to reverse engineer the model, so that it now recommends more often the news from that content provider.

As with static deployment, deploying to a user's device makes it difficult to monitor the model performance.

8.3 Dynamic Deployment on a Server

Because of the above complications, and problems with performance monitoring, the most frequent deployment pattern is to place the model on a server (or servers), and make it available as a Representational State Transfer application programming interface (**REST API**) in the form of a web service, or Google's Remote Procedure Call (**gRPC**) service.

8.3.1 Deployment on a Virtual Machine

In a typical web service architecture deployed in a cloud environment, the predictions are served in response to canonically-formatted HTTP requests. A web service running on a virtual machine receives a user request containing the input data, calls the machine learning system on that input data, and then transforms the output of the machine learning system into the output JavaScript Object Notation (JSON) or Extensible Markup Language (XML) string. To cope with high load, several identical virtual machines are running in parallel.

A **load balancer** dispatches the incoming requests to a specific virtual machine, depending on its availability. The virtual machines can be added and closed manually, or be a part of an **autoscaling group** that launches or terminates virtual machines based on their usage. Figure 8.2 illustrates that deployment pattern. Each instance, denoted as an orange square, contains all the code needed to run the feature extractor and the model. The instance also contains a web service that has access to that code.

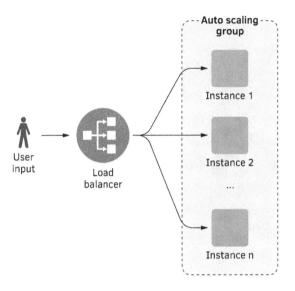

Figure 8.2: Deploying a machine learning model as a web service on a virtual machine.

In Python, a REST API web service is usually implemented using a web application framework such as **Flask** or **FastAPI**. An R equivalent is **Plumber**.

TensorFlow, a popular framework used to train deep models, comes with TensorFlow Serving, a built-in gRPC service.

The advantage of deploying on a virtual machine is that the architecture of the software system is conceptually simple: it's a typical web or gRPC service.

Among the downsides, there is a need to maintain servers (physical or virtual). If virtualization is used, then there is an additional computational overhead due to virtualization and running multiple operating systems. Another is network latency, which can be a serious issue, depending on how fast you need to process scoring results. Finally, deploying on a virtual machine has a relatively higher cost, compared to deployment in a container, or a serverless deployment that we consider below.

8.3.2 Deployment in a Container

A more modern alternative to a virtual-machine-based deployment is a container-based deployment. Working with containers is typically considered more resource-efficient and flexible than with virtual machines. A container is similar to a virtual machine, in the sense that it is also an isolated runtime environment with its own filesystem, CPU, memory, and

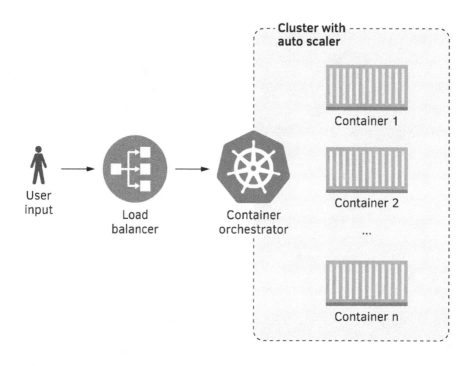

Figure 8.3: Deploying a model as a web service in a container running on a cluster.

process space. The main difference, however, is that all containers are running on the same virtual or physical machine and share the operating system, while each virtual machine runs its own instance of the operating system.

The deployment process looks as follows. The machine learning system and the web service are installed inside a container. Usually, a container is a **Docker** container, but there are alternatives. Then a container-orchestration system is used to run the containers on a cluster of physical or virtual servers. A typical choice of a container-orchestration system for running on-premises or in a cloud platform, is **Kubernetes**. Some cloud platforms provide both their own container-orchestration engine, such as **AWS Fargate** and **Google Kubernetes Engine**, and support Kubernetes natively.

Figure 8.3 illustrates that deployment pattern. Here, the virtual or physical machines are organized into a cluster, whose resources are managed by the container orchestrator. New virtual or physical machines can be manually added to the cluster, or closed. If your software is deployed in a cloud environment, a cluster autoscaler can launch (and add to the cluster) or terminate virtual machines, based on the usage of the cluster.

Deployment in a container has the advantage of being more resource-efficient as compared to the deployment on a virtual machine. It allows the possibility to automatically scale with scoring requests. It also allows us to **scale-to-zero**. The idea of the scale-to-zero is that a container can be reduced down to zero replicas when idle and brought back up if there is a request to serve. As a result, the resource consumption is low compared to always running services. This leads to less power consumption and saves cost of cloud resources.

One drawback is that the containerized deployment is generally seen as more complicated, and requires expertise.

8.3.3 Serverless Deployment

Several cloud services providers, including Amazon, Google, and Microsoft, offer so-called **serverless computing**. It's known under the name of Lambda-functions on Amazon Web Services, and Functions on Microsoft Azure and Google Cloud Platform.

The serverless deployment consists of preparing a zip archive with all the code needed to run the machine learning system (model, feature extractor, and scoring code). The zip archive must contain a file with a specific name that contains a specific function, or class-method definition with a specific signature (an entry point function). The zip archive is uploaded to the cloud platform and registered under a unique name.

The cloud platform provides an API to submit inputs to the serverless function. This specifies its name, provides the payload, and yields the outputs. The cloud platform takes care of deploying the code and the model on an adequate computational resource, executing the code, and routing the output back to the client.

Usually, the function's execution time, zip file size, and amount of RAM available on the runtime are limited by the cloud service provider.

The zip file size limit can be a challenge. A typical machine learning model requires multiple heavyweight dependencies. Python's libraries, to include Numpy, SciPy, and scikit-learn, are often needed for the model to be properly executed. Depending on the cloud platform, other supported programming languages can include Java, Go, PowerShell, Node.js, C#, and Ruby.

There are many advantages to relying on serverless deployment. The obvious advantage is that you don't have to provision resources such as servers or virtual machines. You don't have to install dependencies, maintain, or upgrade the system. Serverless systems are highly scalable and can easily and effortlessly support thousands of requests per second. Serverless functions support both synchronous and asynchronous modes of operation.

Serverless deployment is also cost-efficient: you only pay for compute-time. This may also be achieved with the previous two deployment patterns using autoscaling, but autoscaling has significant latency. While the demand may drop, excessive virtual machines could still keep running before they are terminated.

Serverless deployment also simplifies **canary deployment**, or **canarying**. In software engineering, canarying is a strategy when the updated code is pushed to just a small group of end-users, usually unaware. Because the new version is only distributed to a small number of users, its impact is relatively low, and changes can be reversed quickly, should the new code contain bugs. It is easy to set up two versions of serverless functions in production, and start sending low volume traffic to just one, and test it without affecting many users. We will talk more about canarying in Section 8.4.

Rollbacks are also very simple in the serverless deployment because it is easy to switch back to the previous version of the function by replacing one zip archive.

We've discussed the zip archive size limit, and the RAM available on the runtime. These are important drawbacks to serverless deployment. Likewise, the unavailability of GPU access[1] can be a significant limitation for deploying deep models.

Of course, complex software systems may combine deployment patterns. A deployment pattern appropriate for one model may be less optimal for another one. A combination of several deployment patterns is called a **hybrid deployment pattern**. Personal assistants like Google Home or Amazon Echo might have a model that recognizes the activation phrase (such as "OK, Google" or "Alexa") deployed on the client's device, and more complex models handle requests like "put song X on device Y" will instead run on the server. Alternatively, the deployment on the user's mobile device might augment the video and add simple intelligent effects in realtime. Server deployment would be used to apply more complex effects, such as stabilization and super-resolution.

8.3.4 Model Streaming

Model streaming is a deployment pattern that can be seen as an inverse to the REST API. In REST API, the client sends a request to the server, and then waits for a response (a prediction).

In complex systems, there can be many models applied to the same input. Or, a model can input a prediction from another model. For example, the input may be a news article. One model can predict the topic of the article, another model can extract named entities, the third model can generate a summarization of the article, and so on.

According to the REST API deployment pattern, we need one REST API per model. The client would call one API by sending a news article as a part of the request, and get the topic as response. Then the client calls another API by sending a news article, and gets the named entities as response; etc.

Streaming works differently. Instead of having one REST API per model, all models, as well as the code needed to run them, are registered within a **stream-processing engine** (SPE). Examples are **Apache Storm**, **Apache Spark**, and **Apache Flink**. Or, they are packaged as an application based on a **stream-processing library** (SPL), such as **Apache Samza**, **Apache Kafka Streams**, and **Akka Streams**.

---

[1]As of July 2020.

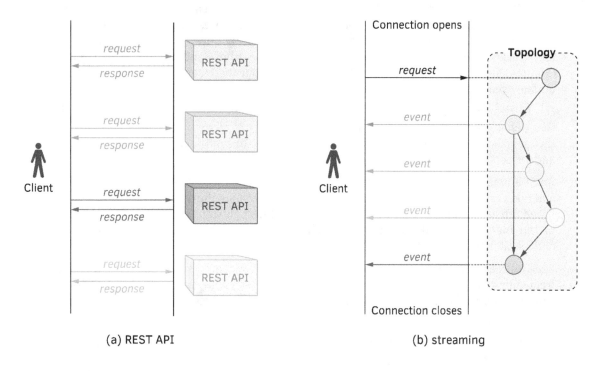

(a) REST API   (b) streaming

Figure 8.4: The difference between a REST API and streaming: (a) to process one data element, a client using a REST API sends a series of requests, one by one, and receives responses synchronously; (b) to process one data element, a client using streaming opens a connection, sends a request, and receives update events as they happen.

The descriptions of these SPEs and SPLs are beyond the scope of this book, but they all share the same property making them different from the REST-API-based applications. In each stream-processing application, there is an implicit or explicit notion of **data processing topology**. The input data flows in as an infinite stream of data elements sent by the client. Following a predefined topology, each data element in the stream undergoes a transformation in the nodes of the topology. Transformed, the flow continues to other nodes.

In a stream-processing application, nodes transform their input in some way, and then either,

- send the output to other nodes, or
- send the output to the client, or
- persist the output to the database or a filesystem.

One node could take a news article and predict its topic; another node could take both the news article and the predicted topic and generate a summary; and so on.

The difference between a REST-API-based application and a streaming-based one is shown in Figure 8.4. Figure 8.4a shows a client using a REST API, processing one data element, such as a news article, by sending a series of requests. One by one, various REST APIs receive requests and produce responses synchronously. On the other hand, a client using streaming (Figure 8.4b) opens a connection to the streaming application, sends a request, and receives update events as they happen.

On the right-hand side of the streaming-based application in Figure 8.4b, there's a topology that defines the data flow in the application. Each input element sent by the client passes through all the nodes of the **topology graph**. Nodes can send updated events to the client, and/or persist data to the database or a filesystem.

An SPE-based streaming application runs on its own cluster of virtual or physical machines, and takes care of distributing the data processing load among the available resources. An SPL-based streaming application doesn't need a dedicated cluster for data processing. It can be integrated with available resources, such as virtual or physical machines, or a container orchestrator (such as Kubernetes).

REST APIs are usually employed to let clients send ad-hoc requests that don't follow a certain frequently-repeated pattern. It's the best choice when the client wants the liberty of deciding what to do with the API response. On the other hand, if each request of the client is:

- typical,
- undergoes a certain pattern of transformations, especially multiple intermediate transformations, and
- always results in the same actions, such as persistence of specific data elements to the filesystem or database, then streaming-based applications provide better resource-efficiency, lower latency, security, and fault-tolerance.

8.4   Deployment Strategies

Typical deployment strategies are:

- single deployment,
- silent deployment,
- canary deployment, and
- multi-armed bandit.

Let's consider each of them.

8.4.1   Single Deployment

Single deployment is the simplest one. Conceptually, once you have a new model, you serialize it into a file, and then replace the old file with the new one. You also replace the feature extractor, if needed.

To deploy on a server in a cloud environment, you prepare a new virtual machine, or a container running the new version of the model. Then you replace the virtual machine image or that of the container. Finally, you gradually close the old machines or containers, and let the autoscaler start the new ones.

To deploy on a physical server, you will upload a new model file (and the feature extraction object, if needed) on the server. Then you replace old files and old code with the new versions, and restart the web service.

To deploy on the user's device, you push the new model file to the user's device, along with any needed feature extraction object, and restart the software.

If you use interpretable code, the feature extractor object can be deployed by replacing one source code file with another one. To avoid redeploying the entire software application, on either the server or the user's device, the feature extractor's object can be serialized into a file. Then, on each startup, the software running the model would deserialize the feature extractor object.

Single deployment has the advantage of being simple; however, it's also the riskiest strategy. If the new model or the feature extractor contains a bug, all users will be affected.

8.4.2   Silent Deployment

A counterpart of the single deployment is **silent deployment**. It deploys the new model version and new feature extractor, and keeps the old ones. Both versions run in parallel. However, the user will not be exposed to the new version until the switch is done. The predictions made by the new version are only logged. After some time, they are analyzed to detect possible bugs.

Silent deployment has the benefit of providing enough time to ensure the new model works as expected, without adversely affecting any users. The drawback is the need to run twice as many models, which consumes more resources. Furthermore, for many applications, it's impossible to evaluate the new model without exposing its predictions to the user.

8.4.3   Canary Deployment

Recall, **canary deployment**, or **canarying**, pushes the new model version and code to a small fraction of users, while keeping the old version running for most users. Contrary to the silent deployment, canary deployment allows validating the new model's performance, and its predictions' effects. Contrary to the single deployment, canary deployment doesn't affect lots of users in case of possible bugs.

By opting for the canary deployment, you accept the additional complexity of having and maintaining several versions of the model deployed simultaneously.

An obvious drawback of the canary deployment is that it's impossible for engineers to spot rare errors. If you deploy the new version to 5% of users, and a bug affects 2% of users, then you have only 0.1% chance that the bug will be discovered.

8.4.4   Multi-Armed Bandits

As seen in Section 7.3 of Chapter 7, **multi-armed bandits** (MAB) are a way to compare one or more versions of the model in the production environment, and select the best performing one. MABs have an interesting property: after an initial exploration period, during which the MAB algorithm gathers enough evidence to evaluate the performance of each model (arm), the best arm is eventually played all the time. It means that after the convergence of the MAB algorithm, most of the time, all users are routed to the software version running the best model.

The MAB algorithm, thus, solves two problems — online model evaluation and model deployment — simultaneously.

8.5   Automated Deployment, Versioning, and Metadata

The model is an important asset, but it's never delivered alone. There are additional assets for production model testing that ensure the model is not broken.

8.5.1   Model Accompanying Assets

Only deploy a model in production when it's accompanied with the following assets:

- an **end-to-end set** that defines model inputs and outputs that must always work,
- a **confidence test set** that correctly defines model inputs and outputs, and is used to compute the value of the metric,
- a **performance metric** whose value will be calculated on the confidence test set by applying the model to it, and
- the **range of acceptable values** of the performance metric.

Once the system using the model is initially evoked on an instance of a server or client's device, an external process must call the model on the end-to-end test data and validate that all predictions are correct. Furthermore, the same external process must validate that the value of the performance metric computed by applying the model to the confidence test set is within the range of acceptable values. If either of two evaluations fails, the model should not be served to the client.

8.5.2 Version Sync

The versions of the following three elements must always be in sync:

1) training data,
2) feature extractor, and
3) model.

Each update to the data must produce a new version in the data repository. The model trained using a specific version of the data must be put into the model repository with the same version number as that of the data used to train the model.

If the feature extractor was not changed, its version still must be updated to be in sync with the data and the model. If the feature extractor was updated, then a new model must be built using an updated feature extractor, and the versions are incremented for the feature extractor, the model, and the training data (even if the latter wasn't changed).

The deployment of a new model version must be automated by a script in a transactional way. Given a version of the model to deploy, the deployment script will fetch the model and the feature extraction object from the respective repositories and copy them to the production environment. The model must be applied to the end-to-end and confidence test data by simulating a regular call from the outside. If there's a prediction error for the end-to-end test data, or the value of the metric is not within the range of acceptable values, the entire deployment has to be rolled back.

8.5.3 Model Version Metadata

Each model version must be accompanied with the following code and metadata:

- the name and the version of the library or package used to train the model,
- if Python was used to build the model, then requirements.txt of the virtual environment used to build the model (or, alternatively, a Docker image name pointing to a specific path on Docker Hub or in your Docker registry),
- the name of the learning algorithm, and names and values of the hyperparameters,
- the list of features required by the model,
- the list of outputs, their types, and how the outputs should be consumed,
- the version and location of the data used to train the model,
- the version and location of the validation data used to tune model's hyperparameters,
- the model scoring code that runs the model on new data and outputs the prediction.

The metadata and the scoring code may be saved to a database or to a JSON/XML text file.

For audit purposes, the following information must also accompany each deployment:

- who built the model and when,

- who and when made the decision of deploying that model, and based on what grounds,
- who reviewed the model for privacy and security compliance purposes.

8.6   Model Deployment Best Practices

In this section, we discuss practical aspects of deploying machine learning systems in production. We also outline several useful and practical tips for model deployment.

8.6.1   Algorithmic Efficiency

Most data analysts work in Python or R. While there are web frameworks that allow building web services in those two languages, they are not considered the most efficient languages.

Indeed, when you use scientific packages in Python, much of their code was written in efficient C or C++, and then compiled for your specific operating system. However, your own data preprocessing, feature extraction, and scoring code may not be as efficient.

Furthermore, not all algorithms are practical. While some algorithms can quickly solve the problem, others are too slow. For some problems, no fast algorithms can exist.

The subfield of computer science called **analysis of algorithms** is concerned with determining and comparing the complexity of algorithms. The **big O notation** is used to classify algorithms, according to how their running time or space requirements grow, as the input size grows.

For example, let's say we have the problem of finding the two most distant one-dimensional examples in the set of examples S of size N. One Python algorithm we could craft would look like this:

```
1   def find_max_distance(S):
2       result = None
3       max_distance = 0
4       for x1 in S:
5           for x2 in S:
6               if abs(x1 - x2) >= max_distance:
7                   max_distance = abs(x1 - x2)
8                   result = (x1, x2)
9       return result
```

or, like this in R:

```
1   find_max_distance <- function(S) {
2       result <- NULL
```

```
3        max_distance <- 0
4        for (x1 in S) {
5            for (x2 in S) {
6                if (abs(x1 - x2) >= max_distance) {
7                    max_distance <- abs(x1 - x2)
8                    result <- c(x1, x2)
9                }
10           }
11       }
12       result
13   }
```

In the above algorithms, we loop over all values in S, and, at every iteration of the first loop, we loop over all values in S once again. Therefore, the above algorithm makes N^2 comparisons of numbers. If we take the time the comparison, abs, and assignment operations take as a unit time, then the time complexity (or, simply, complexity) of this algorithm is at most $5N^2$. At each iteration, we have one comparison, two abs, and two assignment operations $(1 + 2 + 2 = 5)$. When the complexity of an algorithm is measured in the worst case, the big O notation is used. For the above algorithm, using big O notation, we say that the algorithm's complexity is $O(N^2)$; the constants, like 5, are ignored.

For the same problem, we can craft another Python algorithm like this:

```
1    def find_max_distance(S):
2        result = None
3        min_x = float("inf")
4        max_x = float("-inf")
5        for x in S:
6            if x < min_x:
7                min_x = x
8            if x > max_x:
9                max_x = x
10       result = (max_x, min_x)
11       return result
```

or in R, like this:

```
10   find_max_distance <- function(S):
11       result <- NULL
12       min_x <- Inf
13       max_x <- -Inf
14       for (x in S) {
15           if (x < min_x) {
```

```
16              min_x <- x
17          }
18          if (x > max_x) {
19              max_x = x
20          }
21      result <- c(max_x, min_x)
22      result
```

In the above algorithms, we loop over all values in S only once, so the algorithm's complexity is O(N). In this case, we say that the latter algorithm is more efficient than the former.

An algorithm is called **efficient** when its complexity is polynomial in the input size. Therefore both O(N) and O(N^2) are efficient because N is a polynomial of degree 1, while N^2 is a polynomial of degree 2. However, for very large inputs, an O(N^2) algorithm can still be slow. In the big data era, scientists and engineers often look for O($\log N$) algorithms.

From a practical standpoint, when implementing an algorithm, you should avoid using loops whenever possible, and implement vectorization using NumPy or similar tools. For example, you should use operations on matrices and vectors, instead of loops. In Python, to compute $\mathbf{w} \cdot \mathbf{x}$ (a dot product of two vectors), you should type,

```
1  import numpy
2  wx = numpy.dot(w,x)
```

and not,

```
1  wx = 0
2  for i in range(N):
3      wx += w[i]*x[i]
```

Similarly, in R, you should type,

```
1  wx = w %*% x
```

and not,

```
23  wx <- 0
24  for (i in seq(N)):
25      wx <- wx + w[i]*x[i]
```

Use appropriate **data structures**. If the order of elements in a collection doesn't matter, use set instead of list. In Python, the operation of verifying whether a specific example belongs to S is fast when S is a set, and is slow when S is a list.

Another important data structure to make your Python code more efficient is dict. It is called a **dictionary** or a **hash table** in other languages. It allows you to define a collection of key-value pairs with very fast lookups for keys.

Using libraries is generally more reliable — you should only write your own code when you are a researcher, or when it's truly needed. Scientific Python packages like NumPy, SciPy, and scikit-learn were built by experienced scientists and engineers with efficiency in mind. They have many methods implemented compiled C and C++ for maximum performance.

If you need to iterate over a vast collection of elements, use Python **generators** (or their R alternative in the **iterators** package) that create a function returning one element at a time, rather than all elements at once.

Use the **cProfile** package in Python (or its R counterpart, **lineprof**) to find code inefficiencies.

Finally, when nothing can be improved in your code from the algorithmic perspective, you can further boost the speed by using:

- the **multiprocessing** package in Python, or its R counterpart **parallel**, to run computations in parallel; or use a distributed processing framework such as **Apache Spark**, and

- **PyPy**, **Numba** or similar tools to compile your Python code (or the **compiler** package for R) into fast, optimized machine code.

8.6.2 Deployment of Deep Models

Sometimes, to achieve the required speed, it might be necessary to do the **scoring** on a graphics processing unit (GPU). The cost of a GPU instance in a cloud environment is typically much higher than the cost of a "normal" instance. So only the model could be deployed in an environment with one or several GPUs optimized for fast scoring. The remainder of the application could be deployed separately in a CPU environment. This approach allows reducing the cost, but, at the same time, it might add a communication overhead between two parts of the application.

8.6.3 Caching

Caching is a standard practice in software engineering. Memory cache is used to store the result of a function call, so the next time that function is called with the same values of parameters, the result is read from the cache.

Caching helps speed up the application when it contains resource-consuming functions that take time to process, or are frequently called with the same parameter values. In machine learning, such resource-consuming functions are models, especially when they run on GPUs.

The simplest cache may be implemented in the application itself. For example, in Python, the lru_cache decorator can wrap a function with a **memoizing** callable that saves up to the maxsize most recent calls:

```
1   from functools import lru_cache
2
3   # Read the model from file
4   model = pickle.load(open("model_file.pkl", "rb"))
5
6   @lru_cache(maxsize=500)
7   def run_model(input_example):
8       return model.predict(input_example)
9
10  # Now you can call run_model
11  # on new data
```

The first time the function `run_model` is called for some input, `model.predict` will be called. For the subsequent calls of `run_model` with the same value of the input, the output will be read from cache that memorizes the result of `maxsize` most recent calls of `model.predict`.

In R, a similar result can be obtained using the `memo` function:

```
1   library(memo)
2
3   model <- readRDS("./model_file.rds")
4
5   run_model <- function(input_example) {
6       result <- predict(model, input_example)
7       result
8   }
9
10  # Create a memoized version of run_model
11  run_model_memo <- memo(run_model, cache = lru_cache(500))
12
13  # Now you can use run_model_memo
14  # instead of run_model on new data
```

Although using `lru_cache` and similar approaches is very convenient for an analyst, typically, in large scale production systems, engineers employ general purpose scalable and configurable cache solutions such as **Redis** or **Memcached**.

8.6.4 Delivery Format for Model and Code

Recall, serialization is the most straightforward way to deliver the model and the feature extractor code to the production environment.

Every modern programming language has serialization tools. In Python, it's **pickle**:

```
1   import pickle
2   from sklearn import svm, datasets
3
4   classifier = svm.SVC()
5   X, y = datasets.load_iris(return_X_y=True)
6   classifier.fit(X, y)
7
8   # Save model to file
9   with open("model.pickle","wb") as outfile:
10      pickle.dump(classifier, outfile)
11
12  # Read model from file
13  classifier2 = None
14  with open("model.pickle","rb") as infile:
15      classifier2 = pickle.load(infile)
16  if classifier2:
17      prediction = classifier2.predict(X[0:1])
```

while in R, it's RDS:

```
1   library("e1071")
2
3   classifier <- svm(Species ~ ., data = iris, kernel = 'linear')
4
5   # Save model to file
6   saveRDS(classifier, "./model.rds")
7
8   # Read model from file
9   classifier2 <- readRDS("./model.rds")
10
11  prediction <- predict(classifier2, iris[1,])
```

In scikit-learn, it may be better to use **joblib**'s replacement of pickle, which is more efficient on objects that carry large **NumPy** arrays:

```
1   from joblib import dump, load
2
3   # Save model to file
4   dump(classifier, "model.joblib")
5
6   # Read model from file
7   classifier2 = load("model.joblib")
```

The same approach can be applied to save the serialized object of the feature extractor to a file, copy it to the production environment, and then read it from the file.

For some applications, the prediction speed is critical. In such cases, the production code is written in a compiled language, such as Java or C/C++. If a data analyst has built a model using Python or R, there are three options to deploy for production:

- rewrite the code in a compiled, production-environment programming language,
- use a model representation standard such as PMML or PFA, or
- use a specialized execution engine such as MLeap.

The Predictive Model Markup Language (**PMML**) is an XML-based predictive model interchange format that provides a way for data analysts to save and share models between PMML-compliant applications. PMML allows analysts to develop models within one vendor's application, and then use them within other vendors' applications, so that proprietary issues and incompatibilities are no longer a barrier to the model exchanges between applications.

For example, imagine you use Python to build an SVM model, and then save the model as a PMML file. Let the production runtime environment be a Java Virtual Machine (JVM). As long as PMML is supported by a machine learning library for JVM, and that library has an implementation of SVM, your model can be used in production directly. You don't need to rewrite your code or retrain the model in a JVM language.

The Portable Format for Analytics (**PFA**) is a more recent standard for representing both statistical models and data transformation engines. PFA allows us to easily share models and machine learning pipelines across heterogeneous systems and provides algorithmic flexibility. Models, pre- and post-processing transformations are all functions that can be arbitrarily composed, chained, or built into complex workflows. PFA has a form of a JavaScript Object Notation (JSON) or a YAML Ain't Markup Language (YAML) configuration file.

There are open source generic "evaluators" for models or pipelines saved as PMML or PFA formatted files. **JPMML** (for Java PMML) and **Hadrian** are two of the most widely adopted. Evaluators read the model or the pipeline from a file, execute it by applying it to the input data, and output the prediction.

Unfortunately, PMML and PFA are not widely supported by the popular machine learning libraries and frameworks.[2] For example, scikit-learn doesn't support those standards, though side-projects such as **SkLearn2PMML** can convert scikit-learn objects to PMML.

Alternatively, such execution engines as **MLeap** can execute machine learning models and pipelines fast in a JVM environment. At the time of the writing of this book, MLeap could execute models and pipelines created in Apache Spark and scikit-learn.

Now, let us briefly outline several useful and practical tips for model deployment.

---

[2]As of July 2020.

8.6.5 Start With a Simple Model

Deploying and applying the model in production can be more complex than it might seem. Once the infrastructure to serve a simple model is solid, a more complex model can then be trained and deployed.

A simple interpretable model is easier to debug, especially for feature extractors and entire machine learning pipelines. Complex models and pipelines have many dependencies and large numbers of hyperparameters to tune, and are more prone to implementation and deployment errors.

8.6.6 Test on Outsiders

Before putting your model in production, test your model on outsiders, and not just on the test data. Outsiders could be other team members or company employees. Alternatively, you can use crowdsourcing or a subset of your real customers who agreed to participate in experiments with new product features.

Testing on outsiders will help you avoid personal bias, because you, as the creator of the model, are emotionally involved. It will also give your model an exposure to different users (in cases when, for example, your whole team is male or Caucasian).

8.7 Summary

A model can be deployed following several patterns: statically, as a part of installable software, dynamically on the user's device, dynamically on a server, or via model streaming.

The static deployment has many advantages, such as fast execution time, preserved user privacy, and the ability to call the model when the user is offline. There are also a drawback: it's harder to upgrade the model without also having to upgrade the entire application.

The principal advantage of the dynamic deployment on the users' devices is that the calls to the model will be fast for the user. It also reduces the charge on the organization's servers. Downsides include the difficulty to deliver updates to all users and the availability of the model for third-party analyses.

As with the static deployment, deploying the model on a user's device makes it difficult to monitor the performance of the model.

Dynamic deployment on a server can have one of the following forms: deployment on a virtual machine, deployment in a container, and serverless deployment.

The most popular deployment pattern is to deploy the model on a server and make it available as a REST API in the form of a web or a gRPC service. Here, the client sends a request to the server, and then waits for a response before sending another request.

Model streaming is different. All models are registered within a stream-processing engine or are packaged as an application based on a stream-processing library. Here, the client sends one request and receives updates as they happen.

Typical deployment strategies are single deployment, silent deployment, canary deployment, and multi-armed bandit.

In single deployment, you serialize the new model into a file, and then replace the old one.

Silent deployment consists of deploying the old and new versions, and running them in parallel. The user will not be exposed to the new version until the switch is done. The predictions made by the new version are only logged and analyzed. Thus, there is enough time to make sure that the new model works as expected without affecting any user. A drawback is the need to run more models, which consumes more resources.

Canary deployment consists of pushing the new version to a small fraction of the users, while keeping the old version running for most users. Canary deployment allows model performance validation and evaluating the users' experience. It won't affect lots of users in case of possible bugs.

Multi-armed bandits allow us to deploy the new model while keeping the old one. The algorithm replaces the old model with the new one only when it is certain that it performs better.

The deployment of a new model version must be automated by a script in a transactional way. Given a version of the model to deploy, the deployment script will fetch the model and the feature extraction object from the respective repositories and copy them to the production environment. The model must be applied to the end-to-end and confidence test data by simulating a regular call from the outside. If there's a prediction error for the end-to-end test data, or the value of the metric is not within the range of acceptable values, the entire deployment has to be rolled back.

The versions of training data, feature extractor, and model must always be in sync.

Algorithmic efficiency is an important consideration in model deployment. Experienced scientists and engineers built Python packages like NumPy, SciPy, and scikit-learn with efficiency in mind. Your own code may not be as reliable or efficient. You should only write your own code when it's absolutely necessary.

If you implement your own algorithmic code, avoid loops. Implement vectorization with NumPy or similar tools. Use appropriate data structures. If the order of elements in a collection doesn't matter, use a `set` instead of a `list`. Using dictionaries (or hash tables) allows you to define a collection of key-value pairs with very fast lookups for keys.

Caching speeds up the application when it contains resource-consuming functions frequently called with the same parameter values. In machine learning, such resource-consuming functions are models, especially when they run on GPUs.

Chapter 9

Model Serving, Monitoring, and Maintenance

In this chapter, we consider the best practices of serving, monitoring, and maintaining models in production. These are the last three stages in the machine learning project life cycle:

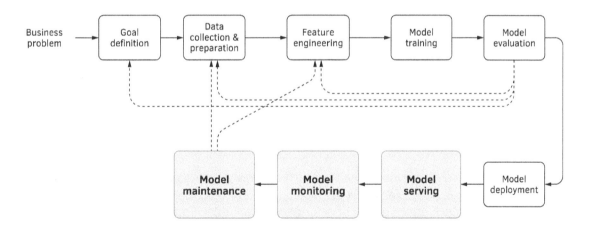

Figure 9.1: Machine learning project life cycle.

In particular, we characterize the properties of a machine learning runtime, the environment in which the input data is applied to the model, and the modes of model serving, such as batch and on demand. Furthermore, we consider three major challenges of serving a model in real world: errors, change, and human nature. We describe what should be monitored in the production environment, and when and how update the model.

9.1 Properties of the Model Serving Runtime

The model serving runtime is the environment in which the model is applied to the input data. The runtime properties are dictated by the model **deployment pattern**. However, an effective runtime will have several additional properties that we discuss here.

9.1.1 Security and Correctness

The runtime is responsible for authenticating the user's identity, and authorizing their requests.

Things to check are:

- whether a specific user has authorized access to the models they want to run,
- whether the names and the values of parameters passed correspond to the model's specification, and
- whether those parameters and their values are currently available to the user.

9.1.2 Ease of Deployment

The runtime must allow the model to be updated with minimal effort and, ideally, without affecting the entire application. If the model was deployed as a web service on a physical server, then a model update must be as simple as replacing one model file with another, and restarting the web service.

If the model was deployed as a virtual machine instance or container, then the instances or containers running the old version of the model should be replaceable by gradually stopping the running instances and starting new instances from a new image. The same principle applies to the orchestrated containers.

Typically, a model streaming-based application is updated by streaming the new version of the model. To enable this, the streaming application must be stateful. Once a new version and the related components (such as feature extractor and scoring code) are streamed into the application, the state of the application changes, and now contains the new version of these assets. Modern **stream-processing engines** support stateful applications. The described architecture is schematically shown in Figure 9.2.

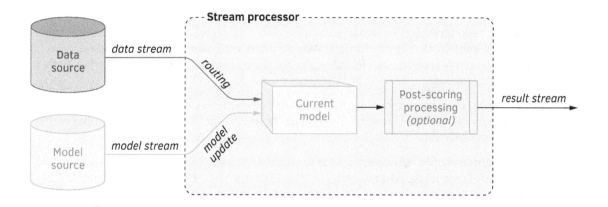

Figure 9.2: Model streaming high-level architecture.

9.1.3 Guarantees of Model Validity

An effective runtime will automatically make sure that the model it executes is valid. Furthermore, it makes sure the model, the feature extractor, and other components are in sync. It must be validated on each startup of the web service or the streaming application, and periodically during the runtime. As discussed in Section 8.5 of Chapter 8, each model should be deployed accompanied by the following four assets: an **end-to-end set**, a **confidence test set**, a **performance metric**, and its **range of acceptable values**.

The model should not be served in production (and must be immediately stopped if it is running) in either of the two conditions:

- at least one of the end-to-end test examples was not scored correctly, or
- the value of the metric, calculated on the confidence test set examples, is not within the acceptable range.

9.1.4 Ease of Recovery

An effective runtime allows easy recovery from errors by rolling back to previous versions.

The recovery from an unsuccessful deployment should be produced in the same way, and with the same ease, as the deployment of an updated model. The only difference is that, instead of the new model, the previous working version will be deployed.

9.1.5   Avoidance of Training/Serving Skew

It is strongly recommended to avoid using two different codebases, one for training the model, and one for scoring in production. When it concerns **feature extraction**, even a tiny difference between two versions of feature extractor code may lead to suboptimal or incorrect model performance.

The engineering team may reimplement the feature extractor code for production for many reasons. The most common is that the data analyst's code is inefficient or incompatible with the production ecosystem.

Thus, the runtime should allow easy access to the feature extraction code for various needs, including model retraining, ad-hoc model calls, and production. One way to implement it is by wrapping the feature extraction object into a separate web service.

If you cannot avoid using two different codebases to generate features for training and production, then the runtime should allow for the logging of feature values generated in the production environment. Those values should then be used as training values.

9.1.6   Avoidance of Hidden Feedback Loops

In Section 4.12 of Chapter 4, we saw one example of a **hidden feedback loop**. Model m_B used the output of model m_A as a feature, without knowing that model m_A also used the output of model m_B as its feature.

Another kind of hidden feedback loop only involves one model. Let's say we have a model that classifies incoming email messages as spam or not spam. Let the user interface allow the user to mark messages as spam or not spam. Obviously, we want to use those marked messages to improve our model. However, by so doing, we risk creating a hidden feedback loop, and here is why.

In our application, the user will only mark a message as spam when they see it. However, users only see the messages that our model classified as not spam. Also, it is unlikely that the user will regularly go to the spam folder and mark some messages as not spam. So, the action of the user is significantly affected by our model, which makes the data we get from the user skewed: we influence the phenomenon from which we learn.

To avoid the skew, mark a small percentage of examples as "held-out," and show all of them to the user without pre-applying the model. Then use only these held-out examples as additional training examples, including those to which the user didn't react.

In a more general scenario, one model can indirectly affect the data used to train another model. Let one model decide the order of books to display, while the other decides which reviews to display near each book. If the first model puts a review of a certain book at the bottom of the list, the absence of a user's response to the second model's review may be caused by its low position on the page, and not by the quality of the review.

9.2 Modes of Model Serving

Machine learning models are served in either batch or on-demand mode. On-demand, a model can be served to either a human client or a machine.

9.2.1 Serving in Batch Mode

A model is usually served in batch mode when it is applied to large quantities of input data. One example could be when the model is used to exhaustively process the data of all users of a product or service. Or, when it systematically applies to all incoming events, such as tweets, or comments to online publications. Batch mode is more resource-efficient compared to an on-demand mode, and is employed when some latency can be tolerated.

When served in batch mode, the model usually accepts between a hundred and a thousand feature vectors at once. Experiment to find the optimal batch size for speed. Typical sizes are powers of two: 32, 64, 128, etc.

The outputs for the batch are usually saved to the database, as opposed to sending them to specific consumers. You would use the batch mode to:

- generate the list of weekly recommendations of new songs to all users of a music streaming service,
- classify the flow of incoming comments to online news articles and blog posts as spam or not spam,
- extract named entities from documents indexed by a search engine, and so on.

9.2.2 Serving on Demand to a Human

The six steps of serving the model **on demand** to a human are as follows:

1) validate the request,
2) gather the context,
3) transform the context into model input,
4) apply the model to the input, and get the output,
5) make sure that the output makes sense,
6) present the output to the user.

Before running a model in production for a request coming from a user, it might be necessary to verify whether that user has the correct permissions for this model.

The **context** represents the user's situation when they send a request to the machine learning system, and in which the user will receive the system's response.

The user can send the request to the machine learning system explicitly or implicitly. An example of an explicit request is when a music-streaming service's user requests recommendations for similar songs to a given song. On the other hand, an implicit request is sent by a direct messenger application for suggested replies to the most recent message received by the user.

A good context may be collected in real or near-real time. It will contain the information needed by the feature extractor to generate all the feature values the model expects. It also contains enough information for debugging, is compact enough to be saved in a log, and contains information that will be used to improve the model over time.

Let's see examples of a good context for several problems.

Device malfunctioning
When detecting device malfunction, a good context contains vibration and noise levels, the task executed by the device, the user ID, the firmware version, the time passed since manufacturing and the last maintenance, and the number of uses since manufacturing and the last maintenance.

Emergency room hospitalization
To decide whether the new patient should be admitted to an intensive care unit, a good context would include age, blood pressure, temperature, heart rate, pulse oximetry level, complete blood count, chemistry profile, arterial blood gas test, blood alcohol level, medical history, and pregnancy.

Credit risk assessment
To make an approval/rejection decision for a credit card application, a good context would include age, education, employment status, country residency status, annual salary, family status, outstanding debts, availability of other credit cards, whether the person is a homeowner or tenant, whether the person has declared bankruptcy, and whether, and how many times, the person missed past credit payments. Even if certain information is not needed for feature extraction, it is still pertinent for logging and debugging: client's ID, date, and time of the day.

Advertisement display
To decide whether a specific advertisement should be displayed to a website user, a good context would include the webpage title, the user's position on the web page, the screen resolution, the text on the webpage and the text visible to the user, how the user reached the webpage, and the time spent on it. For logging and debugging purposes, the context might include the browser version, operating system version, connection information, and date and time.

A **feature extractor** transforms the context into the model input. Sometimes, the feature extractor is a part of the machine learning **pipeline**, as we discussed in Section 5.4 of Chapter 5. However, it's common to build the feature extractor as a separate object.

When the result of the scoring is to be served to a human client, it's rarely presented directly. Usually, the scoring code transforms the model's prediction into a form more easily interpreted, and that adds value to the client.

Before serving the model to a human, it's common to measure the prediction confidence score. If the confidence is low, you can decide to not present anything: users tend to complain less about the errors they don't see. Or, if the user expects an output, inform them about the low confidence. Then prompt, "Are you sure?"

Prompting is especially important when the system might initiate an action based on the prediction. If you are able to estimate the error's possible cost and if the prediction confidence is bounded by $(0, 1)$, then multiply $(1 -$ confidence$)$ by the cost to see the possible impact of making a wrong action. For example, let the cost of making an error is estimated as 1000 dollars and the model outputs the confidence score equal to 0.95, then the **expected error cost** value is $(1 - 0.95) \times 1000 = 50$ dollars. You might put a threshold on the expected cost value for different actions recommended by the model, and prompt the user if the expected cost is above the threshold.

In addition to measuring the model's confidence, calculate whether the value of the prediction makes sense. In Section 9.3, we will further detail what to check, and what the system's reaction should be, if the output doesn't make sense.

It is convenient to log the context in which the model was served, as well as the reaction of the user. This can help both to debug eventual problems, and improve the model by creating new training examples.

9.2.3 Serving on Demand to a Machine

While building a REST API is appropriate for many cases, we often serve a machine by streaming. Indeed, a machine's data requirements are usually standard and pre-determined. A well-designed, fixed topology of a streaming application allows an efficient use of available resources.

Serving on demand, to either machine or human, can be tricky. The demand may vary, from very high during the day, to very low during the night. If you use virtual resources in the cloud, **autoscaling** can help with adding more resources when needed, and then freeing them when demand decreases. However, autoscaling is not nimble enough to cope with accidental spikes.

To deal with such situations, on-demand architectures include a **message broker**, such as **RabbitMQ** or **Apache Kafka**. A message broker allows one process to write messages in a queue, and another to read from that queue. On-demand requests are placed in the input queue. The model runtime process periodically connects to the broker. It reads a batch of input data elements from the input queue and generates predictions for each element in batch mode. It then writes the predictions to the output queue. Another process periodically connects to the broker, reads the predictions from the output queue, and pushes them to

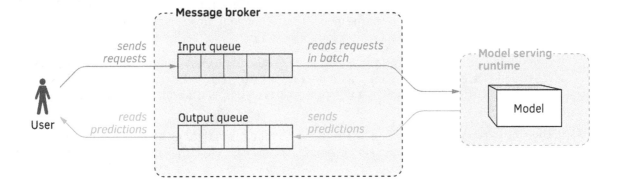

Figure 9.3: On-demand model serving with a message broker.

users who sent the requests (Figure 9.3). In addition to allowing us to cope with demand spikes, such an approach is more resource-efficient.

9.3   Model Serving in Real World

When real people interact with a software system in the real world, serving the model gets complicated. It's usually impossible to predict all user actions and reactions. The architecture of a software system intended for the real world must be ready for three phenomena: errors, change, and human nature.

9.3.1   Being Ready for Errors

Errors are inevitable in any software. In machine-learning-based software, errors are an integral part of the solution: no model is perfect. Because we cannot fix all errors, the only option is to embrace them.

Embracing errors means designing the software system in such a way that when an error happens, the system continues operating normally.

There are three "cannots" we must accept and embrace:

1. We cannot always explain why an error happened.
2. We cannot reliably predict when it will happen, and even a high confidence prediction can be false.
3. We cannot always know how to fix a specific error. If it's fixable, what kind and how much training data is needed?

Furthermore, when an error happens, we cannot always expect that the incorrect prediction will at least be close or similar to the correct prediction. An error can be arbitrarily "crazy." For example, a model for a self-driving car, at the speed of 120 km/h (~74 mph) with no obstacles, may predict that the best action is to stop and drive backward.

Tiny changes in the context may result in unexpected error patterns. For example, the model that recognizes dangerous situations on the factory floor may start making errors after the lightbulb near the camera is replaced. The previous lightbulb was incandescent, and the new one is fluorescent.

Even rare errors may impact users, if the number of users is large. Let the model have a 99% accuracy. If you have a million users, one percent of prediction errors will affect thousands.

It's rare that fixing one error in a model results in new errors. However, there's no guarantee.

How to design a system in the presence of inevitable errors?

9.3.2   Dealing With Errors

First of all, have a strategy that mitigates, at least, partially, a situation in which your system looks or acts "stupid." For example, if your system talks to the user, like a personal assistant or a chatbot, it's better to say, "I don't know," than to say something random. If the error will be directly visible to the user, calculate the **expected cost of the error**, as discussed above, and do not display the prediction to the user if the cost is above a threshold.

Alternatively, train a second model m_B that predicts, for an input, that the first model m_A is likely to make an error on that input. The presence of a "safeguard" model m_B is especially relevant if model m_A is used in a mission critical system.

The error's visibility is an important factor in deciding whether and how to hide it. For example, consider a system that downloads web pages from the internet and extracts some entities from them. Let the user be interested in being alerted when a kind of entity is detected. The model can make two kinds of errors: 1) extract an entity even if the document doesn't contain it (false positive, FP), and 2) not extract an entity that is present in the document (false negative, FN). When the former error happens, the user receives an irrelevant alert and gets frustrated. If the latter, the user doesn't receive any alert, remains unaware of the error, and avoids frustration. In this situation, you might prefer to optimize the model for **precision**, by keeping **recall** reasonably high.

When you train a model, decide which kind of errors you would most like to avoid, and then optimize your hyperparameters, including the prediction threshold, accordingly.

When your confidence for the best prediction is low, consider presenting several options. This is why Google presents 10 search results at once. There are much higher chances for the most relevant link to be among those 10 search results, than for it to be in the first position.

Another way to avoid user's frustration with model errors is to dose the user's exposure to the model. Measure the number of errors your model makes, and estimate how many errors per minute (day, week, or month) a user is ready to tolerate. Then limit the interactions the user will have with the model to keep the number of perceived errors below that level.

For situations when an error happened and might have been perceived, add a possibility for the user to report the error. Once the report is received, log the context in which the model was used, as well as the prediction of the model. Explain to the user what actions will be taken to prevent a similar error from happening in the future.

It's appropriate to measure the user's engagement with the system, log all interactions, and then analyze suspicious interactions offline. This includes:

- whether the user interacts with the system less than before,
- whether the user ignored certain recommendations, and
- whether the user spent adequate time in various settings.

To reduce an error's negative impact even further, if the system allows it, give the user an option to undo an action recommended by the system. Extend this, if possible, to any automated action executed by the system on the user's behalf.

Software applications that act on their user's behalf must be especially limited in their possible actions. Recall that machine-learning models' errors can be arbitrarily "crazy" like in the example of a self-driving car that can suddenly decide to drive backward. Caution must be exercised in other critical scenarios involving health, safety, or money, such as bidding in auctions or prescribing medication. If the model predicts to buy or sell more stocks than the moving average plus one standard deviations, it's a good idea to send an alert and put an otherwise "automatic" action on hold. The same logic should apply if the model predicts to serve an unreasonably high dose of a drug to a patient, or change the speed of the car to a value substantially above or below usual.

If your system can automatically reject the model prediction, it's best to implement some fallback strategy, in addition to informing the user about a failure (Figure 9.4). A less sophisticated model or a handcrafted heuristic may be used as a fallback. Of course, the output of the fallback strategy should also be validated, and also rejected if it seems unreasonable. In this case, an error message should be sent to the user.

9.3.3   Being Ready for, and Dealing With, Change

The performance of a system based on machine learning usually changes over time. In some applications, it can change in near-real-time.

There are two types of model change:

1. Its quality could become better or worse.
2. The predictions for some inputs can become different.

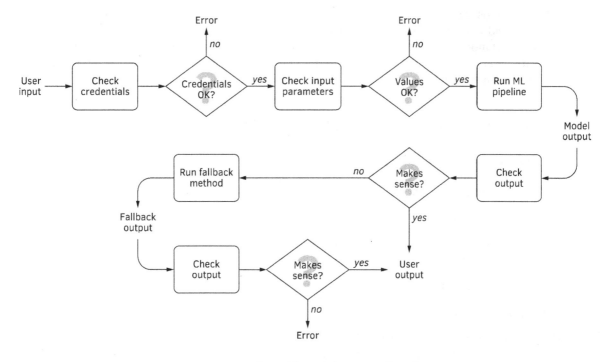

Figure 9.4: Real-world model serving flowchart.

A typical reason for the model performance degradation over time is **concept drift** that we already considered in Section 3.2.6 of Chapter 3. The notion of what is a correct prediction may change because of the users' preferences and interests. This would require retraining the model, using more recently labeled data.

Some change can be perceived by the user as positive. Sometimes, the change can be negatively perceived, even if the system's performance improved, from the engineering point of view. You might have added training examples, retrained the model and observed a better performance metric value. However, by adding new data, you involuntarily induced a data imbalance. Some classes are now underrepresented. Users interested in those classes' predictions see decreased performance, and complain or even abandon your system.

Users become accustomed to certain behaviors. They might know what query to submit to the search engine to get an often-used document or a web application. That query was not necessarily the most optimal for the purpose, but it worked. Suppose you improved the relevancy of your search-result ranking algorithm. Now that query doesn't return that specific document or application, or it puts it on the second page of the search results. The user can no longer find the resource they once found easily, and get frustrated.

If you expect that the user might negatively perceive the change, give them time to adapt.

Educate the user about the changes and what to expect from the new model. Or, it can be done by gradually introducing the changes. You might mix the predictions of the old model and the new model, and slowly decrease the proportion for the old model. Alternatively, you can run both the new and the old model in parallel, and let the user switch to the old model for some time before sunsetting it.

9.3.4   Being Ready for, and Dealing With, Human Nature

Human nature is what makes effective system engineering such a hard endeavor. Humans are unpredictable, often irrational, inconsistent, and have unclear expectations. A solid software system must anticipate that.

Avoid Confusion

The system must be designed in such a way that the user doesn't feel confused interacting with it. A model's output must be served in an intuitive way, without assuming that the user knows anything about machine learning and AI. In fact, many users will assume that they work with typical software and will be surprised to see errors.

Manage Expectations

On the other hand, some users will have too high expectations. The main reason for that is advertisement. To attract attention, a product or a system based on machine learning is often displayed in advertisements as being "intelligent." For example, personal assistants such as Apple Siri, Google Home, and Amazon Alexa are often shown in advertisements as having human intelligence. Indeed, any machine-learning-based system might look very intelligent when inputs are carefully selected. Users can look at such advertisements and extrapolate what they see to situations in which the system isn't designed to operate effectively.

Another common reason users expect something spectacular (even without being promised) is that they worked with a similar (in their understanding) system that looked "very intelligent" to them. Such users would expect the same level of "intelligence" from your system.

Gain Trust

Some users, especially experienced ones, will mistrust any system if they know it contains some "intelligence." The main reason for that mistrust is past experience. Most so-called intelligent systems fail to deliver, and, because of that, some users expect failure when they first encounter your system.

As a consequence, your system must gain each user's confidence, and this must be done early.

A user experienced with "intelligent" systems will most likely make several simple tests of your system's abilities. If your system fails, the user will not trust it. For example, if your system is a search engine, then a user would query their name or a document they authored to test your system. Or, if your system provides intelligence on organizations to corporate customers, a user will check how much your system knows about their organization, and whether the intelligence makes sense. A driver of a self-driving car will most likely test commands like "start the engine," "follow that car," "keep the current speed," or "park on that street." Depending on the nature of the service, you should anticipate such simple tests and make sure that your system passes them.

Manage User Fatigue

User fatigue can be another reason why you see decreasing interest in your system. Make sure that the system doesn't excessively interrupt user experience with recommendations or requests for approval. Avoid showing everything you have to show in one shot. Whenever possible, let the user explicitly express their interest.

Furthermore, not all actions that the system can handle automatically have to be handled this way. For example, if the system automates user's interactions with other people, it might send private or restricted data as an email reply, or post it to an open forum. Before sharing on a user's behalf, it makes sense to evaluate the information's sensitivity. Use a model trained to detect such potentially sensitive texts and images. On the other extreme, a system can be too conservative and automatically filter out relevant information or ask the user to confirm too many decisions which might result in user fatigue.

Beware of the Creep Factor

When users interact with a learning system, there's a phenomenon known as **creep factor**. It means that the user perceives the model's predictive capacity as too high. The user feels uncomfortable, especially when a prediction concerns their very private details. Make sure that the system doesn't feel like "Big Brother" and doesn't take too much responsibility.

9.4   Model Monitoring

A deployed model must be constantly monitored. Monitoring helps make sure that,

- the model is served correctly, and
- the performance of the model remains within acceptable limits.

9.4.1   What Can Go Wrong?

Monitoring should be designed to provide early warnings about issues with the model in production. More specifically, this includes:

- new training data used to update the model made it perform worse;
- the live data in production changed, but the model didn't;
- the feature extraction code was significantly updated, but the model didn't adapt;
- a resource needed to generate a feature changed or became unavailable;
- the model is being abused or under an adversarial attack.

Additional training data is not always good. A **labeler** may have incorrectly interpreted the labeling instructions. Or, one labeler's decisions might be in contradiction with another labeler. Data automatically gathered to improve the model may be biased. Reasons for that could be, for example, a **hidden feedback loop** considered in Section 9.1.6 or a **systematic value distortion** discussed in Section 3.2 of Chapter 3.

Sometimes, the properties of the data in production gradually change, but the model doesn't adapt. It remains based on older data, which is no longer representative. One reason for this is **concept drift** that we discussed in Section 9.3.

A software engineer could fix a bug in the feature extraction code, and update the feature extractor in production. But if the engineer fails to also update the production model, the performance may change in an unpredictable manner.

Even if the feature extraction and the model are in sync, a disappearance or a change of some resource (database connection, database table, or external API) may affect some of the features generated by that feature extractor.

Some models, especially those deployed in e-commerce and media platforms, often become targets of adversarial attacks. Bad actors, such as unfair competitors, fraudsters, criminals, and foreign governments, may actively seek out weaknesses in a model and adjust their attacks accordingly. If your machine learning system learns from the user's actions, then some may act to change the model behavior in their favor.

Furthermore, attackers may want to examine the trained model in order to obtain information about the model's training data. That training data might contain confidential information about people and organizations.

Another form of abuse, which may be the hardest to prevent, is model **dual use**. As any software, a machine learning model can be used for good (as you intended) or for bad (often without your consent). For example, you might create and publicly release a model that makes one's voice sound like a cartoon character. Fraudsters may adapt your result to fake the voice of a bank client, and execute a phone transaction on their behalf. Alternatively, you might create a model that recognizes pedestrians on the street. An automatic weapon manufacturer could use your model to detect people on the battlefield.

9.4.2   What and How to Monitor

Monitoring must allow us to make sure that the model generates reasonable performance metrics when applied to the **confidence test set**. This set should be regularly updated with new data to avoid possible **distribution shift**. Additionally, the model must be regularly tested on the examples from the **end-to-end set**.

While it's obvious that accuracy, precision, and recall are good candidates for monitoring, one metric is especially useful for measuring the change over time: **prediction bias**.

In a static world where nothing changes, the distribution of predicted classes would roughly equal the distribution of observed classes. This is especially true when the model is **well-calibrated**. If you observe otherwise, the model is exhibiting prediction bias. The latter might mean that the distribution of the training data labels and the production's current class distribution are now different. You must investigate the reasons for this change and make the necessary adjustments.

Monitoring allows us to stay alert of abandoned or repurposed data sources. Some database columns might stop being populated. The definition or format of the data in some columns might change, while the unadapted models still assume the previous definitions and formats. To avoid that, the distribution of the values of every feature extracted from a database table must be monitored for a significant shift. A shift of the distribution of both feature values and predictions can be detected by applying statistical tests such as the **Chi-square independence test** and **Kolmogorov–Smirnov test**. If a significant distribution shift is detected, an alert must be sent to the stakeholders.

The **numerical stability** of the model should also be monitored. An alert should be triggered if NaNs (not-a-numbers) or an infinity is observed.

It's important to monitor computational performance of a machine learning system. Both dramatic and slow-leak regression should be detected, and warnings must be sent.

Monitor and send alerts when the usage fluctuations look suspicious. In particular:

- monitor the number of model servings during an hour, and compare it to the corresponding value calculated one day earlier. Send a warning alert to the stakeholders if the number has changed by 30% or more. This threshold must be tuned for your use case to avoid generating excessive warnings;
- monitor the daily number of model servings and compare it to the corresponding value calculated one week earlier. Send a warning alert to the stakeholders if the number has changed by 15% or more. Tune the value for your use case.

Monitoring these numbers helps detect undesirable change:

- minimal and maximal prediction values,
- median, mean, and standard deviation prediction values over a given timeframe,
- latency when calling the model API, and
- memory consumption and CPU usage when performing predictions.

Additionally, to prevent distribution shift, the monitoring automation must:

1) accumulate inputs by randomly putting some aside during a certain time period,
2) send those inputs for labeling,
3) run the model, and calculate the value of the performance metric,
4) alert the stakeholders if there is significant performance degradation.

Recommender systems need additional monitoring. These models offer recommendations to website or application users. It can be useful to monitor click-though rate (CTR), that is, ratio of users who clicked on a recommendation to the number of total users who received recommendations from that model. If CTR is decreasing, the model must be updated.

It's important to note that there is a tricky tradeoff between being too conservative versus frequently alerting stakeholders about small changes in the metrics. If you alert too often, people might become tired of receiving alerts and eventually will start ignoring them. In non-mission-critical cases, it can be appropriate to allow the stakeholders to define their own thresholds that trigger alerts.

Log monitoring events so the entire process is traceable. For visual model performance analysis, the monitoring tool's user interface should provide trend charts showing how the model degradation evolves over time.

One of the monitoring tool's properties should be the ability to compute and visualize metrics on slices of data. A slice is a subset of the data that includes only such examples in which a specific attribute has a certain value. For example, one slice could contain only the examples where the state attribute is Florida; another slice might contain only the data for women, and so on. The degradation of the model might only be observed in some slices, yet remain insignificant in others.

Besides real-time monitoring, it's important to also log data that:

- might help find a problem's source,
- is impossible to analyze in real-time, or
- is helpful for improving existing models or training new ones.

9.4.3 What to Log

It is important to log enough information to reproduce any erratic system behavior during a future analysis. If the model is served to a front-end user, such as a website visitor or a mobile application user, it's worth saving the user's **context** at the moment of the model serving. As discussed in Section 9.2, the context might include: the content of the webpage (or the state of the application), the user's position on the web page, time of the day, where the user came from, and what they clicked before the model prediction was served.

Additionally, it is useful to include the model input, that is, the features extracted from the context, and the time it took to generate those features.

The log could also include:

- the model's output, and time it took to generate it,
- the new context of the user, once they observed the model's output,
- the user's reaction to the output.

The user's reaction is the immediate action that followed the observation of the model output: what was clicked, and how much time after the output was served.

In large systems with thousands of users, where the model is served to each user hundreds of times a day, it can be prohibitive to log every event. It would be more practical to do **stratified sampling**. You first decide which groups of events you want to log, and then you log only a certain percentage of events in each group. The groups can be groups of users or groups of contexts. Users can be grouped by age, gender, or seniority with the service (new clients vs. long-time clients). The groups of contexts could be early-morning, business-day, and late-night interactions.

When you store users' activity data in logs, the users should know what, when, and how it is stored, and for how long. If possible, data should be anonymized or aggregated without loss of utility. Access to sensitive data must be restricted only to those assigned to solve a specific problem during a specific time period. Avoid letting any analyst access sensitive data to solve unrelated business problems. It could lead to legal problems.

Make sure users may opt-out from logging and analysis of their activity data. Different data retention policies will apply to different countries. Each country imposes its own restrictions on what can and cannot be stored about their citizens, or used for analysis.

9.4.4 Monitor for Abuse

Some people or organizations may use your model for their own business. Such users might send millions of daily requests, while a typical user would only send a dozen. Alternatively, some users might want to reverse-engineer the training data, or learn how to make the model produce a desired output.

Ways to prevent such abuse include,

- making users pay per request,
- creating progressively longer pauses before responding to requests, or even
- blocking some users.

To reach their own business goals, some attackers might try to manipulate your model. An attacker might submit data that changes the model in a way that only benefits the attacker. As a result, the overall quality of the model might degrade.

Ways to prevent such abuse include,

- not trusting the data from a user unless similar data comes from multiple users,
- assigning a reputation score to each user, and not trusting the data obtained from users with low reputations, and
- classifying user behavior as either normal or abnormal, and not accepting the data coming from users demonstrating abnormal behavior.

The attackers will try to bypass your defence by adapting their behavior. To effectively defend your system, update your models regularly. Add both new data and new features that detect fraudulent transactions.

9.5 Model Maintenance

Most production models must be regularly updated. The rate depends on several factors:

- how often it makes errors and how critical they are,
- how "fresh" the model should be, so as to be useful,
- how fast new training data becomes available,
- how much time it takes to retrain a model,
- how costly it is to deploy the model, and
- how much a model update contributes to the product and the achievement of user goals.

In this section, we talk about model maintenance: when and how to update the model after it's deployed in production.

9.5.1 When to Update

When a model is deployed in production for the first time, it's often far from perfect. Inevitably, the model makes prediction errors. Some of them could be critical, so the model needs an update. Over time, a model could become more solid, and require fewer updates. However, some models should be constantly updated, so to speak, always be "fresh."

Model freshness depends on the business needs and the needs of the user. The recommender model on an e-commerce website must be updated after each purchase. If the user utilizes a model to get recommended content on a news website, the model might need to be updated weekly. On the other hand, a voice recognition/synthesis or a machine translation model could be updated less frequently.

The speed of availability of new training data also affects the rate of model updates. Even if new data comes in fast, such as the stream of comments on a popular website, it may take time and require significant investment to get labeled data. Sometimes, labeling is automated but delayed, as in **churn prediction**, where the user's decision to stay with or leave the service happens far in the future.

Some models take significant time to build, especially if the **hyperparameter search** is needed. It's not uncommon to wait for days or even weeks to get a new version of the model. Use parallelizable machine learning algorithms and graphical processing units (GPU) to speed up the training. Modern libraries, such as **thundersvm** and **cuML**, allow the analyst to run shallow learning algorithms on GPUs, with a significant gain in training time. If you cannot afford to wait for days or weeks to get an updated model, using a less complex (and, therefore, less accurate) model might be your only choice.

You might decide to update the model less often if an update is costly. For example, in healthcare, getting labeled examples is complicated and expensive, due to regulations, privacy concerns, and expensive medical experts.

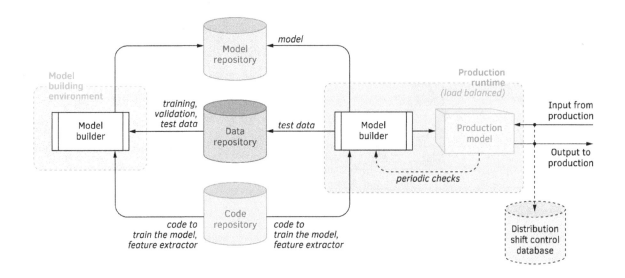

Figure 9.5: A machine learning deployment and maintenance automation architecture.

Not all models are worth deploying. Sometimes the potential performance gain is not worth the user's possible frustration. However, if the user disturbance is manageable, and the deployment is not costly, even a small improvement may result in a significant business outcome in the long run.

9.5.2 How to Update

As discussed, your software ideally allows the new model version to be deployed without stopping the entire system. In virtual or containerized infrastructure, this can be done by replacing the image of a virtual machine (VM) or a container in the repository, gradually closing VMs/containers, and letting the autoscaler instantiate a VM/container from an updated image.

An architecture of machine learning deployment and maintenance automation is schematically shown in Figure 9.5. Here, we have three repositories: data, code, and model; all three repositories are versioned. We also have two runtimes: model training and production. The model runs in the production runtime, which is load-balanced and auto-scaled. When an update of the model is needed, the model training runtime pulls the training data, as well as the model training code, from the data and code repositories, respectively. It then trains the new model and saves it in the model repository.

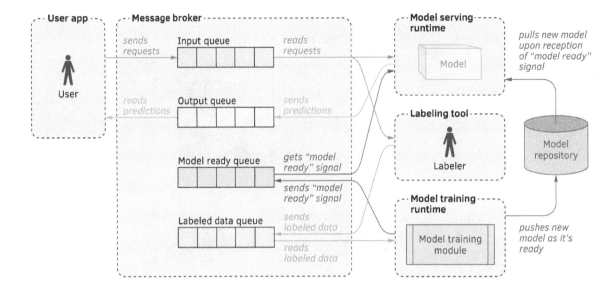

Figure 9.6: On-demand model serving and update with a message broker.

Once a new version of the model is placed in the repository, the production runtime pulls,

- the new model, from the model repository;
- the test data, from the data repository; and,
- the code that applies the model to the test data, from the code repository.

If the new model passes the test, the old model is withdrawn from production. It is replaced with the new one with the appropriate deployment strategy, as discussed in Section 8.4. **A/B testing** or a **multi-armed bandit** algorithm can help make the replacement decision.

The **distribution shift** control database accumulates the inputs received by the model, as well as their scoring results. Once a sufficient number of examples is accumulated, that data is sent for validation to a human[1] with the goal of detecting distribution shift.

In the **model streaming** scenario, the model update happens when the stream processor's state is updated (see Section 9.1.2 and Figure 9.2).

Model update in **on-demand model serving** with a **message broker** architecture is similar to that of model streaming (see Section 9.2.3 and Figure 9.3).

Figure 9.6 illustrates a message-broker-based architecture that allows not just serving the model and updating it, but also contains a human **labeler** in the loop. The labeler receives

---

[1]Or to an automated tool, more accurate than the model, that cannot be deployed in production (e.g., too fragile, costly, or slow).

unlabeled examples, samples some of them, assigns labels to sampled examples, and sends the annotated examples back to the message broker. The model training module reads the labeled examples from a queue. When their quantity is sufficient to significantly update the model, it trains a new model, saves it in the model repository, and sends the "model ready" message to the broker. A model-serving process pulls the new model version from the repository, and discards the current model.

Let's outline a few additional considerations for successful model maintenance.

Many companies use a continuous integration workflow in which the models are trained automatically as soon as new training data becomes available. It is recommended to retrain the model from scratch, by using the entire training data, instead of fine-tuning an existing model on the new examples only.

For each training example, it's recommended to store the labeler's identity. Furthermore, attach the model version used to generate a specific value in the production database, to that value. Should a problem with the version model be discovered, knowing which database values it generated will allow reprocessing of those specific values only.

If a model is frequently re-trained, it is convenient to store pipeline's hyperparameters in a configuration system. Google recommends[2] the following for a good configuration system:

1. It should be easy to specify a configuration as a change from a previous configuration.
2. It should be hard to make manual errors, omissions, or oversights.
3. It should be easy to see, visually, the difference in configuration between two models.
4. It should be easy to automatically assert and verify basic facts about a configuration: number of features used, data dependencies, etc.
5. It should be possible to detect unused or redundant settings.
6. Configurations should undergo a full code review and be checked into a repository.

Make sure that the runtime environment has enough hard drive space and RAM for the updated model. Do not expect that the old version of the model and the new one will only differ in performance. Be ready for the situation where the new model is much larger than the previous one. Similarly, do not expect that the new model will run as fast as the previous one. Inefficiency in the feature extraction code, an additional stage in the pipeline, or a different choice of the algorithm may significantly affect the prediction speed.

Models will inevitably make prediction errors. However, to the business or client, some errors are more costly than others. Once a new model version is deployed, validate it doesn't make significantly more costly errors than the previous model.

Check that the errors are distributed uniformly across the user categories. It's undesirable if the new model negatively affects more users from a minority or specific location.

---

[2]"Hidden Technical Debt in Machine Learning Systems" by Sculley et al. (2015).

If any of the above validations fail, it is not recommended to deploy the new model. Roll it back if the failure is detected after deployment and initiate an investigation. As discussed in Section 9.1, rolling back to the previous model must be as easy as deploying the new model.

Beware of **model cascading**. As discussed in Section 6.7.6 of Chapter 6, if the one model's outputs become inputs for another model, changing one model will affect the performance the other. If your system is using model cascading, be sure to update all models in the cascade.

9.6   Summary

An effective runtime has the following properties. It is secure and correct, ensures ease of deployment and recovery, and provides guarantees of model validity. Furthermore, it avoids training/serving skew and hidden feedback loops.

Machine learning models are served in either batch or on-demand mode. In on-demand mode, a model can be served to either a human client or a machine. A model is usually served in batch mode when it will be applied to big data and some latency is tolerable.

When served on-demand to a human, a model is usually wrapped into a REST API. A machine's data requirements are usually standard and pre-determined, so we often serve it by streaming.

The architecture of a software system intended for the real world must be ready for three phenomena: errors, change, and human nature.

The model deployed in production must be constantly monitored. The goals of monitoring are to make sure that the model is served correctly, and that the performance of the model remains within acceptable limits.

A variety of things might go wrong with the model in production, in particular:

- additional training data made the model perform worse;
- the properties of the production data changed, but the model didn't;
- the feature extraction code was significantly updated, but the model didn't adapt;
- a resource needed to generate a feature changed or became unavailable;
- the model is abused or is under an adversarial attack.

An automation must calculate values of the performance metrics critical for the business, and send alerts to the appropriate stakeholders if the values of those metrics change significantly or fall below a threshold. In addition, the monitoring must reveal the distribution shift, numerical instability, and a decreasing computational performance.

It is important to log enough information to reproduce any erratic system behavior during an analysis in the future. If the model is served to a front-end user, it's important to log the user's context at the moment of the model serving. Additionally, it is useful to include the model input, that is, the features extracted from the context, and the time it took to generate those features. The log could also include the outputs obtained from the model, and time it took to generate it, the new context of the user once they observed the output of the model, and the reaction of the user to the output.

Some users can utilize your model as a basis for their own business. They might reverse-engineer the training data, or learn how to "trick" your model. To prevent abuse:

- don't trust the data from a user unless similar data comes from multiple users,
- assign a reputation score to each user and don't trust the data obtained from users with low reputations,
- classify user behavior as normal or abnormal,
- make users pay per request,
- make progressively longer pauses, and
- block some users.

Most machine learning models must be regularly or occasionally updated. The rate of updates depends on several factors:

- how often it makes errors and how critical they are,
- how "fresh" the model should be to be useful,
- how fast new training data becomes available,
- how much time it takes to retrain a model,
- how costly it is to train and deploy the model, and
- how much a model update contributes to the achievement of user goals.

After a model update, a good practice is to run the model against the examples in the end-to-end and confidence test sets. It's important to make sure that the outputs are either the same as before, or that the changes are as expected. It's also important to validate that the new model doesn't make significantly more costly errors than the previous model.

Check also that the errors are distributed uniformly across the user categories. It's undesirable if the new model negatively affects users from a minority or specific location.

Chapter 10

Conclusion

In 2020, machine learning has become a mature and popular tool for solving business problems. What previously was available only to a handful of organizations, and considered "magic" by others, can today be created and used by a typical organization.

Thanks to open-source code, crowdsourcing, easily accessible books, online courses, and publicly available datasets, many scientists, engineers, and even home enthusiasts may now train machine learning models. If you are lucky, your problem can be solved by writing several lines of code, as demonstrated in many online tutorials.

However, many things can go wrong in a machine learning project. Most are independent of the technology's maturity or the analyst's understanding of the machine learning algorithm.

Machine learning texts, online tutorials, and courses are devoted to explaining how machine learning algorithms work and how to apply them to a dataset. Your success will probably depend on other factors. What data you can get and whether you can get enough of it, how you prepare it for learning, what features you engineer, whether your solution is scalable, maintainable, cannot be manipulated by attackers, and doesn't make costly errors — these factors are much more important for an applied machine learning project.

Yet despite their magnitude, most modern machine learning books and courses often leave these aspects for self-study. Some provide only partial coverage, with just an application to solving a specific illustrative problem.

It's a significant gap in knowledge, and I tried to fill it with this book.

10.1 Takeaways

What do I hope the reader takes away after reading this book?

First of all, a strong understanding that all machine learning projects are unique. There's no single recipe that will always work. Most of the time, the greatest challenges must be solved before you type `from sklearn.linear_model import LogisticRegression`: you must define your goal, select a baseline, gather relevant data, get it labeled with quality labels, and transform labeled data into training, validation, and test sets. The rest of the problem is solved after you type `model.fit(X,y)`, by applying error analysis, evaluating the model, verifying it solves the problem, and works better than the existing solution.

The seasoned analyst or machine learning engineer understands that not all problems, business or otherwise, will be solved with machine learning. In fact, many problems can be solved more easily using a heuristic, a lookup in a database, or traditional software development. You probably should not use machine learning if the system's every action, decision, or behavior, must be explained. With rare exceptions, machine learning models are blackboxes. They will not tell you why they predicted what they predicted, nor why they didn't predict today what they predicted yesterday, nor how to fix these issues.

Furthermore, unless you can find a public dataset and an open-source solution providing exactly what you need, machine learning is not the right approach for the shortest time to market. Sometimes the data needed to train and maintain a model is too hard or even impossible to get.

On the other hand, training data may be synthetically generated by using oversampling and data augmentation. These techniques are often applied when the data exhibits imbalance.

Before you start collecting data, ask these questions: is your data accessible, sizeable, usable, understandable, and reliable? Good data contains enough information for modeling, has good coverage of production use cases and few biases, is big enough to allow generalization, and not a result of the model itself.

Or does your data come with high cost, bias, imbalance, missing attributes, and/or noisy labels? Data quality must be ensured before it's used for training.

The machine learning project life cycle consists of the following stages: goal definition, data collection and preparation, feature engineering, model training, evaluation, deployment, serving, monitoring, and maintenance. At most stages, data leakage may arise. The analyst must be able to anticipate and prevent it.

After data preparation, feature engineering is the second most important stage. For some data, such as natural language text, features may be generated in bulk by using techniques like bag-of-words. However, the most useful features are often handcrafted by the analyst domain knowledge. Put yourself into the "model's shoes."

Good features have high predictive power, can be computed fast, are reliable and uncorrelated. They are unitary, easy to understand and maintain. Feature extraction code is one of the most important parts of a machine learning system. It must be extensively and systematically tested.

Best practices are to scale features, store and document them in schema files or feature stores, and keep code, model, and training data in sync.

You can synthesize new features by discretizing existing features, clustering training examples, and applying simple transformations to existing features, or combining pairs of them.

Before starting to work on a model, make sure that data conforms to the schema, then split it into three sets: training, validation, and test. Define an achievable level of performance, and choose a performance metric. It should reduce the model performance to a single number.

Most machine learning algorithms, models, and pipelines have hyperparameters. They can significantly influence the result of learning. However, these are not learned from data. The analyst sets their values during the hyperparameter tuning. In particular, tweaking these values controls two important tradeoffs: precision-recall and bias-variance. By varying the complexity of the model, you can reach the so-called "zone of solutions," a situation where both bias and variance are relatively low. The solution that optimizes the performance metric is usually found in the neighborhood of the zone of solutions. Grid search is the simplest and most widely-used hyperparameter-tuning technique.

Instead of training a deep model from scratch, it can be useful to start with a pre-trained model. Using a pre-trained model to build your own is called transfer learning. The fact that deep models allow for transfer learning is one of its most important properties.

Training deep models can be tricky. Implementation errors can happen at many stages, from data preparation, to defining a neural network topology. It's recommended to start small. For example, implement a simple model using a high-level library. Apply the default hyperparameter values to a small normalized dataset fitting in memory. Once you have your first simplistic model architecture and dataset, temporarily reduce your training dataset even further, to the size of one minibatch. Then start the training. Make sure that your simple model is capable of overfitting this training minibatch.

Your machine learning system's performance may benefit from model stacking. Ideally, base models used for stacking are obtained from algorithms or models of a different nature, such as random forests, gradient boosting, support vector machines, and deep models. Many real-world production systems are based on stacked models.

Machine learning model errors can be either uniform, and apply to all use cases with the same rate, or focused, and apply to certain use cases more frequently. By fixing a focused error, you fix it once for many examples.

Model performance can be improved using the following simple, iterative process:

1. Build the model using the best values of hyperparameters identified so far.
2. Test the model by applying it to a small subset of the validation set.
3. Find the most frequent error patterns on that small validation set.
4. Generate new features, or add more training data to fix the observed error patterns.
5. Repeat until no frequent error patterns are observed.

The model must be carefully evaluated before deployment, and continuously afterwards. Perform an offline model evaluation when the model is initially trained, based on the historical data. An online model evaluation consists of testing and comparing models in the production environment, using online data. Two popular techniques of online model evaluation are A/B testing and multi-armed bandit. They allow us to determine whether the new model is better than the old one.

A model may be deployed following several patterns: statically (as a part of an installable software package), dynamically on the user's device or a server, or via model streaming. In addition, choose among strategies such as single deployment, silent deployment, canary deployment, and multi-armed bandit. Each pattern and strategy has its pros and cons, and should be chosen depending on your business application.

Algorithmic efficiency is also an important consideration for model deployment. Scientific Python packages like NumPy, SciPy, and scikit-learn were built by experienced scientists and engineers with efficiency in mind. They have many methods implemented in C for maximum efficiency. Avoid writing your own production code, when you can reuse a popular and mature library or package. For high efficiency, choose appropriate data structures and caching.

For some applications, the prediction speed is critical. In such cases, the production code is written in a compiled language, such as Java or C/C++. If a data analyst has built a model in Python or R, there are several options for production deployment: rewrite the code in a compiled programming language of the production environment, use a model representation standard such as PMML or PFA, or use a specialized execution engine such as MLeap.

Machine learning models are served in either batch or on-demand mode. When served on-demand, a model is usually wrapped into a REST API. Serving a machine is often done by using a streaming architecture.

When a software system is exposed to the real world, its architecture must be ready to effectively react to errors, change, and human nature. A model must be constantly monitored. Monitoring must allow us to make sure that the model is served correctly and its performance remains within acceptable limits.

It is important to log enough information to reproduce any erratic system behavior during future analysis. If the model is served to a front-end user, it's important to save the user's context at the moment of the model serving.

Some users can try to abuse your model to reach their own business goals. To prevent abuse, don't trust the data coming from a user, unless similar data comes from multiple users. Assign a reputation score to each user and don't trust the data obtained from users with low reputations. Classify user behavior as normal or abnormal, and make progressively longer pauses or block some users, if necessary.

Regularly update your model by analyzing users' behavior and input data, to make it more robust. Afterwards, run the new model against the end-to-end and confidence test sets. Make sure that the outputs are as before, or that the changes are as expected. Validate that the new model doesn't make significantly more costly errors. Ensure errors are distributed uniformly across user categories. It's undesirable if the new model affects negatively most users from a minority or specific location.

* * *

The book stops here, but your learning doesn't. Machine learning engineering is a relatively new field of software engineering. Thanks to online publications and open source, I'm sure that new best practices, libraries, and frameworks simplifying or solidifying the stages of data preparation, model evaluation, deployment, serving, and monitoring, will appear during the upcoming years. Subscribe to my mailing list on this book's companion website `http://www.mlebook.com`. You will regularly receive relevant links.

Please keep in mind that, like its predecessor The Hundred-Page Machine Learning Book, this book is distributed on the "read-first, buy-later" principle. This means that you may download the entire text of the book from its companion website and read before buying. If you're reading these concluding words from a PDF file, and cannot remember having paid for it, please consider buying the book. You may buy it from Amazon, Leanpub, and other major online book sellers.

10.2   What to Read Next

There are many great books on machine learning and artificial intelligence. Here, I will give you only several recommendations.

If you would like to get hands-on experience with practical machine learning in Python, there are two books:

- "Hands-On Machine Learning with Scikit-Learn, Keras, and TensorFlow" (2nd edition) by Aurélien Géron (O'Reilly Media, 2019), and
- "Python Machine Learning" (3rd edition) by Sebastian Raschka (Packt Publishing, 2019).

For R, the best choice is "Machine Learning with R" by Brett Lantz (Packt Publishing, 2019).

To get a deeper understanding of the underlying math behind various machine learning algorithms, I recommend,

- "Pattern Recognition and Machine Learning" by Christopher Bishop (Springer, 2006), and
- "An Introduction to Statistical Learning" by Gareth James et al. (Springer, 2013).

To get more detailed understanding of deep learning, I recommend,

- "Neural Networks and Deep Learning" by Michael Nielsen (online, 2005), and
- "Generative Deep Learning" by David Foster (O'Reilly Media, 2019).

If your ambitions go far beyond machine learning and you want to sweep the whole field of artificial intelligence, then "Artificial Intelligence: A Modern Approach" (4th Edition) by Stuart Russell and Peter Norvig (Pearson, 2020), known as AIMA, is your best book.

10.3   Acknowledgements

The high quality of this book would be impossible without volunteering editors. I especially thank the following readers for their systematic contributions: Alexander Sack, Ana Fotina, Francesco Rinarelli, Yonas Mitike Kassa, Kelvin Sundli, Idris Aleem, and Tim Flocke.

I thank scientific advisors, Veronique Tremblay and Maximilian Hudlberger, for the review and correction of the Model Evaluation chapter. I'm also grateful to Cassie Kozyrkov for her attentive and critical eye that allowed solidifying the section on statistical tests.

Other wonderful people to whom I am grateful for their help are Jean Santos, Carlos Azevedo, Zakarie Hashi, Tridib Dutta, Zakariya Abu-Grin, Suhel Khan, Brad Ezard, Cole Holcomb, Oliver Proud, Michael Schock, Fernando Hannaka, Ayla Khan, Varuna Eswer, Stephen Fox, Brad Klassen, Felipe Duque, Alexandre Mundim, John Hill, Ryan Volpi, Gaurish Katlana, Harsha Srivatsa, Agrita Garnizone, Shyambhu Mukherjee, Christopher Thompson, Sylvain Truong, Niklas Hansson, Zhihao Wu, Max Schumacher, Piers Casimir, Harry Ritchie, Marko Peltojoki, Gregory V., Win Pet, Yihwa Kim, Timothée Bernard, Marwen Sallem, Daniel Bourguet, Aliza Rubenstein, Alice O., Juan Carlo Rebanal, Haider Al-Tahan, Josh Cooper, Venkata Yerubandi, Mahendren S., Abhijit Kumar, Mathieu Bouchard, Yacin Bahi, Samir Char, Luis Leopoldo Perez, Mitchell DeHaven, Martin Gubri, Guillermo Santamaría, Mustafa Murat Arat, Rex Donahey, Nathaniel Netirungroj, Aliza Rubenstein, Rahima Karimova, Darwin Brochero, Vaheid Wallets, Bharat Raghunathan, Carlos Salas, Ji Hui Yang, Jonas Atarust, Siddarth Sampangi, Utkarsh Mittal, Felipe Antunes, Larysa Visengeriyeva, Sorin Gatea, Mattia Pancerasa, Victor Zabalza, Dibyendu Mandal, and James Hoover.

Index

bootstrapping, 217
Boruta, 100
bucketing, 103

Caching, 239
calibration plot, 185
canarying, 229, 233
capital sigma notation, 3
catastrophic forgetting, 196
Ceph, 73
CephFS, 72
chain rule, 169
checkpoint, 173
chi-square distribution, 208
Chi-square independence test, 259
churn analysis, 106
churn prediction, 40, 262
CIFAR-10, 64
CityHash, 88
class, 4, 11
class imbalance, 24, 66
classification, 4, 11
    binary, 11, 165
    binomial, 11
    multi-label, 133, 165, 177
    multiclass, 11, 133, 141, 165, 177
    multinomial, 11
clipping, 114
clustering, 6, 70, 107
    k-means, 107
clustering algorithm
    centroid-based, 67
CNN, 94, 109, 111, 131, 157, 163, 176
coarse-to-fine search, 152
codomain, 168
Cohen's kappa, 143, 164, 185
collision, 88
compiler, 239
concept drift, 51, 182, 255, 258
confidence level, 216
confusion matrix, 140, 221
container, 200
context, 249, 260
convergence, 170

convolutional neural network, 157
Core ML, 225
correction cascading, 196
correlation, 13, 98, 221
cosine similarity, 65, 67, 108
cost function, 27, 66, 109, 139, 165, 200
covariate shift, 182
cProfile, 239
creep factor, 257
cross-entropy, 177
    binary, 165, 177
    categorical, 165
cross-validation, 9, 60, 152
    five-fold, 152
cuML, 262
cumulative gain, 146
    discounted, 146
    normalized discounted, 147

data
    annotation, 22
    directly-used, 7, 80
    expired, 39
    holdout, 138
    imbalanced, 39, 66, 142, 183
    incomplete, 39
    indirectly-used, 7, 80
    interaction, 55
    labeling, 22
    raw, 7
    sparse, 71
    structured, 73
    tidy, 8
    time-series, 60, 91
    unrepresentative, 39
data augmentation, 62, 77, 160, 173, 188
data imputation, 39, 44
data lake, 73
data leakage, 10, 52, 180, 198
data lifecycle document, 76
data processing topology, 231
data serialization, 71
data structure, 238
database, 73

model training, 12
Momentum, 172
Monte-Carlo simulation, 209
MSE, 139
multi-armed bandit, 212, 264
multi-armed bandits, 234
multilayer perceptron, 107, 109
multiprocessing, 239
MurmurHash3, 88
mutation testing, 219

n-gram, 84
Naïve Bayes, 135
network topology, 163
neural network, 12, 51, 93, 107, 135, 188
    convolutional, 94, 109, 111, 131, 163, 176
    deep, 12, 135
    fully-connected, 109
    gated recurrent, 163
    recurrent, 109, 176
    residual, 163
    shallow, 108
neuron coverage, 219
NFS, 72
noise, 44
    Gaussian, 64
noisy pre-labeling, 42
normalization, 114
    batch-, 160, 173
    mean, 115
    z-score, 115
null hypothesis, 102, 207
Numba, 197, 239
numerical overflow, 114
numerical stability, 259
NumPy, 197, 241

object, 73
object storage, 72
odds ratio, 85
one-hot encoding, 108, 109
one-versus-rest, 11, 186
optimizing and satisficing, 141

outlier detection, 6
overfitting, 44, 139, 156, 193
oversampling, 66

Pachyderm, 75
Packrat, 199
parallel, 239
parameter, 10, 11
parameter-initialization strategy, 167
    ones, 167
    random normal, 167, 175, 193
    random uniform, 167, 175
    Xavier normal, 167
    Xavier uniform, 167
    zeros, 167
PCA, 113, 138
    Incremental, 113
perceptive problem, 13
performance metric, 25, 27, 129, 138, 234, 247
    business-specific, 195
PFA, 242
Pickle, 72, 154
pickle, 240
PII, 36
pipeline, 10, 137, 250, 251
Platt scaling, 187
Plumber, 227
PMML, 242
point process, 93
policy, 6
pqR, 197
precision, 140, 253
prediction bias, 258
prediction strength, 107
predictive power, 95, 97, 156, 188
    low, 50
principal component, 113
Principal Component Analysis, 113, 138
prior probability shift, 182
protected attributes, 221
PULSE, 45
PyPy, 197, 239

www.ingramcontent.com/pod-product-compliance
Lightning Source LLC
Chambersburg PA
CBHW080451010725
28979CB00015B/1037